CAMBRIDGE STUDIES IN LATIN AMERICAN
AND IBERIAN LITERATURE 9

The baroque narrative of Carlos de Sigüenza y Góngora: A New World Paradise

Carlos de Sigüenza y Góngora, one of seventeenth-century Mexico's best-known intellectuals, was a writer of fascinating and complex narratives that exemplify the heterogeneous nature of colonial Spanish American prose. This book is the first critical study to place both the writer and his narrative within the phenomenon of the *barroco de Indias*, or Spanish American baroque. Approaching him as a criollo historian preoccupied with the placement of the New World in a universal context, Professor Ross develops a theoretical framework within which Sigüenza's texts can be read and understood today. She incorporates into her examination such new critical trends in the study of colonial Spanish American literature as the use of narrative theory, the new historiography, and feminist criticism.

Ross focuses on a close reading of Sigüenza's *Parayso Occidental* (1684), a history of the founding of one of Mexico City's first convents. The narrative includes several nuns' life stories – some written by colonial women themselves. Ross examines the strategies at play as a male historian attempts to absorb the writing of women into his universal New World history. Questions of gender, race, and the expression of criollo subjectivity all shed new light on the differences that characterize the Spanish American baroque.

In the Same Series

The baroque narrative of Carlos de Sigüenza y Góngora

A New World Paradise

KATHLEEN ROSS
Duke University

CAMBRIDGE
UNIVERSITY PRESS

Published by the Press Syndicate of the University of Cambridge
The Pitt Building, Trumpington Street, Cambridge CB2 1RP
40 West 20th Street, New York, NY 10011-4211, USA
10 Stamford Road, Oakleigh, Melbourne 3166, Australia

First published 1993

Printed in the United States of America

Library of Congress Cataloging-in-Publication Data
Ross, Kathleen.
The baroque narrative of Carlos de Sigüenza y Góngora : a New
World Paradise / Kathleen Ross.
p.   cm. – (Cambridge studies in Latin American and Iberian
literature ; 9)
Includes bibliographical references and index.
ISBN 0–521–45113–2 (hardcover)
1. Sigüenza y Góngora, Carlos de, 1645–1700 – Criticism and
interpretation.   2. Sigüenza y Góngora, Carlos de, 1645–1700.
Paraíso occidental.   3. Spanish American prose literature – To 1800–
History and criticism.   4. Literature and society – Latin America.
5. Misogyny in literature.   6. Women in literature.   I. Title.
II. Series.
PQ7296.S5Z87   1994
863–dc20   93–3630
                                                               CIP

A catalog record for this book is available from the British Library.

ISBN 0–521–45113–2 hardback

Para Daniel

Contents

Acknowledgments

Many are the friends and colleagues who have worked with me through my years of wrestling with the colonial baroque. Above all I wish to thank Enrique Pupo-Walker, whose work as editor at Cambridge University Press has produced a series of books among which I am truly privileged to include my own. I am grateful to Roberto González Echevarría for nurturing this project in its early stages, and for his steadfast friendship since then. Others whom I would recognize for aiding me with their time, efforts, and expertise include Electa Arenal, Linda Arnold, Robin Dash, Ariel Dorfman, Aníbal González-Pérez, Alice Kaplan, Asunción Lavrin, Marcella Litle, Stephanie Merrim, Jill Netchinsky, Jean O'Barr, Linda Orr, Cynia B. Shimm, Joan Hinde Stewart, William B. Taylor, John Jay TePaske, and Abby Zanger.

Although my conclusions differ from his, Irving A. Leonard through his pioneering research made the foundation on which I have built my work. I salute him as the dean of scholars dedicated to Sigüenza, and thank him for his continued interest in my efforts.

In Mexico City, my work has been facilitated during repeated visits by Karen Cordero, María Agueda Méndez, Manuel Ramos, Nuria Salazar, and Manuel Ulacia. I thank the sisters of the present-day Convento de Jesús María and of the Convento de San José de Carmelitas Descalzas for receiving me and allowing me to consult their manuscript holdings.

In its initial phase as a doctoral dissertation, the Helena Rubenstein Foundation supported this project through a Woodrow Wilson Research Grant in Women's Studies. The Tinker Foundation – through grants to Yale and Duke Universities – and the American Council of Learned Societies sponsored my archival research in Mexico City on Carlos de Sigüenza y Góngora's *Parayso Occidental,* making possible discoveries that

greatly enriched this study. I thank Duke University for grant-
ing me a leave of absence during the 1988–89 academic year.

This book is dedicated to Daniel Szyld, whose love has
sustained me through the process of seeing my project reach
completion.

Introduction

Is the idea of a Spanish American baroque an oxymoron? Is
this combination of a geography and a style one which by definition must be self-contradictory? Was the phenomenon of
baroque writing in colonial Spanish America – the *barroco de
Indias,* or baroque of the Indies, as the colonies were known –
only an imitation of the metropolis, or did it create something
new and different? These are the questions I explore in this
study. They have been posed to me by colleagues in fields of
literature outside Hispanic studies, by students in my classes,
and even by Hispanists not directly engaged in colonial research. In my view, these questions go back to an ambiguity
that is as old as the term itself and has never been convincingly
resolved: What do we mean by the term *barroco de Indias*? Why
not just call it "baroque"? What, finally, is the difference here?

The idea of "difference" has special meaning for literary
criticism. In the terminology of deconstruction, it is a translation of Derrida's *différance,* pertaining to the multiplicity of
meanings inherent in language and the text. This difference,
as it was narrowly defined by early poststructuralists, has little
to do with the author or with historical circumstance. To feminist and cultural critics, however, what makes a text "different"
has everything to do with who wrote it, and where and when.
This creates an impasse that, particularly among feminist
scholars, has defined rival camps of criticism (theoretical or
empirical, French or Anglo-American) that would seem to be
mutually exclusive.

North American and European feminist critics of French literature have done much to bridge this gap and expand the concept of poststructural difference as it relates to the social
construct of gender.[1] As for language-based criticism that takes
cultural and historical difference into account, scholars of Latin

1

American literature have been in the vanguard. Precisely because of the playfulness of language in Latin American texts,
alongside the marginality of the writer whose culture is not
that of the Western center, this intersection of linguistic and
cultural concerns is unavoidable. Critics examining writing in
Latin America since independence have always given history
primary importance; the question of national, regional, or eth-
nic identity is posed over and over again. The experimental,
playful language of the great novels of the 1960s and 1970s –
the "Boom" – is likewise often studied from within a cultural
framework. The heterogeneity of Latin American culture and
the challenge of its literature to European theory of necessity
make the best critical work an enterprise not limited to language alone.

As for colonial Spanish American writing, its study was
largely descriptive until poststructuralist theory came along.
Earlier criticism followed two general routes: the historical, in
which scholars did archival work, and the literary, in which they
looked for telltale signs of modern fictional modes in colonial
texts. In the most influential literary histories, the two routes
merged and defined colonial writing for the majority of readers, as literary histories generally were read in lieu of the texts
themselves.[2] However, since the emergence of theory as an an-
alytical tool beginning in the late 1960s, it is fair to say that
there has been a revolution in the way colonial literature is
read and studied. History and culture, in this case, were never
forgotten – indeed, work on colonial texts is often an interdisciplinary effort closely tied to historical or anthropological
method. But by concentrating on the language of the text, we
have been able to place the writing of sixteenth-, seventeenth-,
and eighteenth-century America in a contemporaneous context. Instead of reading only with twentieth-century eyes, we
have examined what the rules for writing were for authors and
texts in the world they themselves inhabited. Moreover, by inquiring just why colonial writing has been evaluated for so long
according to Romantic or post-Romantic standards, the most
recent colonial criticism is rewriting Spanish American literary
history, enriching the entire field with its findings.[3]

Thus the gap between critical and historical scholarship has
never been so broad as far as Latin American literature is con-

cerned, and difference as a category of inquiry has never been without its cultural component. In a similar vein, the current, hotly debated movement toward revision of the canon of Western literature, which focuses on the value of "nonliterary" texts for study and questions the worth of aesthetic appraisals that emphasize the universal rather than the local, is something already familiar to the field of Latin American literary studies. A canon, largely exclusive of Indian, black, and women writers, exists in our field too, but it is being more rapidly broken down because the underlying foundation is a new one.

It is especially important for scholars of colonial texts to refine knowledge of this foundation in order to further challenge the canon. Built in the nineteenth century and based on the written production of a colonial society far from the metropolis, this tradition is easier to uproot because of its marginal character. Indeed, by examining writing that is not conventional "literature," the very practice of colonial criticism stands for change in the works we read, the way we read them, and the manner in which we historicize them.[4]

My inquiry into American difference challenges modern readings of an important timespan – the seventeenth century. Critical work on the baroque in Spanish art and literature is abundant, since such art was the richest product of a politically and economically depressed era. The contrast between artistic boom and imperial bust is so notable, in fact, that social theories explaining baroque aesthetics and style – principally referring to the religious orthodoxy of the Counter-Reformation – have been advanced by critics for decades.[5] The situation obtaining across the Atlantic is much more problematic. In the New World the phenomenon of the baroque – *barroco de Indias* – arrived a bit late but stayed for a very long time, pervading literature, painting, architecture, and popular art. Yet though the poetry of this century, especially that of Sor Juana Inés de la Cruz, has received attention, the narrative remains neglected. This situation mirrors the state of research in history, which has concentrated on the sixteenth and eighteenth centuries in Spanish America to the detriment of the seventeenth. In the last two or three decades, however, this gap in the historical literature has been steadily addressed from several different angles, especially the economic and social.

I see an acute need for scholarship relating literature, and particularly the narrative, to current historical evidence, and my study is an exercise in such an interdisciplinary approach to the "forgotten century," as it was dubbed by Leslie Byrd Simpson. This era receives short shrift from both camps, for its complexities are daunting. Yet the ferocious polemics raging amongst literary critics and historians alike indicate just what is at stake: an understanding of the forces at work in the first full century of Spanish American colonial life, a time that defined society for many years afterward.

In his now-classic essay "Literatura de fundación," Octavio Paz writes that the Spanish tree planted in American soil has become another, with greener leaves and more bitter sap (Paz 1972, 15). Following this metaphor, we could ask whether the tree of the American baroque is a hybrid or a transplant. Around this issue, critics have expressed almost opposing notions of seventeenth-century writing. The proponents of the hybrid theory – Paz among them – lean heavily toward a symbolic analysis, positing an identification of aesthetic with identity in a heterogeneous society. Those critics who call it a transplant take a materialist view, arguing that the literature of a colonial elite is per se a mimetic exercise based on the class identification of the colonized with the colonizer. Both tendencies claim to describe the baroque literature of the colonies in relation to the world surrounding it; but each sees the relation of the individual writer to the world in a way opposed to the other.

José Lezama Lima postulates in his book *La expresión americana* that the baroque is the foundation of Spanish American literature, for it provided the vehicle to express a new culture that was more a mixture of disparate elements than a synthesis. Since the aesthetic standard of baroque art did not value order, measure, or symmetry, but rather complexity and excess, the cacophony of America could be well represented through such a style (Lezama 1957, 45–52). Lezama, and Paz after him, stand the question of an oxymoronic American baroque on its head: for them the baroque in the New World becomes truly new, breaking with its European master. Far from being a slave to forms defined by the metropolis, the *barroco de Indias* is the point where American writing begins, the place where the tree sends down its own roots.

In contrast, critics of the materialist school see the writers of the colonial period in concrete terms, strive to avoid idealization of the past, and stress the collective over the individual case. John Beverley, for example, examines the literature of sixteenth- and seventeenth-century Spain alongside that of Spanish America during the same timespan, arguing that together they form the corpus of an "imperial era" (Beverley 1987, 13). Literary models imported from Europe are, according to Beverley, part and parcel of a system of domination, and writers are the products of that same system. The production of an author, in turn, depends on the specific material conditions of his or her sociohistorical moment, rather than on individual talent or genius.

In the terms of historical determinism as seen by the critics of this group, the colonial period and its literature respond to changing conditions that lead, eventually, to revolution. An American literature is born through the contradictions created when imposed European styles overlay what remains of indigenous traditions. Different groups and social classes take part in this struggle for American definition, which develops toward liberation as it breaks away from imperial power. Literature is a phenomenon to be explained in material terms.

I contend that both these explanations, the symbolic and the material, are inadequate. They purport a historical analysis, but in the end are informed mostly by modern thought and modernist aesthetics: Paz's analysis, for example, tends toward existentialism, whereas Beverley professes a Marxist, globalizing ideology. Neither accurately portrays the culture of seventeenth-century Spanish America as current historical evidence presents it to us. My own investigation is indebted to these materialist and symbolic critiques, but I wish to go beyond the dichotomy that considers them mutually exclusive paradigms. A literary analysis that takes into account findings from history is a path out of this critical dead end.

The historical scholarship is, however, every bit as disputed as that of literature. In the 1950s, Woodrow Borah in his *New Spain's Century of Depression* raised the issue of whether the European economic crisis of the seventeenth century had extended to Spanish America. Borah believed it had and that the depression was real, the result of various factors, and his hypothesis was generally accepted. Over the years, however, others published divergent views, and the debate has reached a peak since 1981, when John TePaske and Herbert Klein's "The Seventeenth-Century Crisis in New Spain: Myth or Reality?" inspired fierce discussion and a polarization of opinion. The evidence for a "mythical" or a "real" depression has to do with the identification of colonial Spanish America's relative dependency on Spain during the century under examination. Those who argue for the reality of the depression see the colonies as wholly dominated by Europe, suffering through a century of crisis with metropolitan origins; the postulators of a myth of depression hypothesize a gradual lessening of dependency, a growing self-sufficiency that reordered the economy of the Spanish empire. Different kinds of documents and data are called upon to attest to the claims of both sides in the argument. Most of the work has dealt with New Spain, but the rest of Spanish America has also been discussed.

This polemic provides a fruitful model for consideration by critics of colonial literature and culture. When a case is made for a materialist view of baroque writing, it argues for a hypothesis of economic and cultural dependency, whereas the symbolic interpretion looks for signposts of an existential reordering, a new way of seeing the world and Spanish America's place in it. We are discussing the same issues that historians do, although our evidence is based on language and text rather than statistics and documents.

In this book I restate the terms of the literary argument by incorporating some of the historians' dialogue. I do so in an effort to arrive at a broader understanding of the culture that produced the *barroco de Indias,* not because I believe that historical evidence is somehow privileged above textual readings. Indeed, my contention is that history and literature, bound together in the seventeenth century by rhetoric, remain so today, for both rely on language to persuade and convince, and both are subject to the reader's interpretation. By examining the efforts made by Carlos de Sigüenza y Góngora, seventeenth-century historian of New Spain, to disengage from literary models, I show just how much the cultural ideologies of colonial society in the age of absolutism were shaped through baroque literature, making such a discursive separation impossible.

Baroque literature in Spanish America was not a liberating gesture, since those practicing it were colonized. Nor was it merely an exercise in slavish imitation of Spanish style, solely the expression of colonial domination; to say so ignores the evolution of colonial culture throughout three centuries of Spanish rule. Baroque literature in Spanish America was the vehicle through which the criollos, or American-born Spaniards, engaged in an intertextual dialogue with the sixteenth century and the writing of the age of Spanish conquest (*c.* 1492–1580), and thus with a literary history that had become their own as well as Europe's. As this group gained self-sufficiency, so did its literature gradually break from European models. The criollos – some of whom were not totally pure-blooded Spaniards – remained identified with Europe, but as colonized Americans they lived a multifaceted reality ordered by hierarchies of race, class, gender, and religion. Their literature shows a constant wavering of language from dominant to subordinate positions, resulting in subversions of European models even when those models are consciously being imitated. And above all, the great preoccupation is history: rewriting it to include the New World. This foundation was made for themselves and their colonial reality, not for the modern nations of Spanish America that formed after independence; but it was American and not European, even though we cannot yet point to a nationalist impetus.

Moreover, certain individual personalities – creative thinkers – did stand out among the criollos. Their genius, and particularly their literary production, can be recognized without losing sight of the miseries of their age, and of the privileged position they held in it. How did they come to create what they did? Through a dialogue with their particular historical circumstances and society, while at the same time defining that society themselves through their use of historical writing, some writers resisted the Spanish domination of language and culture, and they are the ones we remember today.

Carlos de Sigüenza y Góngora's *Parayso Occidental,* the history of the foundation of one of Mexico City's first convents, is a text where all the defining characteristics of colonial society – religion, race, class, and gender – come into play. Sigüenza y Góngora combines these issues in his narrative as he rewrites the story of the discovery of America from a late seventeenth-century perspective, using the "paradise" of the convent as a metaphor for European colonization. A member of the criollo elite, his position in society has long concerned students of the period, for he was a man of many talents – a historian, mathematician, poet, and ethnographer. He himself studied indigenous civilizations, but was this intellectual a critic of peninsular power, or a collaborator? The same question has been raised with a slightly different cast by both historians and literary critics: was Sigüenza y Góngora a representative of baroque culture and the Spanish state, or a thwarted proponent of the Enlightenment and the nascent America of revolutionary ideas?

These kinds of dichotomous questions do little toward the work of describing the era that produced the *barroco de Indias.* They merely leave us with a portrait of the seventeenth century as a hole in time – a way station on the road to independence for some, the fulfillment of the genocide of the Conquest for others. This century is consistently defined by what went before and after it, and the reception of Sigüenza y Góngora's work offers an illuminating example. My interest is to find new avenues of approach to the complexities of the era, avoiding easy reductions.

As I demonstrate with examples from other colonial writers, the narrative of the *barroco de Indias* can be seen as a product of the complex forces of the dynamic society that surrounded it. My object of study could thus be characterized as the baroque narrative and its cultural milieu. The work to be done here is a revision of literary history that will include the era of American baroque in all its glory and misery, as a time of intense class and racial stratification, religious orthodoxy, and misogyny, alongside new growth at the frontier, expansion in trade, and a wealth of artistic production.

Incorporating the findings of recent historical scholarship is one approach to seventeenth-century literature. Using the tools of inquiry honed by feminist and gender studies across the disciplines is equally crucial. Every field in the humanities and social sciences (as well as some in the biological and physical sciences) has been touched by this radical methodology that asks questions from an angle inclusive of women both as subjects and objects. Such questioning leads not only to knowledge of specific conditions for women, but also to challenges about knowledge as it is constituted in the disciplines themselves. The way in which knowledge is gathered, interpreted, and passed on to succeeding generations is undergoing intense scrutiny, the result being a fresh look at the local traditions of each field.

Parayso Occidental is a good example of a text that remains resistant to interpretation without the tools of feminist scholarship. Written to commemorate the hundredth anniversary of the Mexican Convento de Jesús María, it is largely composed of the *vidas*, or spiritual life stories, of some of the institution's most pious nuns. These vidas appear in various forms: as biography written by male confessors, first-person oral history dictated to either a confessor or another nun, and written autobiography composed by the nuns themselves. All are included within the structure of *Parayso Occidental*, sometimes quoted directly by Sigüenza y Góngora, sometimes heavily edited and paraphrased by him. Being a work that in great part was written by women – though Sigüenza subsumes the nuns' own stories into his broader history – *Parayso* cannot be understood until the sexual politics of the text are brought into full view. By bringing a gender analysis to bear on the narrative, the pieces begin to fall into place: It is no longer a religious anomaly among Sigüenza's works, which deal mostly with more empirical topics such as comets, geography, and exploration, but a stage for the cultural preoccupations of baroque society that inspired all his writing. In establishing that underlying ideology by including women, we provide a new paradigm for questioning the dependency of seventeenth-century life in America. Asking "Where were the women?" – both within the text and without it – takes us into the heart of that daily life. When their story is told, there is a shift in perspective; they are the forgotten voices of the forgotten century.

The criollo elite to which Sigüenza y Góngora belonged was subject to a shifting reality of conformity and subversion, domination and power; it ruled at home but was second-class abroad. Any reading of the *barroco de Indias* must take this into account. The nuns of the Convento de Jesús María were also mostly criollas, but as women they were subordinate to men, and so fit differently into the hierarchy of power. The question

of cultural dependency that I have identified as being of paramount importance to this epoch will necessarily be answered
differently for men and women, but neither answer is complete
without the other.

Thus my approach to the religious life stories that make up so
much of *Parayso Occidental* aims to place them in the context of
a culture of men as well as women. Although the convent provided a place where some women could write, and encouraged
literacy for religious purposes, it cannot be idealized as an autonomous space. I do not believe a community of women apart
from men and the outside world was formed in the convent;
the persistence of class and race divisions within its walls makes
this evident. Postulating that an ideal women's culture could
exist under such repressive conditions as those of seventeenth-
century convents overlooks the reality of the surrounding society, for the convent depended on institutions run by men.

The vidas show us how religious women dealt with their culture through writing or through testimony. This response dif-
fered according to the stations of the individual women; some
were poor, some privileged. Some women resisted the domination of male hierarchies, whereas others conformed. Moreover,
some stories were dictated and so are oral narratives. All have
in common an intensely personal orientation to events, combining autobiography with history. They describe the public
sphere from the vantage point of the private.

In *Parayso Occidental,* the range of life stories recounts different responses to the limitations, and the possibilities, of the
cloister. But matters are complicated by the larger structure of
the text; Sigüenza's history encloses the convent narratives and
uses them to its own ends. The narrative strategies and literary
models called upon to perform this operation of textual domination are at the heart of my study, which lays bare the workings of the criollo historiography that inspires the narrative of
the *barroco de Indias.* But without recognizing the importance of
the feminine text to this process, and the ways in which it differs from Sigüenza's history, the heterogeneity of *Parayso Occidental* remains a mystery.

These women's voices do not exist in a female world cut off
from the outside; they maintain a dialogue with the dominant
sphere of male writing, with men's power and privilege. Besides

looking inward to mystical experience and reflection, they look outward to the world that has shaped their surroundings and controls their space. In teasing out the threads of feminine narrative from *Parayso Occidental,* I expose this dialogue and show how the vidas resist a linear ordering of time as they organize life into language. I use deconstructive methodology here as a tool to uncover layers of meaning, to show how these women's voices cannot be limited within the confines of the convent and church hierarchy. They overflow those boundaries in a struggle for self-definition.

A parallel aim is to better understand the structure of misogyny in colonial Spanish America. Critics of seventeenth-century culture have observed that the restrictions placed on women, the church's extreme fear of them as weak creatures subject to temptation and sin, are hallmarks of the era, which was marked by the prominence of the Jesuits. Thus Octavio Paz and Fernando Benítez – just to mention two prominent, and very different, Mexican thinkers – both see Sor Juana as the victim of a church obsessed with the filthiness of women, with the need to keep them as controlled as possible in all ways. But misogyny in the colonies had another mission as well: to preserve racial divisions in an increasingly mixed society, especially in the urban centers. The theme of miscegenation runs subterranean throughout the narrative of the *barroco de Indias.* Controlling the sexuality of European-blooded women, through marriage or the convent, would ensure the preservation of a criollo group that could continue to dominate the Indian, African, and increasingly mixed-race masses. Misogyny thus served a social purpose beyond religious piety and the ultra-orthodoxy of Counter-Reformation Spain.

And so baroque narratives such as *El Carnero* (1638) and *Parayso Occidental* stress the dangers of the female flesh and the need to securely control woman's desire. How women behave sexually will define the order of colonial society and maintain the separation of the Spanish, Indian, and African races. Mixed-race people – *castas* – upset this neat order. Women, then, are much more than incidental to the baroque era in Spanish America and its literary expression; they are central actors as the encounter of Old and New Worlds moves into its second century.

Feminism and deconstruction intersect here as powerful analytic tools. Feminist theory posits a different structuring of language and plot, a different narrative ordering by women writers. It also asks how women are portrayed by male authors, and to what ends. Deconstruction, in turn, looks for places where the text reveals how language betrays the writer's conscious intent to corral it into one signification. By investigating where the criollo discourse of misogyny leads in *Parayso Occidental,* both the feminine narrative structures and authorial relationships based on power are revealed. The subtexts of miscegenation and repressed sexuality – uncovered as we see how Sigüenza's history attempts to control the vidas – tell us about the criollo culture that looked for ways to exert its own growing self-sufficiency and to integrate the immediate European past of the era of encounter and conquest into seventeenth-century reality.

From all this emerges my conviction that feminist literary and historical methodologies are key to an understanding of baroque narrative, that deconstruction is the most radical way to get at layers of complexity in the text, and that the two can work together. If the writing of the Spanish American baroque has largely defied critical scrutiny, it is because in many cases the wrong questions have been asked, as the work done on *Parayso Occidental* exemplifies. We cannot accept at face value Sigüenza's stated intention (as expressed in the prologue) to rid himself of literary frills and write an "unadorned" history without examining the places where that wish falters. Asking "How much is modern?" begs the question of how language may betray other wishes as well, such as the criollo's hope for racial stratification in an increasingly complex society. This has been the starting point for discussion in the work of literary historians, such as Irving Leonard, and historians, like Elías Trabulse, who portray a modern scientist caught in the dark age of his orthodox century, a rational thinker forced to accept irrational ideas. The symbolic and materialist schools of literary criticism attempt a broader synthesis, but ultimately leave the *barroco de Indias* without definition.

When women are recognized as essential to the story of the story being told, the picture of this century becomes clearer. Although *Parayso Occidental* begins with Sigüenza's announcement of his plan to write an unadorned history "of women and for women," the text he wrote and the book he compiled display a polyphony of narrative voices and strategies for ordering them. Many of those voices belong to women, and without that understanding the text is an enigma.

Convents in the seventeenth century were cultural and social institutions as well as spiritual ones; they played an important role in criollo society as landowning units and dwellings for the daughters of the upper class. Life in the biggest convents of important cities did not generally hold to strict guidelines of poverty or isolation. Sigüenza's effort to praise the Convento de Jesús María, the "western Paradise" that was founded during the sixteenth century for the penniless descendents of Spanish conquerors, contains a subtext lauding a far different institution: the Convento de San José, Mexico City's first Carmelite convent. The nuns who founded this much more rigorous cloister left the Convento de Jesús María precisely in search of a stricter rule. Yet these are the women whose life stories are highlighted by Sigüenza, and their example is meant to encourage conformity and suppression of individuality. In telling the story of the tireless efforts of the founders of San José to enforce orthodoxy in their original convent and of the harassment they faced from their less observant sisters, Sigüenza seemingly undoes *Parayso*'s stated premise: the Convento de Jesús María becomes hell rather than Paradise, its fame resting precisely on those who wished to leave.

However, within the dominant discourse of the seventeenth-century church, praise for the Carmelite founders was also praise for the Convento de Jesús María, which had produced such "saintly" women. Moreover, the Convento de San José was closely identified with Spain and Spanish imperial power, whereas that of Jesús María was, by definition, criollo. But San José's history is embedded in that of Jesús María, and thus the child becomes the mother as the American institution produces that of the Carmelites. The counterpoint of the two convents within Sigüenza's history represents the profound changes at work in seventeenth-century society.

Such changes certainly did not affect the misogynous agenda of church and state, which was shared by Sigüenza y Góngora. *Parayso Occidental*, a retelling of the Conquest of America

dedicated to the king and to the Spanish presence in the New
World, puts forward an orthodox political program in order to
instruct and impress its female audience. In doing so, the text
operates on different levels of discourse while addressing readers both more and less powerful than the author himself. These
shifts between discourses, their dialogue with the Spanish past,
and their political program for the American present, are what
I explore.

Beginning with a detailed review of theories of the *barroco de
Indias*, Chapter 1 is my meditation on the material/symbolic
controversy, taking as its point of departure José Antonio Maravall's *Culture of the Baroque*. Maravall's *mentalité* method of history is taken as authoritative by materialist critics such as
Beverley; I find much of it useful but employ it in a different
way in order to fit the American case. Here I also examine the
currents of historical scholarship dealing with the seventeenth
century in Spanish America, as well as the controversial issue of
economic and cultural dependency in the Spanish colonies.

The critical literature dealing with Sigüenza y Góngora provides a good case history of the trajectory of material versus
symbolic thought concerning the Spanish American baroque.
To that end, I give an overview of several key moments in that
literature and the ideologies they reflect. Through an appraisal
of the body of Sigüenza's texts, I propose a reading based on
different criteria than have previously been suggested.

In Chapter 2 I advance a theory of the narrative of the *barroco de Indias* based on a criollo historiography of shifting discourses. Here enters the question of an intertextual dialogue
between the seventeenth and sixteenth centuries, of the desire
of the criollo author to rewrite the chronicles of Conquest
with a New World focus. Sigüenza y Góngora is my primary
subject, but I make additional reference to other writers of
the period, including Sor Juana Inés de la Cruz and Inca Garcilaso de la Vega. My reading of the two introductory texts of
Parayso Occidental, the "Dedicatoria," addressed to the king,
and the "Prologo al letor," are analyses of the ways in which
language allows multiple interpretations of what is intended
to be "unadorned" history. At this juncture a feminist perspective inclusive of female subjects and objects becomes crucial to

understanding the text, and I introduce such a perspective through close readings.

Chapter 3 continues the reading of *Parayso*, which is composed of three books, or *libros*. The first libro, the convent history written by Sigüenza y Góngora, is examined here. The way in which Libro Primero becomes a metaphor for the Conquest of America and its underlying themes of repressed sexuality and racial division demonstrate the preoccupations of the male criollo writer, representing the dominant voice of his culture. In particular, the late seventeenth-century vision of indigenous culture and the evolution of that vision over more than a century of colonization are paramount to my analysis of Sigüenza's efforts to write an authoritative history of the western Paradise.

The second and third libros, made up of nuns' life stories, are examined in Chapter 4. Here the male author's difficulties as he puts together his larger book become sharper. The vidas take many forms in the text, as biography and autobiography. How they are variously manipulated, the narrative strategies used to contain them, and the models borrowed from history and literature are the subjects of this chapter. The picaresque, Cervantes, and Golden Age theater are some of the literary models I show to be of importance to Sigüenza's project. His paternalism toward the women he writes about, his need to keep their stories in line to fit them to the history he wants to produce, are key elements of these libros.

Finally, Chapter 5 concludes my study with a consideration of the vidas as women's writing. Time and space in the convent are my themes, and poststructuralism combines with feminist theory in my readings. The manner in which Sigüenza deals with mysticism and religious visions within the framework of narrative history is crucial to my argument. The nuns' texts, composed at the behest of confessors, have been the subject of several recent studies written from a feminist perspective, and I inscribe my own arguments within that context. Ultimately, the difference of the feminine text within the history exposes the culture of the baroque in Spanish America.

Forgotten, misunderstood, quiescent, oppressive: all these adjectives have been used to describe the Spanish American seventeenth century. Yet this was a dynamic period of intense cultural change and important literary activity. In many ways, in fact, the literature of the *barroco de Indias* defines the century today for critics and historians alike, in so much as it is taken to be paradigmatic of the era. By inquiring into the work of Carlos de Sigüenza y Góngora and the nuns he wrote about, and by looking at the heterogeneous creations of language, my intention is to bring to light some of the unseen assumptions of that debate.

1

Culture of the Spanish
American baroque

In Mexico City, a metropolis steeped in centuries of history that
honors its cultural figures with monuments and public spaces
dedicated to their memory, the name of Carlos de Sigüenza y
Góngora is nowhere to be found. A perusal of the most recent
edition of the most exhaustive of street guides for the Federal
District yields six streets called Hernán Cortés, twenty-four fea-
turing Columbus (either with or without his first name), and
fifty remembering Sor Juana Inés de la Cruz, but only two
named for Sigüenza, that bring his name into the everyday life
of present-day Mexicans.[1] Carlos de Sigüenza y Góngora, one
of seventeenth-century New Spain's most brilliant intellectuals,
has effectively disappeared from the collective memory of the
modern state that is today's Mexico.

Yet though Sigüenza may be absent from the popular imagination, he is very much alive in the writing of historians and
critics of literature and culture. In the twentieth century he has
come to play a key role for those who work with the history of
Mexican and Ibero-American ideas: the emblem of his age, the
barroco de Indias. Although Sigüenza's name graces almost no
public place, it shows up regularly in the scholarly spaces reserved for very important people, such as anthologies of literature, histories of literature, and critical books and articles.
Much of this scholarship, however, does not focus on Sigüenza
but rather includes him as a peripheral figure, often in counterpoint to his more compelling contemporary, Sor Juana.[2]
Thus a paradoxical situation emerges: A major figure of the
colonial period, indeed one who is seen to embody the very essence of his era, has in reality scarce critical "body" of his own.

My contention is that Carlos de Sigüenza y Góngora has
served as a foil for critics and historians as they advance theories attempting to explain the *barroco de Indias*. By examining
some of the scholarly writing that has made Sigüenza into the

17

emblem of his time, I wish to trace the evolution of critical thought on the Spanish American baroque up to the polemics of the moment. As we shall see, Sigüenza's case is in itself emblematic of the changing ideologies projected by varying critical discourses, particularly those concerning dependency and colonialism, onto the notoriously amorphous category known as the baroque.

More than sixty years ago Irving Leonard opened a new era in the study of Sigüenza with his biography *Don Carlos de Sigüenza y Góngora: A Mexican Savant of the Seventeenth Century.*[3] The book was Leonard's first, and it remains the standard reference for anyone writing about Sigüenza. The fact that it was published in Spanish translation for the first time only in 1984 attests to its enduring value as a piece of exceptional documentary research. Without this book's bibliography, compiled in North and South American archives in the 1920s, we would not have knowledge of many of the texts on which our current readings of Sigüenza are based.

Leonard's *A Mexican Savant,* then, is a foundational work for students of Carlos de Sigüenza y Góngora. Leonard himself, however, wished his book to serve a larger purpose: to fill a laguna in the cultural history of New Spain, the space left unfilled for lack of attention paid to the seventeenth century. Although he most certainly was dedicated to work on Sigüenza per se, Leonard was just as eager to use the criollo intellectual as a vehicle for the depiction of an era. His remarks in the prologue make this clear: "Much valuable work has been done in recent years on the history of New Spain in the seventeenth century ... our knowledge of other aspects of the life and conditions in New Spain has not kept pace" (Leonard 1929a, ix).

We should recall here that *A Mexican Savant* was written at the time that the poets of the Generation of 1927 were beginning their efforts to bring Luis de Góngora, the great Spanish baroque poet, out of the frank disparagement where two previous centuries had placed him. Irving Leonard, in his biography of the Cordoban poet's distant American descendant, is clearly a partisan of the antibaroque sentiments antedating 1927. The Gongoresque aspects of Sigüenza's poetry are ridiculed by Leonard, who nonetheless "forgives" this minor stain on an otherwise sterling record of intellectual achievement:

There is no mistaking the fact that Don Carlos was proud of his verse-writing and he seldom lost an occasion to exercise his muse. . . . But in a life so singularly free of blemishes of the cruder sort, we may be tolerant and forgive him for his little *defectillo* which only proves him to be a very "human" being. Let us, then, turn to the consideration of another phase of his character in which a more admirable trait may be discussed. (28)

The publication of *A Mexican Savant* in California coincided with that of the first twentieth-century Mexican edition of Sigüenza's *Obras*, compiled by Francisco Pérez Salazar in 1928. His edition includes a biography and, like Leonard's book, is still widely consulted. This burst of scholarly activity in the late 1920s marked the first wave of modern work on Sigüenza and was followed in 1931 by Leonard's *Poemas*, an edition of Sigüenza's lyrics including his most extensive poetic compositions, *Primavera indiana* and *Oriental planeta evangélico*. In this 1931 edition a preliminary study by Ermilo Abreu Gómez was published, the first example of textual analysis devoted to the poems. Abreu Gómez's essay, perhaps influenced somewhat by the Generation of 1927, shows respect for the figure of Luis de Góngora, but not for the age that produced him and his criollo relation: "Sigüenza reacciona contra la inercia del período barroco decadente que le tocó vivir" [Sigüenza reacts against the inertia of the decadent baroque period in which he lived] (Abreu Gómez 1931, 21).[4] The analysis goes on to explain that Sigüenza's mediocre poetry was the result of his struggle with a baroque tradition that he despised and could not wholeheartedly practice: "Podría llamársele un preneoclásico" [He could be called a preneoclassicist] (37).[5]

Leonard (1929a) characterizes Sigüenza as a Renaissance humanist, open and enlightened during a dark, closed time: "The study of the life and works of Don Carlos de Sigüenza y Góngora suggests certain analogies with the early humanists of the Italian Renaissance" (182). The criollo's scientific and geographical contributions are stressed, as is his curiosity regarding the surrounding world. Moreover, Leonard shows, through his discussion of Sigüenza's polemic with the Jesuit Father Kino on the nature of comets, that the Mexican's universe was

broader than that of the European. Despite his marginal status
as an American educated in America, Leonard's Sigüenza is a
hero of modernity as he bravely fights the superstition of his
era. His polemical stance demonstrates

that Mexico was not so utterly enveloped in the darkness of ignorance
and intolerance at this time as is still a common belief in some quarters. Not alone on the eastern shores of the great Atlantic was the
light of scientific learning beginning to gleam, and not merely in the
Old World were the shadows of superstition being gradually dissi-
pated. (73)

Thus, this pioneering biography of one of the seventeenth
century's premier writers accomplishes one of its main objectives – that of providing an idea of Sigüenza's surrounding culture – by placing the writer squarely outside his own time.
Sigüenza's ideas identify him with the humanists of the *Quatro
Cento* or with eighteenth-century scientists, but never with the
baroque, that stain on an otherwise admirable career. By defining seventeenth-century culture through a series of oppositions, by pairing it with the periods coming before and after,
Leonard constructs a scheme similar to that proposed in Heinrich Wölfflin's description of Classic versus Baroque in his *Principles of Art History.* Apparently, Leonard was not aware of that
1915 work when he wrote *A Mexican Savant,* for he does not cite
it; but in like manner, his oppositions serve to continue the vision of a seventeenth century rife with neomedieval ignorance
and stagnation of thought, a time when just not much was going on.

Another intellectual important to the *barroco de Indias* who
definitely was aware of Wölfflin's study, and found it limiting,
was the Venezuelan Mariano Picón Salas. In 1944, he had this
to say regarding *Principles:*

No basta en el estilo barroco aislar el rasgo individual: decir, por
ejemplo . . . que es lo "pictórico" en contraste con lo "lineal," como se
determina en las categorías enunciadas por Wölfflin, y que ello en literatura significa oscuridad y primor difícil, frente a la diafanidad y
sencillez del opuesto estilo clásico. Todo esto son expresiones de una
complejidad más hermética. (Picón Salas 1944, 121)

It is not enough to isolate an individual feature of baroque style: to
say, for example . . . as in the categories set out by Wölfflin, that it is
the "painterly" in contrast with the "linear," and that this, in litera-

ture, signifies obscurity and difficulty of workmanship rather than the transparency and simplicity of the opposing classical style. All of this is the expression of a more hermetic complexity.

Picón, like Alfonso Reyes, Pedro Henríquez Ureña and other Latin American thinkers of the middle part of the century, worked toward a different view of the baroque in this study, *De la Conquista a la Independencia*, the book that coined the term *barroco de Indias* in the first place. This view meant to contribute to the ongoing search for a Latin American identity through cultural and literary history, a search begun in the nineteenth century. Here again there is a desire to fill a gap, that of the entire colonial period from Conquest to independence.

Within this space, the *barroco de Indias* occupies a privileged position and a great deal of the book is devoted to it. Picón wants to delve deeper than the formal categories of art history do to explain the "complicación y contradicción" [contradiction and complication] (121) of the Spanish American baroque, what he calls its "vitalidad" [vitality] (123). Moreover, this enigmatic period holds key information for the understanding of the present:

El período barroco que no ofrece al historiador la abundante historia externa de los días de la Conquista . . . es el más desconocido e incompredido en todo nuestro proceso cultural–histórico. Sin embargo, fue uno de los elementos más prolongadamente arraigados en la tradición de nuestra cultura. . . . Pesa en nuestra sensibilidad estética y en muchas formas complicadas de psicología colectiva. (123)

The baroque period, which does not offer the historian the same abundance of external history as does the time of the Conquest . . . is the most unfamiliar and misunderstood period of our entire cultural–historical process. Nevertheless, it was one of the most long-lasting and deeply rooted elements of our cultural tradition. . . . It carries weight in our aesthetic sensibility and in many complicated forms of our collective psychology.

Despite the use of descriptive terms such as "vitalidad" [vitality] (123) and "exuberancia" [exuberance] (123), Picón's relationship to the *barroco de Indias* is ambivalent. For him, it is the expression of a decadent, sedentary culture – "la mar quieta de la existencia colonial en el siglo XVII" [the quiet sea of colonial existence in the seventeenth century] (131) – in contrast with the movement and action of the sixteenth century.

Sigüenza y Góngora is twice referred to by Picón as "un caso monstruosamente ejemplar" [a monstrous example] (137, 150) of the contradictions of baroque culture; here Sigüenza's erudition has been touched by scientific rationalism but remains essentially scholastic in character. For Picón, the titles of Sigüenza's works are "estrafalarios" [extravagant and wild] (137) and equally emblematic of the dilemma of the baroque intellectual who is "un prisionero del laberinto" [a prisoner of the labyrinth] (150). Such a person has information, but no method to guide him or her out of the morass of an era that emphasizes appearance over substance and faith over reason.

Here, then, there is an attempt made to define the *barroco de Indias* as more than an absence between Conquest and independence. Yet the tendency remains in Picón, as in Leonard, to see the seventeenth century as a time of stasis. Although its baroque writing and art overflow with detail and exuberance, according to these scholars nothing much was happening in the society surrounding the artistic production. And Sigüenza, with his wildly titled works, is the distillation of that stagnant culture.

A second peak of work on Sigüenza done in Mexico centers around the tercentenary of his birth. *Don Carlos de Sigüenza y Góngora, erudito barroco,* by José Rojas Garcidueñas, appeared in that year, published by Ediciones Xóchitl in the series "Vidas mexicanas."[6] Much as Leonard's 1929 book provides a résumé of all that precedes it, so does Rojas Garcidueñas's biography remark on significant publications up to the date of the tercentenary. *Erudito barroco* is not itself an extensive scholarly work; it has no bibliography and includes scant notes. Most of the biographical data comes from Pérez Salazar, although Leonard is acknowledged. However, it is clear that the critical moment from which it emerged was completely different from that of fifteen years before, for this book is in many ways a document of growing nationalist sentiment in Mexico. The spirit of President Lázaro Cárdenas's reforms of the 1930s had carried over into literary investigation and had created a national consciousness that claimed Sigüenza as one of its own. The tercentenary was a vehicle through which a whole group of Mexican *literatos* could express not only erudition, but patriotism as well.[7]

The title *Erudito barroco* already tells us that by 1945 the seventeenth century had become accepted – and in Mexico, more than that. It was now a part of the indigenous past, reclaimed by a new generation of scholars. Implicit of Rojas Garcidueñas's book is a critique of Irving Leonard's antibaroque stance as a foreign one. This emerges most notably in Rojas's defense of *Parayso Occidental:*

La obra historiográfica realizada por aquel erudito fue el fruto de larga dedicación . . . y un ánimo generoso por conocer él mismo y dar a conocer a los demás un pasado en que sentía la raíz de esta realidad social que es México, en aquel tiempo todavía informe e imprecisa, y que solamente los espíritus más sensibles y las mentes más indagadoras e inquietas, como el propio Sigüenza, podían percibir y apreciar. (141)

The historiographical work accomplished by that scholar was the fruit of a long-term dedication . . . and a readiness to understand and make it possible for others in that still unformed and imprecise era to understand a past in which he sensed the roots of this social reality that is Mexico, which only the most sensitive spirits and the most questioning and searching minds, like that of Sigüenza himself, could perceive and appreciate.

Alfonso Méndez Plancarte, another Mexican scholar of the 1940s, compiled the important second volume of his anthology *Poetas novohispanos* with a general purpose in mind beyond the presentation of little published poetry: the vindication of the Mexican baroque period as a whole. The introductions to the two parts of this first Mexican anthology of its kind are manifestos that acknowledge their debt to the Generation of 1927 while angrily descrying the continued omission of the New World in that revaluation: "Y hoy todavía, cuando una pléyade eximia de críticos eminentes ha reivindicado al Barroco literario de España, esa nueva justicia no alcanza al nuestro, salvo algún retoque en la alusión a Góngora, sino que todo queda arreglado y 'puesto al día' con declarar bastardo nuestro gongorismo" ["And even today, when a famous pleiad of eminent critics has recovered the literary Baroque in Spain, this new justice does not extend to our Baroque, except for some final touch on an allusion to Góngora; rather, everything is considered taken care of and 'up-to-date' by declaring our Gongorism a bastard"] (Méndez Plancarte 1944, vol. 2, pt. 1, x). As well as extensive commentaries on the many poets included in the anthology, these essays are a first step toward a poetics of the *barroco de Indias* in its New Spain version.

Méndez Plancarte asks the question "¿Contendrían nuestro clima y nuestro terruño, físicos o espirituales, una especial fertilidad barroca?" [Could our physical or spiritual climate and soil have an especially baroque fertility?] (xxvi). Noting the possible influence of the Latin and Indian languages, he considers this of dubious importance; more crucial is the richness of seventeenth-century Mexican architecture and indigenous culture. A parallel is drawn here between colonial churches or buildings and poetry: "Pero nuestra poesía de aquel entonces, no fue sino otra flor del mismo rosal" [But our poetry at that time was only another bloom on the same rosebush] (xxx). The relationship between nascent colonial research and nationalism is stated clearly in a quote from the Mexican poet Ramón López Velarde who had written earlier in the century that "la boga de lo colonial, hasta en los edificios de los señores comerciantes, indica el regreso a la nacionalidad" [the vogue in things colonial, even in the buildings of important businessmen, indicates a return to national customs] (xxx).

Such enthusiasm, when applied to Sigüenza the baroque Mexican poet – as opposed to the enlightened scientist – perhaps errs in its own rather excessive and uncritical praise. Rojas Garcidueñas says of Sigüenza's youthful (1663) composition on the Virgin of Guadalupe: "Ciertamente la *Primavera indiana* es poema artificioso . . . pero ahí hay también fragmentos del brillante gusto barroco" [Certainly *Primavera indiana* is a fraudulently ingenious poem . . . but it also has fragments of brilliant baroque taste] (38). He then goes on to compare the criollo's images of the sea to Rimbaud's "Bateau ivre." Méndez Plancarte classifies Sigüenza as "un grande poeta" [a great poet] (1945, vol. 2, pt. 2: viii) and refutes all opinions up to 1945 to the contrary, including Leonard's. Only in Góngora himself is superiority recognized: "No hay en Sigüenza tanta originalidad y finura, ni el ímpetu y el equilibrio geniales del 'Polifemo'; mas fué, en su escuela, muy auténtico y alto" [Sigüenza's work does not have as much originality or refinement, or genius of balance and impulse as does the "Polifemo"; but for his own school, he was very authentic and eminent] (xi).

It is fortunate that such nationalist feelings were prevalent in Mexico at the time of the tercentenary, or today we would be without editions that remain the only ones available. This explosion of probaroque, procolonial sentiment was a counter to the earlier positivist tradition, and it encouraged criticism with a more literary focus. Sigüenza y Góngora, however, was left with a split personality.

Such a divided view turns up again in Irving Leonard's well-known *Baroque Times in Old Mexico* (1959), written thirty years after *A Mexican Savant*. The relationship between this book by Leonard and Picón's *De la Conquista a la Independencia* is an intimate one; Leonard published a translation of Picón's text in 1962, shortly after having written *Baroque Times*. Indeed, whole paragraphs of the latter work paraphrase Picón. Especially in the idea of a seventeenth-century culture no longer indigenous, but not yet *mestizo*, or of mixed race – that is, not yet with its own identity – Leonard echoes Picón's idea of the baroque as an era of stagnation and stasis. Picón's words: "Los indios han perdido su historia, los mestizos todavía no la hacen, y el acontecer histórico se localiza en un pequeño círculo blanco, todavía semiextranjero, y en el que aún no despierta la conciencia de nacionalidad" [The Indians have lost their history, the mestizos have not yet made any, and historical events are localized within a small circle of whites, still semiforeign, in whom a national consciousness has not yet awakened] (132). And Leonard's: "The Indian majority had, in fact, lost its historical past, while the mixed elements resulting from racial fusion had not yet made any history" (32).

However, as anyone familiar with *Baroque Times* is aware, this text wants to do more than just ruminate on a murky time; it wants to have fun. Even more, it desires to be baroque in its own labyrinth of time and space. As Leonard confesses in his preface: "It is, indeed, a kind of mosaic," he writes, "composed of bits of incident and anecdote . . . it is in itself a kind of Baroque design" (ix). And there is a repetition of the same appraisal noted by Picón: "The Baroque as an historical epoch and a way of life is incompletely assessed" (ix). Thus, Leonard now meets the baroque head-on as a concept useful for a discussion of the seventeenth century, a major change from the focus of *A Mexican Savant*.

Sigüenza, though, remains an emblem, the definition of his age. Leonard proposes another pairing here to illustrate his point: that of Sor Juana with Sigüenza, based in part on the poems each figure addressed to the other.[8] In separate chapters devoted to each writer, Leonard draws parallels and marks divergencies, emphasizing the personal relationship between the "poetess" and the "scholar" (x). There is more than a little romantic invention here; Sigüenza and Sor Juana are rather like star-crossed soul mates, striving to free themselves from the authority of Counter-Reformation society, yet ultimately thwarted in that attempt. In Leonard's fantasy the death of Sigüenza becomes as tragic as that of Sor Juana: "For the nun the pace of death was slower; for the scholar it was speedier. . . . August 22, 1700 brought liberation" (213). The scholar does have a salvation of sorts, however, as he is deemed a precursor of better things to come, a herald of the Age of Reason.[9]

In discussing Leonard and Picón, I have skipped over another key figure in the critical discourse on the *barroco de Indias*, one who finds Sigüenza and his wild and crazy titles irresistable: the Cuban poet and essayist José Lezama Lima. Lezama considers the baroque to be the origin of Latin American literature and the root of the cultural present;[10] it provides a vehicle to express a new culture that is more a mixture of disparate elements than a synthesis. Since the aesthetic of baroque art does not value order, measure, or symmetry, but rather complexity and excess, the cacophony of America can be well represented through such a style. Here the New World baroque becomes truly new, breaking with its European master; it is the point where American writing begins the art of the counter-conquest: "Representa un triunfo de la ciudad y un americano allí instalado con fruición y estilo normal de vida y muerte" [It represents a triumph of the city and an American fruitfully installed there, with a regular style of life and death] (Lezama Lima 1957, 47).

Lezama's discussion of Sigüenza rushes forth enthusiastically:

En Carlos Sigüenza y Góngora se redondea la nobleza, el disfrute, la golosina intelectual, de ese señor barroco, instalado en paisaje que ya le pertenece, realizador de unas tareas que lo esperan, fruitivo de todo noble vivir. . . . Publica libros cuyo solo título tiene de poema y de simpatía ganada por anticipado. (56)

In Carlos de Sigüenza y Góngora become free and clear the nobleness, the enjoyment, the intellectual delicacy of that baroque gentleman, settled in a landscape which now belongs to him, tasks to be

accomplished awaiting him, enjoying everything noble in life. . . .
He published books whose mere titles anticipate their poetry and
charm.

What is especially interesting about this formulation is the way
in which the Cuban writer uses Sigüenza, the urbanized criollo
and quintessential "señor barroco" of the city, to define his own
version of the seventeenth-century American world. What appeals to Lezama is precisely that which was anathema to Picón:
the excess, the frenzy, the complication of it all. Here, the contradictions of a figure such as Sigüenza are no longer a cause
for regret but, on the contrary, give us reason to celebrate. They
signify the richness of a new American culture in formation.

These, then, are the works that defined the *barroco de Indias*
up to 1960. During the 1960s and 1970s, theorists such as Ger-
ard Genette and Michel Foucault turned their attention to the
European baroque, a field particularly neglected in France.
Severo Sarduy, combining among a broad range of readings
French theory with Lezama, produced in his 1974 *Barroco* a
neobaroque manifesto that, although it did not deal specifically
with the American case, celebrated the baroque's subversive or
revolutionary aspects (a position Sarduy had articulated earlier, notably in his 1972 essay "El barroco y el neobarroco").
This became the controversial focus for the coalescence of two
critical orientations to the *barroco de Indias* and its cultural context: the material and the symbolic. Neither orientation is
monolithic and each has its various tendencies, but two rather
clearly delineated stances can be and have been discerned,[11]
and Sigüenza y Góngora continues to be a lightning rod for opposing views.

One of the best-known studies of the 1980s, Octavio Paz's
massive tome *Sor Juana Inés de la Cruz o las trampas de la fe* is
more than a book. It has become a media event, dramatized on
Mexican television and popularizing a neo-Freudian analysis of
the nun's life. Recent articles by Frederick Luciani (1987) and
Stephanie Merrim (1991) have elegantly critiqued the portrait
of Sor Juana that emerges from this biography. From another
angle, I would point out that although separated from them
chronologically, *Las trampas* follows the work of Leonard, Picón,
and Lezama on the *barroco de Indias*. "Not only an attempt at
resolution," Merrim observes, "Paz's study involves an ambitious

project of *re-creation,* being a book of the world, of Sor Juana's world" (12). This suggests a similar goal to that shared by Irving Leonard in his presentation of Sigüenza. And Paz's argument that there is a psychological affinity on the part of the creole writer for baroque complication resonates with Lezama's *señor barroco,* feeling at home with excess and a wealth of detail.

Although Paz's book is a study of Sor Juana, Sigüenza y Góngora makes several important appearances, usually paired with Sor Juana, as he was by Leonard. However, instead of stressing the similarities of the two intellectuals, Paz highlights their differences. The portrait of the baroque intellectual presented by Paz is less flattering than Leonard's, and less romantic. For Paz (1988; 1982), Sigüenza y Góngora's view of Old and New Worlds represents more than anything else the syncretic thought of the Jesuit order: "Sigüenza y Góngora was not unique; his ideas were variations on a prevalent doctrine held, more or less consciously, by other writers of the time, members of the Society of Jesus and those close to it" (154; 211).[12] This presentation of Sigüenza as representative of a group ideology is placed by Paz in counterpoint to Sor Juana's originality, as soon becomes evident.

The analysis based on a contrast of the two writers' triumphal arches, constructed for the entry of the new viceroy, further sets up Sigüenza as Sor Juana's rather pedestrian second banana. Her mind, according to Paz, was synthetic and universal, whereas Sigüenza's was parochial and limited: "It has often been said that Sor Juana is greatly superior to Sigüenza as a writer. It must be stated that this superiority is not merely a matter of style. Sigüenza's mind was not inclined toward synthesis, while Sor Juana's was to a high degree" (178; 240). Here there is a subtext to Paz's work that argues for the importance of a symbolic reading of the baroque. For Sigüenza was a historian, and Paz's relationship to history as method is an uneasy one. History is chance, rhyme, correspondence, in a kind of archetypal construction that resists determinism (473; 611). Culture, on the other hand, is "freedom and imagination" (472; 610), existing alongside historical circumstance but not determined by it.

This is part of an antimaterialist position running throughout Paz's book. The "traps of faith" belong to the twentieth century as well as the seventeenth; in Paz's view, today's intellectuals living in societies that interpret history materially suffer a fate similar to that of Sor Juana. There is a connection between one and the other that history cannot explain; we should only read, and be on guard:

In the twentieth century, by a kind of historical regression, there are abundant examples of writers and ideologues who have become their own accusers. The similarity between Sor Juana's final years and these contemporary examples led me to choose as subtitle of my book *The Traps of Faith*. The phrase is not applicable to all of Sor Juana's life, nor does it define her work; but I believe that it does describe an evil common to her time and our own. The recurrence of the evil is worth emphasizing, and that is why I have used the phrase: as a warning and example. (6; 17–18)

So Sigüenza continues to wick away the ideological stances of his critics, here in Paz's position against material explanations of art. Paz bases his evaluation above all on the individual expression of the writer, as does Lezama. Both the Mexican and the Cuban poets bring to their readings a preoccupation with personality and creativity in relation to a society that repressed (and represses) the individual. Although Lezama's Sigüenza is happier than Paz's, indeed the symbol of baroque exuberance rather than pedestrian history, the portrayals have in common their starting point of individual genius, or lack thereof.

The opposing point of view can be found in José Antonio Maravall's *La cultura del barroco*, a book that has had great impact on diverse scholars of the *barroco de Indias* who approach the question from a materially based perspective. Maravall deals with the European baroque, especially the Spanish case, explaining it in terms of a history of mentalities with evidence accruing from everyday life. The *barroco de Indias* is an extension of absolutist power emanating from Spain; as goes Spain so go the colonies, which are dependent on it both economically and culturally (at least in the urban, criollo milieu). The baroque is a system imposed by a colonial power in America, and far from the liberation or self-realization proposed by Lezama and Paz, or Sarduy's neobaroque, it is a foreign yoke. For materially based criticism, it is precisely the struggle to remove that yoke that is the real story of the *barroco de Indias*.

Critics of the materialist school see the writers of the colonial period in concrete terms, striving to avoid any idealization of the past and stressing the collective over the individual case. John Beverley (1987), as I mention in the Introduction, examines the literature of sixteenth- and seventeenth-century Spain along with that of Spanish America during the same timespan, arguing that together they form the corpus of an "imperial era" (13). Literary models imported from Europe were, according to Beverley, part and parcel of a system of domination, and writers the products of that same system. The production of an author, in turn, depends on the specific material conditions of his or her sociohistorical moment, rather than on individual talent or genius.[13]

Yet there are problems involved when Maravall's work on the European baroque is applied too closely to the American case. In the field of history, a debate comparable to that of literature is taking place, although it is framed in somewhat different terms. Historians of New Spain in particular are divided over the effects of seventeenth-century European economic depression on America. Florescano, Bakewell, TePaske, and others argue that there was, across the century, a gradual move toward economic self-sufficiency, and that the colonies did not sustain the same brutal impact as was the case in Spain. While not denying any of the negative aspects of colonialism, this view asks us to take a closer look at evidence from American trade, mining, and other factors, and also to see the seventeenth century as a period of movement and flux, rather than stagnation. Clearly, to globalize the Spanish experience of economic depression directly to the American colonies leaves out much of the story.

Although such a materialist analysis has not been applied specifically to Sigüenza y Góngora, it calls into question a recent reading by René Jara and Nicholas Spadaccini, who present Sigüenza as a wholly one-dimensional character. They return to the idea of a "pre-Enlightenment figure" (Jara and Spadaccini 1989, 47) outlined three decades ago by Irving Leonard; in fact, this portrayal of Sigüenza is reminiscent of Leonard's *A Mexican Savant,* for nowhere does it mention the criollo in a baroque context. He is depicted not as an ambiguous figure, but as a thinker who has definitely made up his mind on the political question: "Sigüenza y Góngora rejects the European models that are still being imposed on the New World and replaces them with concrete examples of virtue: those of Mexican Emperors. These, according to Sigüenza, were the models that the new Viceroy was supposed to emulate" (Jara and Spadaccini 1989, 45).

Jara and Spadaccini's essay, by ignoring the baroque context of Sigüenza's culture, gives a most limited view of the complex writer. What is evident here, however, is that Sigüenza y Góngora continues to be an emblem for his era, inscribed in this essay within a critical discourse concerned with issues of power and resistance. The picture of the criollo remains at root the same one received through Leonard and Picón, that of an intellectual open to new philosophical and scientific currents, exhibiting an abiding interest in the indigenous history of Mexico while living in repressive times. Shifting critical ideologies once again become evident as Sigüenza now represents a discourse of resistance to the dominant power of metropolitan Spain. The dialectical formation of baroque in opposition to Enlightenment (or independence) remains a substratum beneath these readings. Although Sigüenza's patriotism may be judged to be more or less nationalistic, the image of his life, more than his writing, is the text upon which theories of the baroque are projected.

Other recent examples of criticism have considered, once again as emblematic of the baroque, Sigüenza and his own studies of indigenous American culture. This work attempts to mark out a new path between the idealization of the stylistic flourishes of the *barroco de Indias* on the one hand, and the wholesale rejection of that style as a European imposition on the other. In particular, the manipulation of the dominant code of baroque language by criollo writers is seen as a resistance to authority, the manner in which an emergent criollo consciousness is able to express itself despite the repression of the colonial state. Mabel Moraña (1988), for example, has pointed out in a suggestive argument that "el gongorismo lejos de ser en todos los casos la 'lengua muerta' del poder imperial, dio a muchos intelectuales del Barroco indiano un motivo de lucimiento y autoafirmación, actuando, paradójicamente, como pretexto en el proceso de conformación de la identidad cultural hispanoamericana" [Gongorism, far from being in all cases the "dead language" of imperial power, gave many of the intellectuals of the Baroque in the Indies a motif for self-affirmation and splendor, paradoxically acting as a pretext in the process of shaping a Spanish-American cultural identity] (242). Moraña says of Sigüenza:

En la obra de Sigüenza y Góngora . . . aparece concretamente el concepto de "patria" casi siempre en contextos donde sirve como elemento diferenciador con respecto a la indiferencia arrogante de los europeos, y para identificar un proyecto cultural que no se extendía mucho más allá de los límites reivindicativos del sector criollo ni descartaba todavía la matriz española. (244)

In the work of Sigüenza y Góngora . . . the concrete concept of "homeland" appears almost always in contexts where it serves as a differentiating element with respect to the indifferent arrogance of Europeans, and to identify a cultural project that did not extend much beyond the grievances of the criollo sector, nor reject as yet the Spanish matrix.

Such an evaluation points toward a more fruitful discussion of Sigüenza and the *barroco de Indias.* Yet we must go further in revising our idea of Sigüenza if we are to reconceptualize his baroque culture, and for that we need to examine his texts, too often forgotten. Irving Leonard wrote *A Mexican Savant* after carrying out much careful textual documentation and archival research; his work laid a truly solid foundation for others to build on. Yet his portrayal of the criollo, laced with a positivist bent, laments that "the works of Sigüenza of greatest value, at least to the general historian, were in most cases never published. Aside from his *Astronomical Libra* . . . scarcely any of his works of genuine erudition came out in book form" (Leonard 1929, 16). Although Leonard then goes on to examine the published texts and admits their value as "veritable mines of miscellaneous information" (17), the idea that we have lost forever what truly defined Sigüenza as an intellectual has endured to the present moment almost unchallenged from any quarter. According to this assessment, as readers we are handicapped from the start, and our point of departure must be the life, not the text.

In truth, what we read today as Sigüenza's work is but a fraction of what he actually wrote. In a recent book on Sigüenza's lost manuscripts, the Mexican historian Elías Trabulse demonstrates through brilliant historiographical sleuthing how one of the finest personal libraries of seventeenth-century New Spain – Sigüenza's collection of his own work and that of others – was dispersed over the course of the centuries, its components lost, sold, disappeared. For Trabulse, this represents the more general dispersal of written Mexican history, the chapters of a national story lost to subsequent generations. He writes of Sigüenza's manuscripts:

Todos esos papeles tienen una historia que contarnos, no sólo la de su contenido, sino la de su largo viaje desde el último tercio del siglo XVII hasta hoy. Algunos desaparecieron en el camino, otros quedaron irremisiblemente mutilados, otros más fueron copiados y anotados. En suma, esos manuscritos tienen su propia vida y su propia historia independiente de lo que llevan escrito. (Trabulse 1988, 11–12)

All these papers have a history to tell us, not only that of their own content, but also that of their long journey from the last third of the seventeenth century to today. Some disappeared along the way, others were left irremissibly mutilated, still others were copied and annotated. In sum, these manuscripts have a life and history of their own, independent of what is on their written pages.

The approach of literary historians to Sigüenza's work, both extant and missing, has been to invent a taxonomy based on two criteria: chronology and genre.[14] Sometimes these two are combined, as in *A Mexican Savant,* where chapters have titles such as "Earlier and Lighter Writings" and "Sigüenza, Antiquarian and Historian." In general, Sigüenza's texts have been typed into four broad categories: historical chronicles, including *Parayso Occidental* and *Infortunios de Alonso Ramírez;* scientific treatises, most of which have disappeared; accounts of voyages and explorations, a blending of the first two categories; and poetry, both lyric and epic.

These generic and chronological criteria, which strive to complement the portrait of a multifaceted intellectual of many interests and talents, obscure a more sober reading of Sigüenza's work as we know it today, and as it must have been at the time of his death in 1700, judging from Trabulse's evidence. It is the idea of history that encompasses all others throughout Sigüenza's work, looming larger than religion (the traditional marker of Counter-Reformation literature) or science (an appreciation for which, in Leonard's view, differentiates Sigüenza from his baroque contemporaries). History – written history –

reifies the past and gives it the status of a series of events worthy of perpetuity, something particularly important to criollo writers, for these intellectuals needed an ancient history to which they could point as proof of tradition and parity with Europe. If Sigüenza became an ethnographer and collector of books on indigenous culture, it was not so much due to feelings of nascent nationalism in the modern sense, as to a desire for justification of his own New World existence (and this is a point to which I return in my reading of *Parayso Occidental*).

References to the myths and legends of the Aztecs and other indigenous groups are dispersed throughout Sigüenza's writings, and an effort is often made to merge Indian gods with Christian saints. A particularly striking example is that of the 1680 *Theatro de virtudes políticas que constituyen a un príncipe*, in which an arch built for the entry into Mexico of the new viceroy, the Marqués de la Laguna, is illustrated with portraits of Aztec rulers. (The same entry, but a different arch, is the subject of Sor Juana's *Neptuno alegórico*, which employs classical mythology.) Octavio Paz's chapter "Political Rites" in *Las trampas* explains the antecedents of both the ceremonial entry and the triumphal arch, tracing the latter to a Roman custom revived by the Renaissance. Paz observes that Sigüenza rejects the martial connotations of the arch, yet overlooks the fact that New Spain exists only through war and conquest; equating Rome with Mexico, the criollo bypasses Spain's role in the colonization of America and moves directly from paganism to Christianity.

Religious themes permeate Sigüenza's work at all times, as befits the work of a man who aspired, unsuccessfully, to the Jesuit priesthood. However, his is not an uninterested sort of faith, but one always related to a historical vision. *Primavera indiana* and *Glorias de Querétaro*, very much in the vein of other seventeenth-century Mexican tracts, are examples of *guadalupanismo* – the cult of the Virgin of Guadalupe – at its height. The specifically American character of the Virgin of Guadalupe is central to these compositions. In *Primavera indiana*, an epic poem of seventy-nine *octavas reales*, or eight-line stanzas, "sagrada Inteligencia" [sacred Intelligence], sent from heaven to earth, "termina el vuelo donde yace altiva / La gran Tenochtitlan en aureo trono" [ends her flight where the great Tenochtitlan proudly lies on its golden throne] (in *Obras*, 1928,

stanza xxxvi). Inteligencia goes on to explain that she has
found Germany, France, and England inhospitable territories
(xxxvii–ix), but Mexico a worthy and innocent land (xli). The
apparition of María, the Virgin Mary, to a humble peon follows. Clearly, the innocent New World location of Mexico,
along with its status as a territory recently conquered for the
church, is the deciding factor in Inteligencia's choice. The
American miracle changes a formerly heathen land into a fully
Christianized one through a providential design that was commonly celebrated in New World historiography of the sixteenth
and seventeenth centuries.[15]

San Francisco Javier, "apóstol de las Indias" [apostle of the
Indies] is another religious subject with added historical overtones. The Indies in question are the Asian ones, namely China
and Japan, but the association with their American namesake
cannot be missed. As Columbus sailed out to find the Orient by
going west, so San Francisco, the martyred Jesuit missionary,
was another kind of explorer to the east. *Oriental planeta evangélico,* a paean to the missionary and to the Society of Jesus,
which he helped found, takes advantage of the baroque fascination with the exotic to explode in *silvas* – stanzas mixing
seven- and eleven-syllable lines – adorned with a sensuousness
not to be seen in the criollo's later works:

> No con fragrante salve
> De destilados ambares suaves,
> No con voz dulce, que afectaron graves
> Consonancias retóricas del Alva
> Le recive en su seno
> El oriental terreno
> Si con admiración, pues ve a su mano
> Ser todo el Orbe feudo soberano.
> (*Poemas* 1931, 129)

The eastern land welcomes him to its bosom, not with a flagrant
greeting of filtering soft ambers, or the sweet voice of dawn affected
by grave rhetorical harmonies, but with amazement, as it sees the entire universe a fief to his sovereign hand.

Once again Sigüenza's religious topic harks back to more secular concerns. Not only a pious epic in praise of an important
proselytizer, the poem includes the added detail of an Eastern
setting and all the possibilities for embellishment that this

offers. Sigüenza has found a way to work in the baroque conceits of shadow and light, and East and West, while remaining within a context both sacred and historical (the poem is called an *epopeya sacro-panegírica,* or sacro-panegyric epic). Such conventions, however, take on new force when used by a poet born in the western Indies, for a fundamental shift in perspective occurs that causes all terms to be redefined.

Geography, intimately related to this redefinition, is an overriding passion of Sigüenza y Góngora. The voyages and explorations of which he writes in *Mercurio volante, Trofeo de la justicia española,* and *Infortunios de Alonso Ramírez* are an affirmation of New World existence: they effectively put the western hemisphere on the map. Sigüenza made literal maps, also, such as that of the Valley of Mexico included in chapter 5 of Leonard's *A Mexican Savant.* The presence of geographic terms in other works – *Parayso Occidental, Oriental planeta* – underscores this preoccupation with terrestrial placement. It was another way, this time on a physical level, to work out the problem of a land with no Christian past.

Sigüenza is striving, in as many ways as possible, to situate Mexico within the universe as he conceived it. Providing a history meant establishing not only indigenous traditions and a religious background, but also the unique position of America with respect to Europe on the actual face of the earth.[16] The idea of exploration implies the new and unknown, whereas a *viaje,* or voyage, can be a return to the past. Both elements are at play in Sigüenza's geographic scheme as New and Old Worlds intersected for the criollos. *Mercurio volante* tells in journalistic style of the Spanish reconquest of New Mexico from rebellious Indians; certainly Sigüenza identifies here with the soldiers of the Crown, as he does in *Alboroto y motín de los indios de México.* Yet in *Infortunios,* a Puerto Rican circles the globe only to wind up in Mexico, back in the Caribbean where he started. Although this is a pessimistic conclusion in the picaresque mode, at the same time Alonso Ramírez's final salvation rests in the New World, not the Old.

Libra astronómica y philosóphica is the ultimate example of Sigüenza's "balance." This work has been used by Leonard and others to prove the Enlightened state of its author's scientific thinking, but it is better understood as baroque science in the service of a historical idea rather than as a piece of objective research. As Octavio Paz notes in his study of *Theatro de virtudes:* "Two currents combined in Sigüenza's attitude. The ideas came from the syncretism propagated by the Jesuits; the sentiments, from the confused aspirations of criollo society" (154; 211). Paz is referring here to religious ideas; a thorough study of Sigüenza's cosmographical work in the *Libra* would also take into account seventeenth-century attempts by the Jesuits to combine American and Asian cultures with Christianity in the scientific realm.

The "confused aspirations" of which Paz speaks are a point of departure for my study rather than a conclusion. The attempted resolution through language of such confusion, the establishment of a synthetic picture of history that extends from the ground (mapmaking) to the sky (comets), furnishes the basis upon which Sigüenza's texts can be read and interpreted today. The fragmentary nature of Sigüenza's surviving texts results in a portrayal of the criollo that is analogously divided into bits and pieces. Yet I believe it is possible to reconcile Sigüenza the scientific rationalist with Sigüenza the baroque poet and Sigüenza the criollo partisan by exploring the synthetic historiography that is attempted in each one of these texts.

Leonard's presentation of a personality torn between modernity and medievalism appeals to our modern sensibility. We are attracted to the Romantic concept of an intellectual out of step with his times, a writer who could not publish most of his writing for lack of funding, a professor unable to live on his meager salary. Lezama's baroque gentleman, reveling in the diversity of colonial society and putting down the roots of modern Latin America, is equally passionate and compelling, and likewise distorting. Paz's identification of Sigüenza's patriotic sentiments with Jesuit syncretism, although perceptive and certainly correct, also paints only a part of the whole.

It is by reading Sigüenza's texts as part of a discourse obsessed with matters of history, geography, and, above all, societal change – a criollo discourse – that we can escape the temptation to characterize those texts and their surrounding culture through the life of one figure. In particular, it is important to think of seventeenth-century Spanish America as more of a churning current than a quiet sea, as a period of growth and

conflict rather than a calm interlude. Historical evidence reflects such change. Beneath the smooth exterior of a well-
ordered colony peek through the difference of people and
poetry repressed by the Inquisition, new racial groups in formation, a popular culture which grew in spite of the penalties
meted out to transgressors.[17] While our vision of the culture
that spawned the *barroco de Indias* remains static, so too will
our portrait of a figure such as Sigüenza y Góngora stay stuck
in place.

All of Sigüenza's works demonstrate these characteristics of a
society in flux. I include poetic compositions such as *Primavera
indiana* and *Oriental planeta evangélico*, letters like *Carta al Almirante Pez* (*Alboroto y motín de las indios de México*), the history of
Parayso Occidental, the cosmography òf *Libra astronómica y philosóphica*, and the biography–travel narrative of *Infortunios de
Alonso Ramírez*. All demonstrate an awareness of America as different from Europe and an attempt to place it within various
systems, principally biblical, cosmological, and historiographical. Moreover, these works are written in dialogue with the
sixteenth-century chronicles of Conquest, continuing the work
begun one hundred years earlier by historians such as Bernal
Díaz del Castillo and Inca Garcilaso de la Vega. The reworking
of the chronicles using baroque language can be seen as well in
other writers of Sigüenza's era, such as Juan Rodríguez Freyle.
It could be called criollo historiography, an exercise in redefin-
ing the American past through a language often at odds with
the task of truthfulness, indeed a language that attempts to dis-
tort and deceive. Delineating this historiographical practice is
the topic of my Chapter 2.

Sigüenza, operating within an elite group of criollos close to
the uppermost levels of the court and the church, was keenly
sensitive to the prejudice directed at American-born Spaniards.
His works reflect the search for a sense of place in a changing
society, one in which the growing prominence of criollos on the
social scale was threatened both from above by European scorn,
and from below by continued racial blending, or *mestizaje*. Much
of Sigüenza's language bespeaks this search as he maps out a
universe where America will no longer be eccentric. Sigüenza's
own love–hate relationship with the baroque is an integral part
of that process of change.

Thus it is limiting to confine Sigüenza's baroque culture – and that of Spanish America – to the dialectics of ignorance and enlightenment, colonizer and colonized, power and resistance. Both historians and literary critics are arguing about issues of dependency, whether it be economic or cultural. But as long as we continue to see history and literature through a post-Romantic lens, whether positivist, existentialist, or Marxist, whether looking for colonial roots from a cyclical perspective or globalizing from the case of Europe to that of America, we will not get much of anywhere in our understanding of the *barroco de Indias*. To read the Spanish American baroque in a new way, we need to place its writing and writers in a historical context that will assume the ambiguities inherent in a discourse that represents a criollo class in ascendence, looking for its own history not only toward the poles of Spain and indigenous culture, but also to the sixteenth-century chronicles of Conquest.

2

A New World Paradise

A passion for history, rather than for science and reason, is the marker I take as paradigmatic in my reading of Sigüenza y Góngora's texts. In this chapter I explore what history meant to Sigüenza's efforts as a criollo writer and advance my own theory of baroque historiographical practice in Spanish America. To do so, my first goal is to situate this reading in a matrix of current critical thought that considers colonial writing as a key element of a discourse broader than the rigid categories of literature versus history allowed in the past. Within such a concept of colonial discourse, I propose the notion of a specific criollo historiography demonstrating a language of shifting power relationships and polyphony, as seen through close textual readings. In this chapter, my objects of study will be two introductory texts of *Parayso Occidental*: the "Dedicatoria" addressed to the Spanish king and the "Prologo al letor" addressed to the reader. I will also analyze the first chapter of Libro Primero, leaving the rest of the larger text for subsequent chapters of my study.

In the 1980s the concept of colonial discourse in Spanish American culture emerged as a new critical paradigm for the field of colonial literature. Rolena Adorno and Walter Mignolo, among other critics, have presented eloquent arguments for broadening the idea of literature – the written word defined by European tradition – into that of a discourse embracing the aggregate of synchronic cultural practice.[1] Such a broadened term shifts emphasis away from the kind of traditional criticism I mention in the Introduction, where a search for traces of literary detail leads the reader on a critical treasure hunt for nuggets of stories or novels buried in colonial texts, and toward an approach that avoids dichotomizing the narratives of history and literature.

The advantages of such an approach to the work of Sigüenza are easy to appreciate, for this method allows us as readers to get away from the conundrums posed by traditional generic categories. Taking in different modes of narration, we can explore Sigüenza's discourse as that of a criollo intellectual consumed by the need to define New World history in American terms – at a point in time when "America" signified a perspective on the world somewhere between that of New and Old Spain, to paraphrase Octavio Paz's (1988; 1982) felicitous description (151; 207). Moreover, working toward an understanding of the criollo discourse in Sigüenza y Góngora's texts restores his own lost present, absent in the judgments that would place him outside of his own time.

Such an understanding also separates Sigüenza's figure from that of Sor Juana. In truth, the comparison has never been helpful for either writer. Sigüenza was a historian and Sor Juana a philosopher; they both used the media of poetry and letters and lived lives inseparable from the ruling institutions of church and court; in short, they shared a common culture by writing in the same place at the same time. But Sor Juana's experience as a woman intellectual indelibly marks her texts (and her life) with the agony of struggle and self-defense, giving them a character different from that of Sigüenza's.

The nun did work within the same criollo discourse that maintained a certain fascinated distance from the complicated racial blending of the viceregal capital (a topic I return to in later chapters in my reading of *Parayso Occidental*), and she was a member of the same colonial intellectual elite to which Sigüenza belonged. Nevertheless, the religious, intellectual, and personal barriers she faced as a woman of her time were not the same ones with which he had to contend, and this reality is evident in the life and the texts of each. What is more interesting than a pairing of these two intellectuals is the posing of other critical questions. One query would ask which models each writer followed in his or her intellectual trajectory; another, what they have come to represent, separately, for readers today. Others have asked these questions in regard to Sor Juana,[2] and in this book I posit them for Sigüenza y Góngora.

I begin with the assumption, then, that history during Sigüenza's era still followed the rhetoric of Renaissance historiography, rather than the more objective tenets of the Modern period. The importance of historiographical tradition in the works of sixteenth-century colonial historians such as Inca Garcilaso de la Vega (1539–1616) or Gonzalo Fernández de Oviedo (1478–1557) has been fruitfully examined,[3] but Sigüenza has not been approached from this angle. As I have already discussed, critics have placed emphasis on what separated him from his era – postulated scientific or patriotic thought – and not on what he shared with his intellectual milieu. I pointed out in Chapter 1 how Paz's delineation of a Jesuit ideology of syncretism effectively places Sigüenza back in his own time; this is a good basis from which to proceed and I wish to build on its demythification of Sigüenza's "modernity." But my approach is to define a historiographical present for Sigüenza – a baroque, criollo historiography – stressing rhetorical currents as well as religious or psychological ones.

It is the criollo's writing of history that opens the door to our understanding of baroque prose in Spanish America. To read Sigüenza's texts as representative of the conflicts and trends of their own era is to radically question his identification as a modern, preneoclassic, scientific, or Enlightenment figure. At the same time, it is a way to approach the difficult writing of the colonial seventeenth century without ending up in utter confusion. It is clear that *Parayso Occidental* is a narrative history very much of its time and, moreover, that it is not exceptional within the body of Sigüenza's work for being so. Once *Parayso* is considered entirely apart from the idea of modernity, it looks like another example of the manner in which European narrative forms were challenged in America and forced to change, alongside the works of other New World historiographers such as those mentioned in the previous paragraph.

Seventeenth-century historiography in Spain and the American colonies is invariably linked to baroque, rather than Renaissance, style. If we consider, for example, the case of Antonio de Solís y Rivadeneyra, a Spanish historian of the Indies whose *Historia de la conquista de México* was published in 1684 – the same year as *Parayso Occidental* – the question of baroque style immediately emerges. Solís was named *cronista oficial* in 1661 when he was fifty years old and had enjoyed fame as a poet, dramatist, and gentleman of the court;[4] in 1667 he took his final vows as a member of the Jesuit order. The *Historia de la conquista* was the only work of history he composed during his twenty-five-year tenure as government chronicler.

As Luis A. Arocena's 1963 study convincingly shows, in Solís's history a distinct baroque historiography is evident in the book's style and philosophy. Arocena discusses in this regard the important theoretical works of Luis Cabrera de Córdoba (1611) and Fray Jerónimo de San José (1651), who wrote instructive treatises for historians,[5] and mentions as well Baltasar Gracián's influence as a moralist (in books such as the 1637 *El héroe* or *El criticón* of 1651–7). The changes wrought in Renaissance historiography during the seventeenth century were numerous, including greater detail in descriptive passages, a self-conscious use of language for ironic effect, and a general emphasis on moral teaching.[6]

Critics have not considered the importance of baroque precepts for the writing of history in Sigüenza's work because his own contribution to the genre of *historia* – that is, *Parayso Occidental* – has never been considered as such. On the contrary, it has been used to substantiate claims of Sigüenza's modern, antibaroque stance, claims based on the text of the prologue, which I examine in this chapter. But *Parayso* is a baroque history, planned and carried out by its author according to accepted rules of writing, which in the late seventeenth century still made history part of rhetoric. Moreover, it is a text inscribed within the particular subgenre of historiography that dealt with the subject of the New World, a group of texts established with the works of Pedro Mártir de Anglería (1459–1526) and Fernández de Oviedo, which were written in the 1520s. It is to this legacy of sixteenth-century histories – commonly referred to as the chronicles of Conquest and discovery – that we must look to understand their criollo descendents, of which *Parayso Occidental* is a notable example.

By the end of the sixteenth century, American-born writers were joining the ranks of an elite corps: the learned historians. *Historia*, tracing its precepts back to the classical age, was a vehicle for Renaissance humanists who strove to interpret a harmonious, balanced universe through harmonious, balanced prose. In this way, the very act of writing an aesthetically pleasing history replicated the philosophical principles that informed it.[7] How the European discovery of America challenged this notion of harmonious universality, making historians out of unlettered eyewitnesses, is a key topic in present-day research on colonial writing; indeed, it would be accurate to say that it is at the heart of the important studies I have already cited in this book. The manner in which histories following the old models gradually changed, or were resisted by new voices and perspectives, is the story of the formation of a historical discourse on, and in, the New World.

Within that discourse historians read and cited one another, and eventually set themselves the task of rewriting accounts of the foundational events of discovery and Conquest. Rewriting, of course, was a prominent feature of Renaissance historiography. Each text inscribed itself in the tradition of those that went before it, and it was this repetition that lent the weight of authority to the interpretation. From the very start in the histories written about the New World this tradition was coupled with an authority bestowed on the eyewitness informant – informants who sometimes were not trained historians, for instance, Cortés's soldier Bernal Díaz del Castillo (1492–1580).[8]

By the time of the final decades of the sixteenth century, a new generation of writers who owed their very existence to the encounter of Europe with what became known as America began to write histories about the New World. These were the mestizo and criollo writers – two notable examples would be Inca Garcilaso and Juan Suárez de Peralta (1540?–?) – who contributed to the chain of texts a perspective that at once criticized Spanish abuses of power, and accepted the Conquest as a providential event in universal history. The discourse of colonialism had begun to be recycled through the writing of colonial subjects themselves.[9]

Sigüenza y Góngora did not belong to this first generation of criollo writers. His late seventeenth-century world was one far removed from that of a century before, when colonization was a process in its earliest stages. By Sigüenza's time, the midpoint of Spain's four-hundred-year presence in America had been reached, and a distinct colonial culture had formed in each region of the Indies. Yet his own New World history, *Parayso*

Occidental, continues to refer back to the traditions of Renaissance historiography, following the European model for the narration of past events. Above all, it repeats the theme of divine will as a determinant for the Spanish Conquest of the Indians.

As Sigüenza rewrote the histories preceding his, he changed the language employed so as to fit the style and mentality of his era, which today we call the *barroco de Indias*. Not only European Renaissance historiography and its classical sources, but also the New World chronicles of Conquest undergo a transformation in this criollo discourse. Sigüenza builds on the foundation of these works of the first century of discovery and colonization, altering them through narrative strategies that create a polyphonic text and draw from literary, as well as historiographic, models. The importance of digression, moral teaching, allegory, and *conceptismo* (the intellectualization of reality through conceits of language), all hallmarks of baroque style, are notable throughout the text. The culture of absolutist power – Maravall's definition of the baroque era – is clear in this history that is dedicated to the king. At the same time, however, a fundamental shift of perspective puts the center in America and makes the New World better than the Old, indicating the growing consciousness of a separate, less dependent colonial subjectivity on the part of the historian.

What I posit as criollo historiography in Sigüenza y Góngora's text is its inscription within the tradition of the New World chronicles, using baroque language to rewrite the story of the Conquest and European discovery of America. The use of such language in and of itself is not a revolutionary act, such as that imagined by Lezama Lima's postulated *contraconquista* [counter-conquest] of complexity. Nor is it a mere imitation of metropolitan style, a pat imposition of the aesthetics of Spanish absolutism. Instead, the baroque prose of the Indies results from a mixture of discourses, some expressing the privileged status of a criollo elite, some a second-class status at the viceregal court. The American nature of this baroque prose rests not in its usage of conceits, digressions, and other standard tropes, but in the manipulation of previous histories of conquest through the employment of language borrowed from literature. The polyphony of narrative voices in the prose, its

fluid and changeable character, and an obsession with the reinterpretation of American history put a stamp of difference
on the criollo historiography of the *barroco de Indias*. It is a way
of retelling the past through a discourse of shifting power relationships, represented by a complicated, self-contradicting
language.

Through this formula we can understand what transpires
when we as readers today approach baroque colonial prose.
The doubt created by a fluctuating discourse echoes through
our own reading, undermining whatever sense of security we
may seek in static categorizations. Moving beyond an uncom-
fortable feeling of shifting ground to more stable territory requires a qualitative leap: the acceptance of the synthetic,
polyphonic narrative itself, with all its inherent contradictions.
The crosscurrents of varying discourses that rely on many models produce a heterogeneous historiographical narrative defying simple definition. It is this defiance that makes the work so
difficult and elusive for today's reader. Yet the resistance to set
types is also where we may locate a criollo discourse of history,
a rewriting of the events of the Conquest from a New World
perspective that does not fit into old categories.

Sigüenza y Góngora thus follows sixteenth-century models
for New World historiography as he writes *Parayso Occidental*,
his own natural and moral history of America. The Convento
de Jesús María and its environs are first placed in a broader historical context; subsequently, the text goes on to discuss the
manner in which the convent was founded, moving from the
universal to the local situation. Sigüenza pulls together his history through archival research, interviews, and eyewitness accounts, including his own. All of this is designed to show how
New Spain, and its criollo convent, fit into the providential plan
that brought Christianity to America via (Old) Spain.

In truly baroque style, the convent and its founding are allegorical representations, as is indicated by the title of the book
itself. This New World Paradise, located in the western Indies,
is not only the repository of chastity and faith, but also a metaphor of divine will in America. As in Sigüenza's *Primavera indiana*, it represents the perfection of a virgin land where the
word of God can be propagated. By the time of Sigüenza's era,
America represented as utopia or Paradise had already become

a commonplace historiographical figure.[10] Through readings of two texts that introduce the body of *Parayso Occidental* to two different audiences, I will show how the criollo text interpreted that figure according to a reformulated concept of the universe and its centers of civilization.

The two preliminary texts – the "Prologo al letor," or prologue to the reader, and the "Dedicatoria" – are directed to Sigüenza's two audiences: the nuns and the king of Spain, respectively. These are two distinctly different discourses, that of a criollo subject of the Crown addressing his sovereign, and that of a member of the male criollo elite addressing a female audience. In the body of *Parayso*, the two combine in the oscillating pattern that constitutes a criollo historiography written from an American perspective, but still fundamentally identified with Spain.

The "Prologo al letor" has achieved a notoriety that the complete *Parayso Occidental* has never enjoyed, for this short text has been used by scholars such as Irving Leonard to prove Sigüenza's distaste for the excesses of baroque style. It furnishes important ammunition for those who would read in Sigüenza the cries of an early scientific rationalist, unable to escape the decadent complication of his era. Another interpretation emerges, however, when the prologue is read in the context of baroque New World historiography. And by taking into account the female audience to which the text is directed, my reading changes the panorama considerably.

Sigüenza's opening statement could not be clearer: "No ha sido otro mi intento en este Libro sino escrivir historia observando en ella sin dispensa alguna sus estrechas leyes" [My only intention in this Book has been to write history, observing without exception its strict rules] (lines 1–2),[11] a reference to his familiarity, as a scholar, with the rhetorical demands of the vehicle he has chosen. The *historia*, as I noted in the previous discussion, was a form of narrative discourse reserved for the educated precisely because of its identification as a branch of rhetoric (the "estrechas leyes"). The theme of a discursive mode privileged by tradition is expanded in lines 2 through 5: "Assi lo hazen quantos despues de haver leydo las antiguas, y modernas con diligencia, hallan ser las que solo se aplauden las que son historias" [All those will do so who, having diligently read both ancient and modern works, find that the only ones worthy of praise are histories]. To ensure that the reader is equally aware of what constitutes such a *historia*, Sigüenza offers a definition – "Es el fin de estas hazer presente lo pasado como fue entonces" [Their goal is to present the past as it was at that time] (lines 5–6) – followed immediately by a comment on the proper way to accomplish this goal: "y si entonces no se exornaron los sucesos humanos con adornos impertinentes de otros asuntos, como puede ser plausible en la historia lo que por no ser en ella à proposito suele causar à los que la leen notable enfado?" [and if at that time human events were not embellished with the impertinent adornments of other subjects, how can things not proper to a history, that often cause readers considerable annoyance, be plausible there either?] (lines 6–9). In this formulation, history and its exigencies of verisimilitude come into direct conflict with superfluous ornamentation that belongs instead to other, less demanding forms of writing, which are the prologue's next focus.

Between lines 9 and 20, Sigüenza differentiates between the three main rhetorical categories of sermon, history, and poetry, noting that although learned quotations are suitable to sermons, and "florido estilo" [flowery style] is proper for poetry, neither will do for *Parayso Occidental* – and not only because of purely rhetorical considerations. For the first time in the prologue the presence of women as subjects and audience emerges: "Y aunque me huviera sido en estremo facil embarazar el texto, y ocupar los margenes de este libro con semejantes cosas, siendo mi asunto el escrivir historia de mugeres par mugeres, claro està que hiziera muy mal en hazerlo assi" [And although it would have been extremely easy for me to encumber the text, and fill the margins of this book with such things, since my purpose here is to write a history of women for women, clearly I would be very wrong in doing so] (lines 17–20). Thus it is the female potential readers of this history who serve as Sigüenza's excuse for an unadorned text, an important point to which I will return later.

This first paragraph, then, establishes Sigüenza's philosophy of historical discourse. The second addresses the parallel issue of style. "Por lo que toca al estilo," states Sigüenza, "gasto en este Libro el que gasto siempre; esto es, el mismo que observo quando converso, quando escrivo, quando predico, assi por que quizàs no pudiera executar lo contrario si lo intentase" [As for matters of style, in this Book I use the same one I always do; that is, the same one I observe when conversing, writing, or sermonizing, perhaps because I could not accomplish the contarary even were I to try] (lines 24–7). A more truthful assertion would be hard to imagine, for *Parayso* does in large part follow Sigüenza's other writings stylistically. But this statement has been understood by various scholars to be a good example of wishful thinking on Sigüenza's part, and an example of his penchant for simplicity (e.g., Leonard 1959, 202).

This evaluation bypasses the question of the complexities endemic to the writing and language of *Parayso Occidental* as a text fully inscribed within the historiographical controversies of the late seventeenth century. As William Nelson (1973) has shown in his study of Renaissance storytelling, all through the sixteenth and seventeenth centuries the distinction between truthful and false narration was a much debated topic (38–72). There were many different lines of thought as to the best way a historian could truly represent the past. European writers of narrative fiction, as opposed to poetry or theater, likewise debated what made their creations different from those of historians, for the limit between one type of work and the other was unclear and subject to interpretation.

According to Renaissance precepts the historian was to report events as they had happened, without distortion, without venturing into the inventions of fictive accounts or poetic license, but how the historian was to do so was not decided. How much a writer could follow ancient models, inventing speeches for heroes and descriptions of battles, was, in particular, a contested subject (Nelson 1973, 40). In the context of Sigüenza's Counter-Reformation, colonial culture, it was even more important to avoid the modes of prose fiction that were prohibited from circulating (with only partial success) by the authorities and the Inquisition. Thus when Sigüenza declares his history to be entirely separate from the adornments of "poetry" – which represents fiction as well – he is abiding by the rhetorical, religious, and legal rules of New Spain in 1684.

But by that time, as I mentioned in the case of Solís, baroque language – which by definition complicated and embroidered plain speech – was also being employed in Spain to present the

events of the past. The tropes of poetry had invaded history
and its telling. Official language in absolutist Spain, and in its
colonial cities, was couched in a stylized rhetoric of ceremony
and strict morality. Thus the relationship of fact and fiction, or
truth and falsehood, in the narrative was even more complex
that it had been in the earlier part of the century. Sigüenza
would bring to this complication his own desire to elevate the
tradition of a criollo New Spain to a level surpassing that of
its Old Spanish metropolis, while still remaining part of the
empire.

Such complexities are seen further in lines 29 to 33, which
offer a satirical sample of late baroque prose – an involved description of a dead woman's appearance – and Sigüenza's tart
commentary: "Escrivir de una difunta. . .y servir todo este cir-
cumloquio para dezir que conservaba despues de muerta los
mismos colores que quando viva, que otra cosa es sino condenar un Autor su libro. . .à que jamàs se lea" [To write this about
a dead woman. . .when all the circumlocution serves just to say
that she maintained the same color dead as when alive, is nothing more than an Author condemning his book. . .never to be
read] (lines 29–36). This is followed by a long list of the typical
figures of baroque style: the vocabulary of the spheres, jewels,
and flowers (lines 38–42). Finally, poetic style is tied together
with history: "y como quiera que no es esto lo que se gasta en
las comunes platicas, debiendo ser el estilo que entonces se usa
el que se debe seguir quando se escriven historias, desde luego
afirmo el que no se hallarà el cathalogo de essas cosas en la presente" [and since this is not the usage of everyday conversation,
which should be the style one should follow when writing histories, naturally I affirm that a catalogue of such things will not
be found in this one] (lines 44–7).

The enumeration of the scorned tropes, clearly a satirical
commentary by the author on the poetry of his day, produces a
text baroque in the sense that its very protest adds on yet another layer of excess detail and paradoxical ornament. Although Sigüenza is at pains to separate his history from
poetry – in consideration of both traditional historical truth
and his female subject and audience – the history will still be
pervaded with baroque style in the writing, and baroque mentality in the balance of discourses employed for different audi-

ences by a criollo historian. Moreover, it cannot be assumed that
Sigüenza identifies normal, everyday conversation with the
"simple and natural," given that even daily interactions in
seventeenth-century New Spain were governed by an elaborate
code of ceremony, particularly among the elite group to which
Sigüenza belonged. What the prologue presents is a statement
critical of bad poetry, but not one that automatically rejects baroque language in all instances.

The writing of history, then, is shown by Sigüenza to exist in
uneasy balance with poetry. What kind of language does he use
to tell the story of his western Paradise? That of historical
truth, which he claims for his work in paragraph three: "En su
verdad, puedo afirmar no haver perdonado para conseguirla
diligencia alguna, leyendo quantos libros impressos podian
contener algo para mi asunto" [As for truthfulness, I can state
that I have left no task undone in order to obtain it, reading all
published books that might contain something for my subject]
(lines 49–51). However, such sources are unreliable, for "todos
necessitan de emmienda" [all are in need of emendation] (line
51). So Sigüenza consults the convent archives themselves,
leading him to boast that "no ay [historia] sino la que aquí se
dirà, sacada de los mismos papeles originales que se escrivieron
etonces, y que refiero en parte" [there is no other history than
the one told here, taken from the same original papers written
at the time, which I mention in part] (lines 54–6).

This is where the gendered character of *Parayso Occidental* becomes vitally significant. The female audience has forced an
abandonment of the usual rhetorical complications and tropes,
including quotations that would display the author's erudition.
At the same time, the inclusion of women's texts – the nuns' life
stories, taken from convent archives – is required for historical
truth. For these reasons *Parayso Occidental* has been understood
as a throwback to hagiographical models rather than as history,
declared to be naively uncritical and deeply enbedded in the
mire of prerational philosophy. In his *Ciencia y religión en el
Siglo XVII*, for instance, Mexican historian Elías Trabulse
(1974) wonders at the apparent contradictions of *Parayso*: "Las
maravillas aquí narradas nos parecerían incompatibles con el
intelecto del autor de la *Libra*, sobre todo cuando él mismo
afirma haber indagado lo suficiente come para considerar vale-

deros los testimonios" [The marvels narrated here would seem to be incompatible with the intellect of the author of the *Libra*, above all since he himself affirms he has done enough research to consider the testimonies truthful] (119).

In Chapter 5 I discuss the models of hagiography and their importance to the nuns' life stories and to the efforts of women telling their own tales. My point here is that *Parayso* is neither medievally pious nor antibaroque in a modern sense. The contradictions noted by Trabulse are what constitute criollo history for a seventeenth-century writer, not at all incompatible with an intellectual whose text attempts to blend the differing discourses of his era: those of religion and state in a colonial society that was rapidly changing. I agree with Trabulse's evaluation of Sigüenza as "un autor entre dos épocas" [an author between two eras], but take issue with the historian's portrait of Sigüenza as a budding empiricist "que. . .pertenece más al futuro que al pasado" [who belongs more to the future than to the past] (31).[12] Sigüenza's research in the convent archive was the same type of research carried out by other American chroniclers, a continuation of the New World historiographical tradition of privileged eyewitness testimony. Moreover, there is no reason to doubt Sigüenza's belief in the religious miracles or visions he relates, marvels that only fueled the identification of New Spain with Paradise.[13]

Because this text must be structured to include women both inside and outside it – both as subject and audience – the configuration of criollo historigraphy is laid bare. The rhetoric of both history and poetry have been reexamined, reevaluated, and rearranged in a pattern that ultimately leaves them in an unsteady balance. The need to reconcile the discourse of history with a female topic and readership exposes with startling clarity the narrative strategies of writing during the Spanish American baroque period. For it is the language of *Parayso Occidental* that reveals its connection with Sigüenza y Góngora's other texts, be they historical, scientific, or poetic. The connection lies in the blending of types of discourse, which in *Parayso* are that of a criollo subject directed to the Spanish king or to his representatives, and that of "everyday conversation," the language of a changing, heterogeneous society. Everyday speech, for a writer such as Sigüenza, meant a baroque language with which he himself wielded the limited power of the criollo establishment, identified with Spain and yet aware of its American difference. The gendered text of *Parayso*, identified with female subjects and readers, demands that the writer make changes in the old models. It shows us how the prose narratives of colonial Spanish America had to expand narrow categories to include their own difference from Europe, even when such expansion was overtly resisted by the author, as in Sigüenza's protests that he followed strict, classical rules of writing.

In his study *El prólogo como género literario*, Alberto Porqueras Mayo notes the permeability of the prologue vis-à-vis the text it precedes. Thus the introduction to a book of poetry takes on lyrical qualities, those of a novel or drama, novelesque or theatrical aspects, respectively. In Sigüenza's prologue, both historical and literary purposes are at work shaping the use of language, just as they will be in the four hundred pages that follow. *Parayso Occidental*, because of its special status as a history "about women and for women" and the doctrinal character of much of the nuns' writing, requires a prologue that will prepare the reader – perhaps a nun herself, or perhaps a man to whom the book's exemplary quality is paramount – for a text that fits no one rhetorical category. Sigüenza here defends his combination of history and women's life stories, elements in the text that will pull the narrative in different directions.

This prologue would fit in the category designated "prólogo doctrinal" by Porqueras Mayo (1957): "El prólogo doctrinal suele acompañar a un libro también doctrinal. . . . De aquí, que los prólogos doctrinales. . .solamente, por lo común, existían adosados a obras de tipo meramente discursivo y no de pura intención literaria" [The doctrinal prologue usually accompanies a doctrinal book. . . . This is why doctrinal prologues . . . usually only existed in connection with works of a solely discursive type, not those of pure literary intent] (116). However, the "prólogo preceptivo" category also describes Sigüenza's text. Its definition reads:

El novelista, el poeta, el dramaturgo. . . . son "creadores" pero su experiencia profesional les vuelve teorizante sobre la novela, la poesía, el teatro. . . . El marco adecuado para expresar sus ideas preceptivas es el prólogo. De aquí, la importancia del material ideológico en general, y preceptivo en particular, que se encuentra en los prólogo. (114)

The novelist, the poet, the playwright. . . . are "creators" but their professional experience makes them theorize about the novel, poetry, the theater. . . . The appropriate framework in which to express their preceptive ideas is the prologue. This is why the ideological material in general, and the preceptive material in particular, that is seen in these prologues is so important.

Sigüenza expands on literary theory as well as history, for to him they are part of the same rhetorical study. Indeed, this prologue is the distillation of Sigüenza y Góngora's poetics, his own system of criollo discourse. The stinging parody of derivative baroque poetry mocks a lack of talent, without rejecting the underlying precepts of seventeenth-century style. The unclassifiable quality of this text in such a rigid scheme as that offered by Porqueras Mayo only points out the limitations of a purely generic, structural analysis, and, in particular, the uselessness of such an approach in colonial textual scholarship. That the prologue is thoroughly permeated with the text, there can be no doubt, but upon examination such a flow between parts of a text must be declared a gratuitous observation. The prologue is not merely permeated with the text: it is text, written by the same author and subject to all the same multiplicities of language as the pages it introduces.

The polemicization of questions of rhetorical style in the prologue results in a caveat to the reader that, paradoxically, warns more by adherance than by avoidance. The paradox is carried through in the larger text as well, in the very architecture of *Parayso Occidental*. There is an important clue in the prologue when Sigüenza writes of "emmienda," which we can read with two different meanings: correction or proposed variation. Sigüenza informs the reader that he has consulted all the sources at his command to ensure the truth, but that "todos necessitan de emmieda" (line 51). By the first definition, error is implied in the sources, thus calling into question their reliability (and enhancing that of *Parayso*). At the same time, by suggesting a variation, "emmienda" makes doubtful the historical truth of Sigüenza's own text. For if the word proposes a variation, an interpretation, a rereading of prior histories, how can the author claim exclusive rights to truth ("no ay [historia] sino la que aqui se dirà" [line 54])? Moreover, the idea of a variation brings up once again visions of the hated and derisory catalog of baroque excess, making us aware of the process of adornment and layering in progress even as Sigüenza denies it. In this manner, baroque language combines with Renaissance historiography in a constantly shifting pattern within the criollo chronicle. This prologue to a baroque history epitomizes the mixture of rhetorical models to be found in the larger history itself, which will both follow and resist the earlier chronicles of conquest that serve as a reference.

Surveying Sigüenza y Góngora's work, we find only one prologue to compare with this one. In most other texts the prologue is omitted entirely (as in *Infortunios de Alonso Ramírez*) or written by someone else (as in *Libra astronómica*). The *Theatro de virtudes políticas*, however, has an extensive, three-part *preludio*, a term that Porqueras Mayo recognizes as synonymous with "prologue" (74). Preludios 1, 2, and 3 address issues that Sigüenza knew were bound to be controversial: his use of indigenous figures on the viceroy's triumphal arch, the idea that Neptune was Noah's great-grandson and progenitor of the Indians, and any implied criticism of the classical representations of Sor Juana's arch that might be inferred from his own, very different approach (*Obras* 1928, 5–39). These preludios are peppered throughout with quotes in Latin from the ancient classics, biblical scripture, patristic writers and Renaissance scholars, along with references to such sixteenth-century chroniclers as Francisco López de Gómara and Bernal Díaz, demonstrating the "encumbering" common to learned histories.

Sigüenza included prologues, then, in two texts that broke established molds for the writing of history: *Parayso Occidental*, with its lack of critical substantiation and its everyday language, and *Theatro de virtudes políticas,* with its inclusion of Aztec deities. In both cases, the prologue serves as an attempt to fill the gap left by the text, that is, an attempt to define and justify its difference. The prologue to *Parayso* offers a display of baroque language to supplement a supposedly unadorned text; the preludios include citations from European sources to back up the Jesuit syncretism elucidated by Octavio Paz in his *Las trampas.*

In the *Theatro*, Sigüenza attempts to incorporate Aztec rulers in his world vision without fundamentally challenging the nature of the narrative. The indigenous presence, although suspiciously heterodox, has a direct parallel in the classical gods celebrated by Sor Juana and in the biblical heroes of the Old Testament. The writer of the *Theatro* can use the models of Renaissance historiography and make them work to his own patriotic ends through the figure of the prince; despite their strangeness, New World names and legends are absorbed into a syncretic view of the universe that operates within learned history. The preludios speak to formal and thematic, rather than rhetorical, changes: "Escollo en que peligrase el acierto pudiera jusgarse de mi idea en la disposicion formal del Arco, que aqui descrivo lo extraordinario, como si apartarse de las trilladas veredas de los Antiguos fuera acercarse al precipicio y al riesgo" [My idea for the formal disposition of the Arch, where I describe extraordinary subjects, may be judged a reef putting prudence into danger, as if to stray from the beaten track of the Ancients were to draw near the risks of a precipice] (12). Even though its topic enters into the murky politics of criollo patriotism, and breaks the mold of classical symbols, the changes at work in the writing of history do not affect the deep structure of the *Theatro*.

It is really in *Parayso Occidental* that the old categories are split wide open, for the female presence requires a more radical rhetorical adjustment. In *Parayso Occidental*, the rhetoric of classic history must change to accommodate the difference of religious heroines, rather than Aztec heroes. What is required for *Parayso* is an expansion of the lofty language of classic history, which focused on male heroes, so that women may be included in the narration. It is Sigüenza's desire to draw his female sources into an American history – a rewriting of the earlier chronicles of Conquest that will make the convent a New World Paradise – that makes both the language and structure of *Parayso Occidental* a baroque text. In the prologue, in the Dedicatoria and in the many-layered narrative voice, baroque style emerges in the service of an interpretation of the Conquest from a criollo perspective. For it is baroque language – the models of poetry – that can include women, rather than the elevated language of classical history. Although Sigüenza may resist the presence of literary language in his history, it must be called on to narrate the allegory he wants to present.

Examining a text of Sigüenza's comparable to *Parayso* in its historical goals such as *Piedad heroyca de don Fernando Cortés* (1693?), it is clear that to narrate the founding of the Hospital de la Inmaculada Concepción de Nuestra Señora – a charitable institution founded by Cortés – no such change in language is noted, or necessary. *Piedad heroyca*, a paean to the conqueror of Mexico and a rewriting of Bernal Díaz's *Historia verdadera*, is another one of Sigüenza y Góngora's fascinating baroque histories. But the telling of Cortés's exploits fits perfectly within the boundaries of Renaissance historiography, as Francisco López de Gómara's 1552 biography had already demonstrated with elegant assurance. Cortés was, after all, a hero and conqueror. Thus, the text can be safely complicated with quotes in Latin, layered with citations from Cortés's will and other sources, such as papal bulls, and still make a claim to succinctness:

Oblíganme ocupaciones continuas *reducir a compendio* en lo que quiero escribir quanto antes me ocupaba en la idea mucho papel: Y assi fuerza que fuese, siendo de magnitud primera el asunto de ello; y no pudiera ser sino assi, quando es su objeto manifestarle al mundo, *reducidas a perfección*, piadosas disposiciones del invencible Marqués del Valle D. Fernando Cortés, cuyas menores acciones seran digno empleo de la Fama mientras durare el mundo, y que sin duda huviera perpetuado la ethnica antigüedad, dibujando con oro de estrellas en el papel del cielo un retrato suyo . . ..(*Piedad* 1960, 1; emphasis added)

My continual tasks oblige me to *reduce to a summary* all I want to write before I take up too much paper with my idea. And so it must be, since my subject is of the first magnitude; it could not be otherwise, when the goal is to demonstrate to the world, *reduced to perfection*, the pious acts of the invincible don Fernando Cortés, Marqués del Valle, whose smallest actions will be a worthy use of Fame for as long as the world exists, and who without a doubt the Gentiles of antiquity would have perpetuated, drawing his portrait with gold stars on a map of the sky . . ..

This perfectly reduced compendium is a far cry from the "emmienda" of *Parayso Occidental*. Here, the brevity of the narrative is presented as an asset to its historicity: a great deal of material has been sifted through in order to come up with a concentrated version of the truth. Both texts are presented as histories, yet their results are widely divergent; indeed, one often noted aspect of a *Parayso Occidental* is its lengthiness. Why the difference in criteria employed for the writing of the two texts? Why should so much excess material make *Parayso Occidental* more of a history, when the paring down of *Piedad heroyca* can claim the same achievement?

To answer this question, I must first pose another: Who is the author of *Parayso Occidental?* In the Introduction I described the text's division into books, or Libros, and the concerns each one addresses. The case Sigüenza makes for these three Libros as the one true history of the Convento de Jesús María, an assertion based on exhaustive scholarship and substantiation by witnesses, is set out in the prologue. If the three taken together as a single corpus are to be considered, then Sigüenza y Góngora emerges as the person who has united them, and he is also the architect of the entire book's structure. But on another level, that of the individual Libros, the authorship of *Parayso Occidental* is not so obvious.

Sigüenza, in his quest for truth, has included texts that are not his own. Indeed, without such a guarantee of truthfulness, his very role as historian would be called into question, and *Parayso Occidental* would not so readily be identified with the rules of history. Yet Sigüenza's authorial relationship to the nuns he writes about is unclear, and deliberately so. Time and again he interrupts the narrative to reclaim authority, to exercise his control as researcher, scholar, and editor, not only of the sisters but of their confessors as well. In a vein similar to the conclusion of Sigüenza's 1690 text *Infortunios de Alonso Ramírez* – which is another life story retold – the writers of these various vidas are not permitted to narrate their own stories. Rather, Sigüenza always intercedes, his own "I" offering commentary that is at times moral but often stylistic as well.

For example, the first chapter of the second Libro states: "Este Libro. . .se compondrà de lo que el buen licenciado. . .sin mètodo, ni estilo escrivio en el suyo, añadiendo lo que, o por tradicion, o por relacion de las que conocieron a la Venerable Madre se conserve en la memoria de las antiguas Religiosas" [This Libro. . .will be composed of that which the good licentiate. . .without method or style, wrote in his own, adding to it that which, either by tradition, or through the accounts of those who knew the Venerable Madre, is preserved in the memory of the past Nuns] (fol. 52v).[14] But since the convent tradition (presumably an oral one) and the accounts are not noted – since this narration of history is to be simple and un-adorned – the final result is murky. The writing belongs to the nuns and their confessors, but the rewriting – the inscription within history – is Sigüenza's: ultimately, the two cannot be told apart.

In Chapters 3 and 4 I look further at the ways in which Sigüenza manipulated his textual sources, many of which were the life stories of nuns. They were dealt with in different ways with varying results, cited or excerpted according to their position in the historian's overall design. What interests me here is how the text, lacking citations – a less learned scholarly apparatus – is trumpeted as true history because it is unlike embellished baroque poetry. To be truthful, the nuns' texts must be reproduced free of encumbrance, but at the same time everything must be emended by additional commentary, as well as correction of errors. The prohibition against citation, meant to improve the text's historiographical value by simplifying it, removes a critical marker and leaves a text undefinable by rigid European standards.

In a history such as *Piedad heroyca*, the citations, the erudition, and the critical approach function to satisfy at the same time the demands of criollo historiography (a presentation of New World perspective through baroque language) and the requirements of truthful narration. For *Parayso Occidental*, the discourses of Renaissance and criollo historiography, with their conflicting views of the world, must be reconciled in another way. Clearly, the narrative strategies always mentioned in conjunction with this text, that is, its length and unquestioning inclusion of religious visions, are employed by Sigüenza in order to include women while remaining truthful in a classical sense and baroque in structure. The length of the text and the layering of narrative voices stand in for the elevated style omitted by necessity for the female audience. In this manner *Parayso Occidental* can be understood as a colonial baroque narrative, a rewriting of the chronicles of Conquest through the compilation and appropriation of convent sources. Rhetorical tools of the Old World are stretched by Sigüenza to a new limit in *Parayso* in order to accommodate the American reality of a colonial convent, the allegorical Paradise.

A reading of another preliminary text will further demonstrate the path the narrative follows on the road to criollo historiography. The "Dedicatoria" addressed to King Charles II is actually the very first text of *Parayso Occidental*. Its language is certainly fit for a king: given over to the grand gesture, the sweeping assertion, the hyperbolic, and the superlative, none of the self-reflexion or sarcastic parody of the prologue is present here. The style is formal and the grammar impersonal, in contrast with the first-person voice used in the prologue. Whereas the latter speaks directly to rhetorical polemics, the Dedicatoria addresses the subject matter of the convent itself, placing this theme in a broad, indeed, cosmic context. If, in the prologue, the reader of *Parayso Occidental* is to be prepared for a text "about women and for women" and all that qualification implies, the Dedicatoria presents the criollo Convento de Jesús María as one of the crown jewels of the monarch's empire and a glory of the New World.

Yet the two texts have much in common. By manifesting all the problematic features of *Parayso Occidental*, especially its struggle to absorb the female presence of subject and audience into the space of history, both provide lucid commentary on the book that follows. The "Prologo" and the "Dedicatoria" not only address those problems, but suffer from them as well. Their example sets the tone for the larger text, demonstrating the complex criollo discourse of shifting power relationships, of dependency and autonomy.

José Lezama Lima (1957), as I discussed in Chapter 1, was fascinated with Sigüenza y Góngora for his wonderfully imaginative titles alone: "Publica libros cuyo solo título tiene de poema y de simpatía ganada por anticipado" [He publishes books whose mere titles anticipate their poetry and charm] (56). A reading of the Dedicatoria illuminates this history entitled *Parayso Occidental* and shows how that title reveals criollo attitudes toward the Conquest of America, just as the prologue demonstrates an ambivalence toward European rhetorical tradition. In the Dedicatoria, Sigüenza clearly sets out the thoughts, goals, and incentives that have brought him to write about a "western Paradise" planted within the cloister of a colonial nunnery.

That Sigüenza y Góngora meant "Paradise" in a biblical sense – the terrestrial Paradise, the Garden of Eden – is evident immediately in his reference to "aquel delicioso Parayso, con que en las niñezes del mundo se engrandeciò el Oriente" [that delicious Paradise, with which the East was exalted in the infancy of the world] (lines 3–4).[15] The story of the Fall is recounted in this first paragraph with four vivid strokes. The original Paradise "se componia de lo que experimentò la voracidad del tiempo por vegetable" [was made up of that which, because it was immature, experienced the voracities of time] (lines 5–6), and was the scene where "triunfò de la original pureza la primera culpa" [the first sin triumphed over original purity] (lines 8–9). In addition, this imperfect garden provided a place in which "conducidos de la inobedencia se enseñorearon de la humana naturaleza todos los vicios" [the vices, driven by disobedience, became the masters of human nature] (lines 10–11), and finally, when sin had won out, "de aquel desterrò un Cherubin à una sola muger, que lo habitaba, por delinquente" [a Cherub exiled the only woman who inhabited it for her delinquency] (lines 12–13).

Contrasted with this capsule summary of the fall from grace as related in Genesis is the Convento Real de Jesús María, which meets and surpasses Eden on all counts. Rather than "lo vegetable," the convent "se forma de flores, que se han de immortalizar por racionales" [is made of flowers which will be immortalized for their rationality] (lines 6–7), and within its walls "tiene pacifica habitacion la divina gracia" [divine grace inhabits peacefully] (line 9), untroubled by evil. As for human nature, "la reducen à su ser primitivo las virtudes todas" [all the virtues reduce it to a primitive state] (lines 11–12), while the female inhabitants, "innumerables Virgenes" [inumerable Virgins], "viven como Serafines abrazadas en el amor de su Esposo" [live like Seraphim embraced by the love of their Bridegroom] (lines 13–15).

Thus does Sigüenza set up his western Paradise. It is, however, not only of the nunnery that he sings, moving into the second paragraph. The nuns bring honor to their own abode, but more important, to the monarchy and the empire, for they represent the triumph of the Conquest and the conversion of the infidel. God had caused this to be so in the days of the Austrian monarchs – "entregò las sombras de este Ocaso à sus triunfantes armas" [he delivered the shadows of this West to his triumphant arms] (lines 21–2) – and Philip II repaid the debt "no con otra cosa que con empeñarse en debelar perfectamente las sombras de la infidelidad, con que se infamaban estas provincias desde su antiguo origen" [by his insistent efforts to completely defeat the shadows of infidelity that dishonored these provinces from the time of their ancient origin] (lines 25–7).

Whereas the first paragraph retells the story of the original Creation, the third addresses itself to the second genesis, the discovery of the New World. Sigüenza explains why Columbus's ships erred in their course: "Afanandose su discretissimo zelo en que sojusgasen los resplandores del Evangelio à las denegridas tinieblas del gentilismo, equivocò el Ocaso con el Oriente, trasladando quanto havia de claridad en el Oriente al obscuro Ocaso'" [His eager intelligence enthused with the subjugation of the soiled darkness of heathenism by the splendors of the Gospels, he mistook West for East, transferring all the light of the East to the dark West] (lines 32–5). And so that knowledge of God, obtained in the first Paradise and lost through sin, "en esta Occiseptentrional America se convervase estable" [would be kept stable in this occiseptentrional America] (lines 38–9), a New World Paradise – "el mejorado Parayso" [the improved Paradise] (line 41) – was founded and funded.

It was a commonplace in medieval and Renaissance literature to locate the earthly Paradise by means of its biblical description: a garden in the East from which flow four rivers.[16] Indeed, it is to these specifications that Columbus ([1498] 1946) attempts to tailor the land he has discovered, when in his letter of the Third Voyage he tells the Catholic kings: "Tengo sentado en el ánima que allí es el Paraíso Terrenal" [I feel in my soul that the Earthly Paradise is there] (188). The admiral has to bend and twist things around a bit, giving detailed reasons for his definition of river, lake, and sea. Finally, he attributes the whole matter to the mysteries of God, saying that if the body of water he has found "de allí del Paraíso no sale, parece aún mayor maravilla, porque no creo que se sepa en el mundo de río tan grande y tan fondo" [does not flow from Paradise, it is an even greater marvel, for I do not think there is known in all the world such a large, deep river] (184).

When the colonial epic poet Bernardo de Balbuena takes up the theme in *La grandeza mexicana*, he exploits another biblical attribute of Paradise: that of eternal spring. "En este paraíso mexicano," he relates, "todo el año es aquí mayos y abriles, / tiempo agradable, frío comedido, / crielo sereno y claro, aires sutiles" [In this Mexican paradise, the entire year is Mays and Aprils, agreeable weather, a gentle cold, the sky serene and clear, the winds light (Balbuena [1603] 1975, 94). Balbuena expands the wonders of New Spain in a frenzy of sensuous detail, but although his style is baroque, his vision of nature is more akin to that of the Renaissance: it is a beautiful thing to behold and to experience, a manifestation of God on earth.

Sigüenza y Góngora's *Parayso* depicts a truly baroque garden, where light and shadow have replaced, through metaphorical representation, the trees of life and knowledge. This is a garden of the soul in which nature, both plant and animal, must be controlled and suppressed. In Eden, "lo vegetable," that is, an immaturity subject to temptation and corruption, causes the Fall. The flowers that form the occidental Paradise – nuns in their habits of black and white – are rational ones. In them, divine grace triumphs and human nature is kept strictly in check by virtue. Nature becomes the enemy in a garden of pleasure and color, and the *locus amoenus* of classical and Renaissance imagery is no more; in its place we have the landscape of baroque *conceptismo*, owing as much to Calderón as to Góngora.

Perhaps the best comparison to Sigüenza's paradise would be the terrain explored by thought and reason in Sor Juana's "Primero Sueño," which was written some time before 1691. Here too the primary motif is the contrast of light and darkness, represented by day and night. As Sor Juana's flight of understanding takes place in a dream and is dispelled upon awakening – thereby turning around the usual association of knowledge with light – so too does Sigüenza invert the sixteenth-century garden by making it one of artifice and abstraction rather than fauna and flora.

At the same time, a geographical inversion occurs, for Paradise is no longer east, but west. Columbus, approaching what he took to be India, thought his new Paradise was situated in the East. His conception of the world, of course, was based on a world map with Europe at its center. As Edward Said (1978) observes in his study on Orientalism, Christianity finalized the setting up of two Orients, Near and Far (58). The Near Orient was a land one could return to; it was already known through military campaigns and the Bible. The Far Orient was the mysterious East; representing the entirely new, it was unknown and unexplored, the *oriente* of Columbus's new earthly Paradise. Sigüenza y Góngora shared this double view, for his East was not only that of Eden, but also the China and Japan of *Oriental planeta evangélico*, his epic poem praising San Francisco Javier's mission to those countries. To a seventeenth-century criollo, the world center was still Europe.

However, a difference in orientation was inescapable, for intellectuals such as Sigüenza knew they were natives of neither center, nor East, but of a West with no Christian past. Their very existence was an excess, unplanned and unforeseen, a case of geographic overkill. The *barroco de Indias* heaped excess upon excess, carrying to extremes what the Europeans had begun. Thus the conceit of *ocaso* [West] and *oriente* [East], of shadow and light – used throughout Hispanic baroque writing – here takes on new meaning. The East is not only the source of clarity, revelation, and Christianity: it is a conquering power that moves westward to banish darkness and convert the heathen. Seen from the criollo perspective, Europe itself – the Old World – becomes the East. At this point in the text, the Conquest occurs, predicated on confusion – "equivocò el Ocaso con el Oriente" [he mistook West for East] (line 34) – and it effectively causes a major upheaval in the balance of power, "trasladando quanto havia de claridad en el Oriente al obscuro Ocaso" [transferring all the light of the East to the dark West] (lines 34–5). Upon its conversion to Christianity, West becomes East and is able to "blazonarse Oriente" [emblazon itself as the East] (line 44).

The colonization of the Indies altered global relationships for all time by adding another hemisphere to the map. Sigüenza y Góngora operated in a universe of overlapping spheres: New and Old Worlds, New and Old Spains, Aztec gods and church fathers, neoscholastic doctrine and Cartesian rationalism. East and West blurred where the spheres met; in *Parayso Occidental* they do so in the garden of the convent. The two elements of the title reflect baroque concepts of nature and geography, which amount to inversions of what preceded them in the more harmonious Renaissance. The criollo perspective undermines European concepts of cosmic order, while at the same time it attempts to integrate them into another sort of structure that emerges as the very unstabilized text we read.

There is another dimension to this text that ties together the many strands of meaning and makes sense of them. Sigüenza's New World Paradise, the representation of Christianity and light triumphant over the darkness of the infidel, is located within the walls of a convent. This garden is inhabited not by one lone, delinquent woman, but by inumerable females, brides of Christ all. An important contradiction poses itself: How can women both lose and regain Paradise? How can they be responsible for two such opposite outcomes in the story of humanity on earth? Sigüenza seems to have recognized this issue as a problematic one, for in lines 43–50 is his disclaimer: "Las primeras luzes de la Fè" [The first lights of faith], which have caused West to become East, have not come out of this particular Paradise, he writes, "por ser funcion que solo fia la Iglesia Catholica à varoniles animos" [since that is a function the Catholic Church entrusts only to male souls]. Nevertheless, the convent is the place where "se recabò, y recaba de el Altissimo el que ilumine con los resplandores de su noticia, y mantenga en el conocimiento de su divinidad à las nuevas gentes" [the highest Lord was, and is, entreated to illuminate the new peoples with the splendors of His news, and to maintain their knowledge of His divinity] (lines 47–9). In addition, from the cloister "con exercicios santos se le solicitan, y consiguen à la Española Monarquia felicidades, y duraciones" [continuance and joy are sought and obtained for the Spanish Monarchy through holy exercises] (lines 49–51).

Despite Sigüenza's attempted reconciliation, the relationship between the biblical account of Eden and the chronicle of its Mexican counterpart remains uneasy. The dilemma becomes even more acute when, three separate times in the text, the Convento Real is declared to surpass its forerunner. From its very foundation it was superior: "mejorando en el su magnificencia aquel delicioso Parayso, con que en las niñezes del mundo se engrandeciò el Oriente" [bettering in its magnificence that delicious Paradise, with which the East was exalted in the infancy of the world] (lines 2–4). After the four-point comparison, when the convent has been demonstrated to better Eden, Sigüenza refers to the virgins of the occidental Paradise in the following way: "Mejoras son estas, que, en parangon de el Oriental Parayso, no solo le grangean al Occidental del Convento Real de Jesus Maria antelaciones bastantes, sino que tambien le forman à los gloriosissimos progenitores de Vuestra Magestad panegyricos, que desde oy llevarà la immortal Fama de gente en gente" [In comparison with the Oriental Paradise, they are better, for not only do they obtain much prominence for the Occidental Convento de Jesús María, they also form a panegyric to the most glorious progenitors of Your Majesty, that from this day forward immortal Fame will carry from one people to another] (lines 16–20). And finally, after establishing the parallel between the Creation and the Conquest, the orthodoxy of faith in the formerly pagan West must be assured: "Por preciso tubo el prudentissimo Rey ilustrar su Imperial Metropoli de el nuevo mundo con el mejorado Parayso" [The most prudent King felt it necessary to enlighten the Imperial Metropolis of the new world with a better Paradise] (lines 39–41).

The convent is not only equal to Eden, it is better. West not only becomes East, it surpasses it. There is a final inversion inherent in the concept of Paradise within a community of women, and specifically a community of nuns. For rather than relying on innocence, the occidental Paradise is founded on virginity, on the conscious suppression of desire. Much as the plants in this garden are controlled and rational, so are the bodies and natures of the women who inhabit it. Planting a better Paradise in a convent supposes an essential dichotomy in female sexuality, the vision of woman as either virgin or temptress. If Eve lost the original Paradise, Mary will regain it in the New World, and in so doing will elevate it to a higher level, beyond the corruptions of the flesh.

The preservation of virginity and the conquest of nature is a metaphor for the Conquest of the New World. Light and the East move in to displace shadow and the West; Christianity defeats its heathen enemies; and Eden is transformed into a garden of purity. In true baroque fashion, the innocence of the women in the occidental Paradise is artificial, even excessive. As Sigüenza notes later, in the second chapter of the first Libro, the convent was founded for those "que anhelaban con fervorosas ansias por consagrarse a la divina Magestad en virginal holocausto" [who desired with feverish anxiety to consecrate themselves to the divine Majesty in a virginal holocaust] (fol. 5v).

The opening chapter of *Parayso Occidental* develops further, through the theme of virginity, the syncretic idea of pre-Conquest Mexico as a land with direct parallels to Western history. This chapter is entitled "Refierese el modo con que en el tiempo de su gentilidad consagraban los Mexicanos, a sus Vestales Virgines" [In which is mentioned the ways in which the Mexicans consecrated their Vestal Virgins in heathen times] (fol. 1v). Here, the indigenous virgins of the Mexican, or Aztec, temples are considered as equals to their Roman cousins. Sigüenza, realizing the shock this was likely to provoke in conservative readers, explains that since virginity is a virtue "tan en estremo excelente, no es indignidad en las Christianas narraciones ilustrarlas aun con exemplos gentilicos, siendo los que se hallaron en estas Naciones Occi–Septentrionales, dignos de perpetuidad en la comuna estima" [so extremely excellent, that it is not an indignity for a Christian narrative to be illustrated with heathen examples, being that those found in these Occi-septentrional Nations are commonly esteemed to be worthy of perpetuity] (fol. 1v).

"Perptuity," of course, means written history. This inclusion of Indian vestal virgins in such a history is accomplished by basing their worth on two factors. The first is the didactic: the story of these pure young women should serve to inspire its readers. And, once again, Sigüenza presents a disclaimer (and example) of baroque excess:

Y aunque la excelencia del estado Virginal, tiene sobrada recomendacion en lo intrinseco de su bondad, sin que se le de nuevo valor a lo estimade [sic] sus quilates con los adornos postizos; con todo parece que excitando las personas, que lo professan, con los antiguos exemplos, es suavizarles lo arduo de lo que emprenden. (fol. 1v)

And although the excellence of the Virginal state has more than sufficient recommendation is its intrinsic goodness, without giving more value to its estimable worth with false adornments, even so it seems that to excite the persons who profess it with ancient examples is a way to ease the arduousness of what they have undertaken.

The "false adornments" of this text, descriptions of the lives of indigenous girls, can be justified because the audience – also female – will learn from the example. The historical value makes the story more than a mere embellishment, but, once again, the protest itself plants a seed of doubt, especially when it is repeated a few pages later: "Puede server esta veridica narracion no tanto de adorno con que se ilustre mi Historia, quanto de estimulo eficacissimo para avivar el espiritu" [This veridical narration may serve not so much as an adornment to illustrate my history, as a most effective stimulus to enliven the spirit] (fol. 4v). The criollo narrative that aspires to be a history denies inventive language, while at the same time demonstrating it.

By placing Mexican vestal virgins in the opening chapter of a book lauding a convent founded for the descendents of the European conquerors, Sigüenza y Góngora makes a conscious statement about his estimation of pre-Christian Mexico: it occupies a place in the history of New Spain equal to that of Rome for the Europeans. "Antigua historia" [ancient history] (fol. 1v) is redefined as seen from the American perspective, and this is the second reason why the virgins are admitted to perpetuity: they provide an even better example than the foreign Romans do. Sigüenza asserts: "Y si hasta agora al repetido exemplo de las Vestales Romanas le conmovian los animos piadosos de las Christianas Doncellas, no se yo porque no ha de ser mas eficaz, y activo el que aqui he propuesto" [And if up to now the pious souls of Christian Maidens have been moved by the repeated example of Roman Vestals, I do not see why the example I have proposed here should not be more effective] (fol. 4v). Following this is a patriotic statement typical of Sigüenza's criollo sentiments, in which the writer avers that it is the domestic character of Mexican virgins that has caused their low standing relative to the Roman variety, "como si la bondad de las cosas no la distribuyese Dios indefinitamente a todas las partes donde llego su poder" [as if God had not distributed the goodness of things without limits, to all places where his power reached] (fol. 5r).[17]

Superficially, then, as an "adornment," the syncretism here is performed by drawing a parallel between East and West, and between two pagan cultures. Indeed, by appropriating the Roman reference of "Vestales" and applying it to Mexican priestesses, Sigüenza creates the hybrid "Doncellas." However, the underpinnings of this combination, the historical evidence on which it is based, suggest something else. The heart of this chapter is Sigüenza's transcription of a selection from the manuscripts of Fernando de Alva Ixtlilxochitl, the early seventeenth-century historian and descendent of Texcocan nobility whose papers Sigüenza had acquired in the 1670s.[18] Introducing his source, Sigüenza makes this declaration: "La oracion siguiente, que se halla entre las que de boca de los Antiguos conservo en sus Manuscritos el Ciceron de la lengua Mexicana D. Fernando de Alva, la cual referirè con las mismas palabras, que la tradujo por corresponder a las originales con propriedad muy precissa" [The following oration is found among those that the Cicero of the Mexican language, don Fernando de Alva, preserved in his Manuscripts from the mouths of the Ancients; I will report it using the same words he translated, since they correspond to the originals with a most precise correctness] (fol. 2v).

Thus it is a third-hand text that the reader must accept as fact and as history. Reading this excerpt of Alva Ixtlilxochitl, what immediately stands out is its extremely European language and Catholic theology, as several examples will demonstrate. The Vicario [vicar], presiding over the ceremony of initiation, tells the eight-year-old girl about to enter the temple: "En el dia de tu nacimiento votaron tus Padres tu asistencia en este lugar de espinas, y de dolores, para que en el estes, y vivas, pidiendo al Criador de todas las cosas, te dè de sus bienes" [On the day of your birth, your parents vowed your attendence in this place of thorns and pain, so that you may live here, petitioning the Creator of all things to give you His goodness] (fol. 3r). Then, in a most baroque oxymoron, he explains that "con este presupuesto, determinese desde agora tu coraçon a sufrir con alegria, la hambre de los ayunos" [with this assumption, your heart must decide from now on to suffer with joy the hunger of fasting] (fol. 3r). Finally, he issues a terrible warning against trangression:

Y quando llegares a la edad en que la sangre se enciende, mira Hija muy preciosa, como cuydas de tu pureza, pues solo con que tengas deseo de pecar, ya abràs pecado, y por esso seràs privada de tu buena fortuna, y castigada rigurosamente con que tus carnes se pudran. (Fol. 3r)

And when you reach the age when your blood is on fire, precious Daughter, watch carefully how you guard your purity, for just by having the desire to sin you will have already sinned, and for that your good fortune will be taken away, and you will be punished rigorously so your flesh may rot.

Sigüenza follows with his own description of daily life in the temple, all the while emphasizing the sacrificial nature of a life thus dedicated to religious service. Although the decoration of this chapter of *Parayso Occidental* with a detail from the Aztec period relocates ancient American history back to its own soil, the real historical synthesis occurs between Indian and criollo nuns. This chapter is Sigüenza's baroque, Jesuit interpretation of Alva Ixtlilxochitl's Christian interpretation of indigenous life. Comparing the facts as Sigüenza tells them with the 1590 *Historia natural y moral de las Indias* by another Jesuit, Joseph de Acosta, we find more or less the same data, although Acosta says the girls entered the temple for a space of only one year, between the ages of twelve and thirteen (240–4). Sigüenza's narrative version is much more passionately related, its hyperbole befitting a baroque history.

Interestingly, these Aztec keepers of the flame do offer a much truer example for the criollas of New Spain than could the vestal virgins of Rome. The latter were highly prestigious members of Roman society whose vow of chastity was linked to the maintenance of their autonomy and political power. Later, Christian commentators ascribed ascetic motives to classical requirements of virginity, but pagan priestesses were not consecrated as such for moral reasons.[19] The philosophy behind the Aztec practice is unclear from Acosta's description, but although the Mexican virgins practiced penitence, mortification of the flesh, and poverty, their main purpose was to serve the gods by keeping the temple clean and the idols fed. After their period of service, as noted by both Sigüenza and Acosta, the women were married off by their families. But even if the ideology for demanding the preservation of purity was divergent, the way of life in the Indian convent was similar enough to that of the Criollo institution to make the parallel plausible.

Thus this first chapter of *Parayso* is an excellent example of the manner in which a criollo history attempts the management of several discourses. The discourse of history must be dealt with by proffering evidence, which in this case means Alva Ixtlilxochitl's manuscript rather than Acosta's *Historia natural*, a source Sigüenza certainly knew. Perhaps he felt that the descendent of Indian nobles offered a truer picture of indigenous life than the Jesuit priest could, or that Alva's description was more complete. Whatever Sigüenza's rationale, the text makes a clear choice on the side of complication, in a story greatly embellished with a Christian overlay of detail and moral interpretation. The drama and passion of baroque language is better served by Alva than Acosta. At the same time, Sigüenza uses the presence of women in the history to advantage, by transforming the Convento de Jesús María into a New World Paradise that stands as a symbol of the conquest of sin and paganism. In the text, this is accomplished through the fusion of two American convents, the Mexican and the criollo.

The Convento de Jesús María was founded to house the penniless daughters and granddaughters of the Spanish conquistadors, women without the money to pay the dowry required to enter a religious order. Until a cloister was set up especially for them, such colonial women were destined to lives of misery and unhappy marriages, or sin in the eyes of the church. Indeed, the sources used by Sigüenza y Góngora in the second and third Libros of *Parayso* document life histories whose protagonists are like picaresque characters, moving from husband to husband (rather than master to master) until finally gaining redemption as brides of Christ. In a very material way the metaphor of Conquest became reality: bodies that usually would have been sold to the highest bidder because of economic necessity were ransomed for God and placed in a controlled environment where their purity was assured.[20]

In the case of *Parayso Occidental* the metaphor of Conquest extends from the sexual to the textual. Sigüenza y Góngora has appropriated the writings of the sisters and called them his own – "los. . .refiero en parte" ("Prologo," lines 55–6) – and, more important, literary history has evaluated them on this basis. Without acknowledging the female presence of author, subject, and audience in *Parayso Occidental*, this work cannot be analyzed effectively, for the text's baroque variation on Renaissance historiography is to be found in the changes made to include women. Ignoring the crucial role played by women both inside and outside *Parayso Occidental* has caused this text to be considered antibaroque, a misreading of criollo historiography. At the same time, examples of colonial women's writing have been buried and ignored.

Recognizing the female presence in *Parayso Occidental* makes possible an analysis of the text from two perspectives: that of the historiographical rhetoric of the Indies and that of women writers/readers. The former has, by now, been sufficiently drawn out to enable me to pose one more question: What is a criollo classic? That is, what are the sources, authorities, texts, and examples on which seventeenth-century historiography in New Spain models its practice?[21]

Defining a criollo classic defines the essence of the *barroco de Indias*, for it is the baroque that reinvents the classics. Indeed, to establish a meaning for "classic" in seventeenth-century colonial Mexico is to explain why this writing is baroque at all. It maps out the difference of baroque American-style, that is, how *de Indias* changes the essential component of the text to fit its New World existence. Criollo baroque historiography, exhibiting simultaneous impulses to European truth and excessive embellishment, moves between the discourses of colonial subjectivity and growing autonomy with a constant ambivalence as it refers back to classic texts.

In reading through Sigüenza's works, the establishment of a canon of classics seems like a fairly easy task to accomplish. In *Theatro de virtudes políticas*, in *Libra astronómica*, in *Piedad heroyca*, all the references are there before us. Indeed, Sigüenza's works are thought to be characterized by this ponderous, erudite style, considered critically enlightened by some readers and frivolously baroque by others. The standard authorities are summoned for evidence on all matters historical, stylistic, moral, and religious. In the *Theatro* the ancients of Greece and Rome such as Euripides, Ovid, and Seneca are quoted liberally and in Latin. There are references from both the Old and New Testaments, as when Genesis is used to substantiate the claim for Neptune's kinship to Noah (*Theatro de virtudes* [1680] 1928, 25). The church fathers, especially Augustine, and the thinkers of the Renaissance are represented in force. Sometimes all these references are presented together, with a baroque insistence:

Confiesso con ingenuidad despues de lo que aqui é discurido, ser verdaderissima la asercion de Horacio lib.2 Epist.2. *Non omnes eadem mirantur, amantque.* Y mucho mas indubitable la de S. Ambrosio lib.7 Epist.40 ad Sabin. . . . Conque poniendome parte de la razon, no dudo el que no faltara quien se desagrade de lo que para mi tengo por bueno, como dixo con discrecion juyziosa Sidonio Apolinar lib.9 Epist. II. . . . pero no por esse dexaré de dezir con Sedulio Epist.ad Macedon. citado como el de arriba. (20)

I admit, following what I have discussed here, that the assertion of Horace in book 2, Epistle 2, *non omnes eadem mirantur, amantque*, is totally true. And even more undoubtedly that of Saint Ambrose, book 7, Epistle 40 ad sabin. . . . Therefore, taking the side of reason, I do not doubt that there will be those who will be displeased by that which I hold as good, as was said with discrete judgment by Sidonio Apolinar, book 9, Epistle 2 . . .but not because of this will I fail to state with Sedulio Epistle ad Macedon, as cited above.

José Gaos (1959), in his presentation of *Libra astronómica*, notes:

Los autores citados en la *Libra* son casi dos centenares. . . . Los hay citados como autoridades específicas en temas como los de los monstruos, la edad del mundo, la ciencia de Adán y los patriarcas. Los hay citados como recurso literario o polémico o como autoridades acerca de la polémica misma o del tema de la autoridad.(xv)

There are almost two hundred authors cited in the *Libra*. . . . Some are cited as authorities on specific topics such as monsters, the age of the world, the science of Adam, and the patristics. Some are cited as a literary or polemical device, or as authorities on the polemic itself or on the topic of authority.

This gives a perfect idea of the excessive, obsessive quality of Sigüenza's citations and an example of why his works have the reputation of being tedious and boring to read.

However, there is another set of classics present in the texts of Següenza y Góngora: the sixteenth-century chronicles and histories of the New World. The references Sigüenza makes to the chronicles are sometimes noted and sometimes left unmentioned, but they are always there as an undercurrent of classicism, an essential element of the text, a subtext that Sigüenza strives to rewrite. The sixteenth-century chronicles provide the essence that the seventeenth-century baroque of the criollo needs to exist in a tradition of written history. The prose of the *barroco de Indias* puts the chronicles of discovery into action through its complicated, ambivalent discourse, makes them real, and adds life to what, by the late 1600s, had become classic and dead. It shifts the geographical West to the New World.

Chapter 4 in the *Theatro*, for example, exalts the virtue of hope in a ruler as personified in the figure of Acamapich, the first Mexican king. Acamapich is portrayed on the triumphal arch handing bamboo stalks to Hope ("Acamapich" means *cañas*, or stalks). The stalks signify those used to construct the first huts and temples of the Aztec center, Tenochtitlan. Sigüenza, making a characteristically syncretic leap, remarks that he is reminded of the bamboo tree of the biblical Seth, supposedly still extant in the fourteenth century. He continues:

Acuerdome, digo, porque me persuado han de competir duraciones con ella [la caña de Seth] las que dieron principio a México, y mas haviendola promovido el comun cuydado a la grandeza presente (que en algun tiempo será assumpto en que se remonte mi pluma) de que dizen mucho, aunque siempre quedan en ello cortos, varios Autores que pudiera citar en prolija serie. (*Theatro de virtudes* [1680], 1928 82)

I am reminded of it [the bamboo tree of Seth], I say, because I am persuaded that its duration will be matched by that of the stalks with which the city of Mexico was begun, even more so because of the general effort that has brought the city to its present greatness (which someday will be a subject for my pen), about which various authors whom I could cite in abudant succession say much, although never enough.

Among these works subsequently mentioned are those by the historians Juan Torquemada and Antonio de Herrera, and Bernardo de Balbuena's epic *Grandeza mexicana*.

Sigüenza must elaborate on these authors because to him their works lack vitality. By the standards of the baroque, even the frenzy of *Grandeza mexicana* is too classic, too cold, too lifeless. The sixteenth-century epics, chronicles, and histories were written by Spaniards who had come to the New World as soldiers, priests, or representatives of the king; the criollo text, with its added measures of complication and excess, departs from another reality altogether. The *barroco de Indias* inverts the classic chronicles, making east into west, embroidering and gilding the historical discourse of the sixteenth century in order for it to exist in baroque America.

In *Piedad heroyca*, Sigüenza y Góngora's text performs a complex maneuver that could be taken as archetypal for the classic-into-baroque strategy of historiography that I propose. The immediately "classical" reference here is Bernal Díaz del Castillo's *Historia verdadera*, which is criticized soundly, its author cited as Cortés's "mal contento Coronista" [malcontent chronicler] (*Piedad heroyca* 1960, 4). Díaz del Castillo is not the only one whose head rolls under Sigüenza's axe; all historians who did not give Cortés due credit for establishing the Hospital de la Inmaculada Concepción are taken equally to task.

Jaime Delgado (1960) asserts in the introduction to his edition of *Piedad heroyca*: "La Historia trata, en consecuencia, de dar a conocer objetivamente lo que aconteció en el pasado. Para ello, es necesario reunir la mayor cantidad posible de información documental y que ésta sea fehaciente, de probada veracidad, pues todo dato falso o no comprobado debe rechazarse" [The History consequently attempts to make known objectively that which happened in the past. To do this, it is necessary to gather the greatest possible quantity of documentary information, and for that information to be of proven veracity, because any false or unproven fact should be rejected] (CV). But to read *Piedad heroyca* as an objective history is to miss a crucial point: the motive behind a criollo text written in praise of Cortés, and by extension, of the Conquest. Here, the baroque text takes the colonial classics and examines, judges, and ultimately turns them inside out by using them in the service of criollo claims to power. For in written history, in what will survive in perpetuity as truth, lies power. By embracing Cortés and the power he represents, while employing a baroque discourse to do so, Sigüenza's text ignores Spain as an enduring, dominant presence in America. Making Hernán Cortés the hero of a criollo history converts him into a New World – not a European – figure.

Like all criollo production, however, this outcome is ambivalent at best. The criollo patriot remains allied with the charitable Cortés while conveniently ignoring the violent conqueror. Mexico City is lauded as a place that will last for thousands of years, yet the destruction of Tenochtitlan by the Conquest

is never mentioned. And the use of baroque language as a vehicle for narrating history is scorned, even while the text embraces complication as a way to represent New Spain's reality.
Sigüenza y Góngora's histories do not waver on the cusp of modernity; they are wholly baroque in their tension, contradictions, and ambiguities. The attempt to gain power by rewriting
the chronicles, by inscribing New Spain into Old Spain's history
of triumphant conquest, ultimately remains suspended in a
state of colonized ambivalence, between the discourses of dependency and autonomy.

3

The discourse of paternity

In Chapters 1 and 2 I built a foundation of literary history and theory on which to base my reading of the three Libros comprising *Parayso Occidental*. My object in this chapter is to tell the story of how the story was told, but first a question from the last chapter must be posed once more: Who is the author of *Parayso Occidental*? My previous answer was that although the architecture and design of *Parayso* are Sigüenza y Góngora's, much of the writing, and the oral testimonies, belong to the sisters of the Convento de Jesús María. Or, in more precise terms, the book is Sigüenza's and the vidas are the nuns'.[1] They must be read both together and separately to understand the text we today call *Parayso Occidental*.

The crucial problem for Carlos de Sigüenza y Góngora, criollo historian, is how he will tell the story of a convent, built for the criolla descendants of conquistadors and identified with the criollo elite, while directing his narrative to two different audiences: the Spanish king and the nuns themselves. An appeal is made to the Crown for the convent's continued material support, while a message of orthodox religious ideology and example goes to the female readers. Simultaneously, as a historian and intellectual, Sigüenza has his own agenda in mind: the inscription of *Parayso Occidental* in a tradition of New World historiographical discourse narrated from a criollo perspective. As I show in this chapter and Chapter 4, these numerous goals are often in conflict within the text, and Sigüenza's writing demonstrates how his differing discourses come to an unsteady coexistence. My contention, then, is that in *Parayso Occidental* we have an example of the way in which colonial prose narratives were written. By melding various strategies drawn from historical rhetoric and literary language, Spanish American authors portrayed a New World subjectivity through a writing that lay outside standard boundaries and genres.

Sigüenza's solutions for the resolution of conflicting demands on the text are baroque language, a lack of critical references, and a wealth of excess layering. As I have shown, these strategies are made possible by the presence of women as subjects and audience. The female readers and subjects inside and outside this history justify recourse to less scholarly models, such as mystical tracts or hagiography, but these same sources – the nuns' own texts – are held to be proof of truth and accuracy, as required of a classic history. The contradictions inherent in this approach to historical discourse ultimately challenge its own claim to veracity through what I call criollo historiography: the oscillating, unresolved pattern of language that makes up the text.

Parayso Occidental can be read and approached in at least three different ways. First, as a history written by a criollo during the colonial period, the main question is one of authority. From this angle, the principal story to be told is one of a reconquest of New Spain's history through baroque language, a retelling of the sixteenth-century chronicles of discovery. This is the book, composed of three component Libros, I examine here in Chapter 4. Second, as a narrative history by colonial women, as a collection of the records of women's lives through the nuns' own writing or words, *Parayso Occidental* is largely a text written or narrated by women, and not by Sigüenza. My approach to reading these vidas is different from the way I read Sigüenza's history, and is the topic of Chapter 5. Third, the text we read today through the prism of intervening centuries, belonging neither to Sigüenza y Góngora nor to the sisters of the convent but to ourselves as readers, is one of multiple meanings and ambiguous language. I am interested in those ambiguities and have already mentioned several; they continue to be the basis of my close reading of the text and will be directly addressed in my Epilogue.

I begin this reading of *Parayso* with some formal considerations. The full title of the book reads:

Parayso Occidental,
PLANTADO, Y CULTIVADO
por la liberal benefica mano de los muy Catholicos,
y poderosos Reyes de España Nuestros Señores
en su magnifico Real Convento de

JESUS MARIA de Mexico:
DE CUYA FUNDACION, Y PROGRESSOS,
y de las prodigiosas maravillas, y virtudes, con que exhalando
olor suave de perfeccion, florecieron en su clausura
la V.M. MARINA DE LA CRUZ,
y otras exemplarissimas Religiosas
DA NOTICIA EN ESTE VOLUMEN
D. Carlos de Sigüenza, y Gongora
Presbytero Mexicano.

Parayso Occidental, PLANTED AND CULTIVATED by the liberal
and beneficent hand of the most Catholic and powerful Kings of
Spain, Our Lords, in their magnificent Real Convento de JESUS
MARIA of Mexico City: OF WHOSE FOUNDATION AND
PROGRESS, and prodigious marvels and virtues, with which the Venerable Madre MARINA DE LA CRUZ and other exemplary religious
women, giving off sweet smells of perfection, flowered in its cloister,
don Carlos de Sigüenza y Góngora, Mexican Presbyter, GIVES
NOTICE IN THIS VOLUME.

Clearly set out here is the tripartite division of the history to
follow. Libro Primero (47 folios in length) treats the founding
of the Convento de Jesús María, starting with the chapter on
Aztec "vestal" virgins and continuing on through the inception,
founding, and establishment of the new cloister in 1580. This
first Libro ends with the founding, in 1616, of another convent,
the Convento de San José de Carmelitas Descalzas. The first
discalced Carmelite convent in the viceregal capital, it was begun by several of the nuns of Jesús María, who left their original convent in search of a stricter way of religious poverty and
contemplation as set forth in the reforms of Teresa of Avila,
who was canonized in 1618.

Libro Segundo (80 folios) traces the life of Madre Marina de
la Cruz, mystical visionary and convent reformer. Madre Marina's story is taken from documents left by her confessor, Pedro
de la Mota, and from the writings of her protégée and spiritual
daughter, Inés de la Cruz. Marina lived a full life, complete
with two husbands and a daughter, before entering the cloister.
Sigüenza's history describes both those early years and the ones
spent as a nun in the western Paradise of the Convento de Jesús
María. Libro Segundo ends with several chapters on Marina's
virtues, and with the miracles attributed to her after her death.

The third and final book, Libro Tercero (77 folios), is a potpourri of vidas. The autobiography of Inés de la Cruz, a founder of the discalced Carmelite Convento de San José, occupies the first seven chapters, and Inés's disciple Mariana de la Encarnación is the subject of the following two. Single and double chapter accounts of the lives of various nuns and servants of the convent make up the rest of this Libro to the point of its final five chapters. There, María Antonia de Santo Domingo, a personal friend of Sigüenza's who was instrumental to the writing of *Parayso Occidental,* is awarded four chapters. Lastly, there is the life of a man, Matías de Gámez, chaplain of the convent. This concluding chapter ends *Parayso* with the miracle of Matías's intact and uncorrupted body, disinterred thirty-two years after his death.

Thus, three-fourths of the work's length is concerned with the life stories of Marina and her sisters, with the opening section (Libro Primero) accounting for the other fourth. Together they comprise *Parayso Occidental,* a title undoubtedly invented by Sigüenza for what otherwise is called *La fundación del Convento Real de Jesús María de México.* This more prosaic appellation would be in keeping with other conventual documents of the era for, as Irving Leonard (1929) notes, such chronicles were indeed common (103).

However, although convent chronicles were ubiquitous in the religious seventeenth century, in her 1982 study *Cultura femenina novohispana* the Mexican historian Josefina Muriel remarks that whereas male religious orders regularly published their accounts of institutional foundations, those by nuns saw print only through the interventions of confessors or chaplains. Muriel has done exhaustive archival work on New Spain's convents and their chroniclers, and is very familiar with *Parayso Occidental.* In her view, Sigüenza is one of the few male authors even to acknowledge that his material is taken from the nuns' writings, a difference Muriel ascribes to his great love and admiration for sisters whom he knew personally.

Such a distinction, however, can be better understood by placing Sigüenza's *Parayso* in the context of his other histories. Sigüenza was a professional scholar, scientist, and writer; although he aspired to join the Society of Jesus, he was never ordained and remained a member of the laity until his death. The perspective and training he brought to the writing of *Parayso Occidental* – as evidenced by its poetic title – was that of an intellectual who lived close to the Jesuit order, but not within it.

Although *Parayso* may be categorized with other convent chronicles on the basis of its subject matter, a textual analysis beyond simple description must be carried out against the kind of theoretical and historical background I have developed. Compared with a less learned priest who views the nuns as his spiritual daughters, as brides of Christ who demonstrate the will of God through their sacrificial example, Sigüenza's citation of sources is notable. Contrasted with other erudite histories, and especially other histories of his own, *Parayso* comes out wanting. Sigüenza's affection for the sisters, real as it may have been, cannot serve as an explanation for the complexities of *Parayso Occidental*.

Muriel (1982) substantiated her assertion regarding Sigüenza's devotion to the nuns with a citation from the prologue, stating:

Entre todos los cronistas es éste el que escribe con más amor y respeto por la obra de las mujeres. En desacuerdo con los hombres de su época dice:"no ignoro el que de ordinario las desprecian los varones [sic] ingenios, que son los que cuidan poco de Poliantheas." (46)

Among all the chroniclers, this is the one who writes about the work of women with the most love and respect. In disagreement with the men of his era, he says: "I am aware that ordinarily they are scorned by masculine wits, who care little for Poliantheas."

Here there is a misreading of "las" (in "las desprecian" [they are scorned]) as a reference to women. Sigüenza is actually discussing "mis marginales anotaciones" [my marginal annotations] in this part of the prologue (lines 21–22), and sarcastically commenting that not only female readers, but careless male readers as well, have no need for them. His opinion of women, as expressed here, is a denial of their intellectual capability completely in line with the prevailing attitudes of his era.

The demonstration of the divine blessing afforded the convent surely served as a principal incentive for Sigüenza's writing of *Parayso*, as he affirms throughout the "Dedicatoria," "Prologo," and the first chapter of Libro Primero. But in the first book, by virtue of his position as a criollo educated entirely in the New World, the topic of Providence acquires a whole new dimension. And that is why the convent becomes a western Paradise: Sigüenza wants his history to be Mexican, as well as pious. Such patriotism emerges through explicit references to New Spain's pre-Conquest history (e.g., the Aztec vestals), and in the narrative strategies employed in an attempt to gain authority over the text of the past. I focus now on those strategies at work in the first Libro by examining the narrative voice of authority it presents.

It is in Libro Primero that the voice of Carlos de Sigüenza y Góngora, historian, most clearly emerges. First-person interventions and editorial comments constantly appear to remind the reader of his roles as writer, archivist, and ultimate arbiter in matters historical and stylistic. Chapter 1 begins with one such declaration:

Asuntos, que devieran despreciarse por repetidos, suelen tal vez conseguir la dicha de no vulgares, quando por la singularidad de las circunstancias con que se adornan, no se hazen indignos de los comunes aprecios; y aunque en otros pudieran ser effectos estos de nimio estudio, en mi solo quiero se tengan por consequencia del amor grande que me ha devido mi Patria, quando por averlas elegido por asunto de mis tareas, me hallo bastantemente capaz de sus antiguas historias; razon potissima para que sin valerme de las remotas, y estrañas, pueda ilustrar con aquellas, lo que tuviere necesidad de semejantes apoyos. (fol. 1v)

Topics that should be scorned for their repetitiveness sometimes become, perhaps, happily less vulgar when, because of the singularity of the circumstances adorning them, they become not unworthy of general esteem; and although for others this may be the effect of excessive study, as for me, I want it to be taken as the consequence of the great love I owe to my Country, since I find myself knowledgeable in its ancient histories, having chosen them as the topic of my work; this is the strongest of reasons why I may illustrate with those histories whatever needs such support, without relying on remote or foreign ones.

This is the first example of a type of narrative interruption that will occur again and again in *Parayso Occidental:* that of Sigüenza establishing territorial domain over his discourse through the medium of expertise in indigenous Mexican history. The founding of the convent is thus immediately placed in the realm of that history, rather than in the context of Spanish or other European traditions. By writing about indigenous history – of which he was a recognized master – Sigüenza immediately claims authority for *Parayso* as the one true story of the Convento de Jesús María. Others, as it were, start in medias res: not built on indigenous foundations, they are destined to be incomplete and therefore lacking. This is an aggressive beginning to the criollo account.

Chapter 2 continues in this vein with a comment on the transition from paganism to Christianity: "siendo entonces la populosissima Ciudad de Mexico, el mayor theatro de abominable impiedad: como no havia de ser agora un delicioso Parayso de religion, y virtud?" [the heavily populated city of Mexico being back then the greatest theater of abominable impiety, how could it not now be a delicious Paradise of religion and virtue?] (fol. 5r). The "Parayso" here is not only a convent, but the city of Mexico itself. The histories of both institutions are intertwined and interrelated so completely in this Libro that they merge into one.

Sigüenza goes on to observe that whereas male religious orders were present from the very first, there was in this Paradise a sad paucity of cloisters for female virgins. He has a practical, realistic explanation that announces another aspect of this Libro: its concentration on the material, rather than the spiritual, side of the foundation. This explanation is short and to the point: "Efectos quisas de la novedad de la tierra, cuya poblacion era entonces por lo que mas se miraba" [Perhaps it was due to the newness of the land, whose population was then the greatest concern] (fol. 5v). The European women imported to New Spain were destined to be the wives of conquerors and the mothers of criollos, not the founders of convents.[2]

Skipping over the first fifty years of colonial rule, Sigüenza next introduces us to the two men who carried out the dream of a convent for poor, dowryless women. However, Pedro Tomás de Denia's past was somewhat of a mystery, and here the narrator's voice interjects the first of another type of comment, one that establishes editorial alongside historical authority: "se hallaba avezindado en esta ocasion Pedro Tomas de Denia, hombre à lo que nos podemos persuadir de ajustado proceder, y religiosas costumbres, cuyo origen, y sucesos de su vida, à pesar de la solicitud con que pensè conseguirlos, me los ha negado el tiempo, sin esperança de hallarlos" [Living there at that time was Pedro Tomás de Denia, a man whom we may be persuaded was of correct conduct and religious custom, whose origins and life story have been denied to me by time, with no hope of finding them, in spite of the solicitousness with which I tried to obtain them] (fol. 5v). Here there is a lack of hard data, freely admitted by Sigüenza since he doesn't need it in any case. Later on, the editorials regarding the text remark on too much material rather than too little as Sigüenza picks and chooses from among his sources. The effect of all such authorial asides, however, is similar. Meant to increase confidence in Sigüenza's own methodology, skill, and judgment, they introduce a doubting note of lacking material and cumulatively result in a layering of ghostlike sources that haunt the history but are never cited by name. The text seesaws back and forth from credibility to disbelief, from an excess to a paucity of fact.

The other crucial actor in the story is Pedro Moya de Contreras, the archbishop of Mexico. He is strongly supportive of Pedro Tomás's effort to found "un Monasterio, en que sin dote alguna se les diese el estado de Religiosas à Doncellas nobles Hijas, y Nietas de Conquistadores" [a Monastery where noble Maidens who are Daughters and Granddaughters of Conquistadors may be granted the status of Religious, with no dowry whatsoever] (fol. 6v), and gives permission for fundraising and the subsequent founding. The third chapter continues the laying of a physical groundwork for both the convent and the narrative, as it lists the names of the first group of *capellanas* (the women given dowries) and those of the nuns who became officers, and goes into detail on the subject of the houses that were to be transformed into a cloister.

This history, devoid of the ponderous quotations and allusions that weigh down Sigüenza's other chronicles, is written in well-paced and sometimes vivid prose enlivened with emotion. This can be seen, for example, in the following description of the festivities surrounding the convent's first days:

No son ponderables las avenidas de regocijo con que se inundo la Ciudad, viendo ya perficionada la fundacion de un Convento, que solo se erigia para el remedio de pobres; y para que el aparato exterior fuese indice de lo que havia en los animos, rara fue la casa, que no se coronase aquella noche con luminarias alegres discurriendo por las calles, y lugares publicos una costosa, y lucidissima encamisada, que dispusieron los Cavalleros mosos con magestoso aparato. (fol. 10v)

The flood of joy that innundated the City, seeing the perfected foundation of a Convent raised only for the assistance of the poor, cannot be exaggerated; and so that the exterior pomp would indicate what was in their souls, rare was the house that was not crowned that night with festive lights, and a costly, most splendid procession, running through the streets and public places, was arranged with magestic pomp by the young Gentlemen.

Besides typically baroque hyperbole and a description of colonial ceremony, this passage demonstrates a preoccupation with the conflicts of body and soul, exterior and interior lives, flesh and spirit that also echoes a narrative problem. What should be a book devoted to the religious – in an orthodox sense – from the very beginning has emphasized instead the material, economic foundation of the convent. Sigüenza is well aware of the contradiction, for he begins the first chapter of Libro Segundo: "Ya desde aqui se le previenen à mi pluma mayores vuelos tanto mas sublimes quanto và de lo perecedero a lo perdurable, y de la tierra al cielo" [From here on are forseen for my pen loftier flights, as sublime as the distance between that which perishes and that which endures, and between the earth and the heavens] [fol. 48r). Libro Primero, however, is firmly rooted in worldly soil.

This is a problem related to the question of authority. It is the material, quantitative data Sigüenza finds in the convent archives that he can use to back up claims to truth. The spiritual side leads to a fuzzy area not so readily proven, as is indeed the case with the miracles and mystical visions of the nuns. Teresa of Avila's *Libro de las fundaciones*, to mention a sixteenth-century model for this type of narrative that was important to religious writers such as the nuns, places no such importance on details and lists of names, dates, and documents. In the most literal sense, then, Sigüenza wants his convent history to be grounded on fact.

But like everything else in *Parayso Occidental*, this material scheme has its inversion. Two of the most crucial junctures of Libro Primero, involving the voice of an omniscient narrator, use the physical presence of a body in order to demonstrate the will of divine Providence. The first occurs in chapter 5. Pedro Tomás de Denia has gone to Spain in quest of a *Real Cédula* [royal decree] (fol. 16r) from King Philip II. During his absence, the convent becomes unfit for habitation; it leaks, is easily broken into, and is located in an unsafe, unpopulated area of the city. Archbishop Moya de Contreras, while not wishing to offend Pedro Tomás, decides to approve a move of the cloister to more spacious and sumptuous quarters near the center of the capital. Sigüenza quotes verbatim the prelate's *auto*, or official declaration. The nuns move with all the predictable "indecible alegria" [unspeakable joy] (fol. 14v) accompanying their entry.

Meanwhile, Pedro Tomás spends two years in Spain with no luck in penetrating the state bureaucracy because he lacks the money to bribe greedy officials; as Sigüenza notes, Denia's petitions are sent "al tribunal del olvido" [to the tribunal of oblivion] (fol. 15v). Finally, Denia decides to use his last recourse: a letter written by the archbishop directly to the king, "con advertencia, de que solo entonces la pusiese en [sus reales manos], quando reconociese, no conseguia sus intentos con los papeles restantes" [with the warning that he should only place it in (the royal hands) when he realized he would not obtain what he wanted with other papers] (fol. 15v). Within six days a royal decree is produced, the text of which is also included by Sigüenza. The *cédula* awards royal patronage to the convent explicitly in order that it be a place

que en el se recojan, y remedian, hijas, y nietas de los Descubridores y antiguos Pobladores de essa tierra, pobres, y virtuosas . . . porque nuestra intencion, y deseo siempre ha sido, y es de aumentar en quanto nos fuere posible, el culto divino, y las cosas tocantes à la honra, y servicio de Dios N. Señor. (fol. 16r–v)

in which the poor, virtuous daughters and granddaughters of Discoverers and former Colonizers of that land will be cloistered, and assisted . . . because our intention and desire has always been, and is, to increase public worship and all things having to do with honoring and serving our Lord God, to the extent possible for us.

Sigüenza dutifully and accurately records all this, then, in the name of "Historia," feels compelled to intervene:

Faltara à las leyes de la Historia, si omitiera la enodacion [sic] del misterioso enigma, que contenia la carta del Arcobispo de Mexico, cuya

eficacia recabo en casi solos seis dias, lo que no pudieron tantas in-
formaciones en muchos meses; y mas resultandole de ello al Convento Real de Jesus Maria, su mayor lustre, que es al que unicamente
devo atender en lo que voy escriviendo. (fol. 17v–18r)

I would neglect the laws of History were I to omit to note the mysterious enigma contained in the letter of the Archbishop of Mexico,
whose effectiveness gained in only six days what much more information could not in many months; and even more so, since it resulted in
great luster for the Convento Real de Jesús María, which is the only
thing I should attend to in my writing.

According to Sigüenza, it is doña Michaela de los Angeles, a
young girl who has taken up residence in the convent, who is
the cause of this good fortune. Doña Michaela is the archbishop's niece and she had come to América with him ten years before, in 1572, at the age of two. Her uncle's letter informs the
king of her new home, says Sigüenza y Góngora, "la qual noticia mas que el pretexto, que se refiere en la Cedula, fue el unico
motivo del voluntario empeño, y liberalidad magnifica con que
haziendose especial Patron de este Convento . . . le dono la
Magestad Catholica tan excesiva riqueza" [news of which, more
than the pretext mentioned in the Cédula, was the sole motive
for the voluntary obligation, and magnificent liberality with
which, making himself the special Patron of this Convent . . .
his Catholic Majesty donated to it such excessive riches] (fol.
18r). And who is Michaela, inspiration for this "misterioso
enigma"? According to Sigüenza, she must be the illegitimate
child of Philip II, treated from the start "con mas altos respec-
tos de los que a la nobleça, y merecimientos del Tio se le de-
vian . . . los que no eran sino devidos aprecios à su Real Sangre"
[with greater respect than that owed to her because of the nobility and position of her Uncle . . . respect that was nothing
more than the proper appreciation of her Royal Blood] (fol.
18r).

Thus the voice of the narrator has broken in to clear up a
mystery in the pursuit of truth, yet his explanation hinges on
an absent document, one that is not included here (of course,
we would not expect it to be). The reader is left to wonder just
how Sigüenza obtained his information. Moreover, it turns out
that what we have carefully read, and what Sigüenza has carefully researched, is mere pretext. The text – the real story – is

missing and, as a final blow, it is illegitimate: money comes to the convent, a haven of virtue, only because of the presence of the king's natural child.

The narrator's own explicit goal, another pretext, also marks the hidden text of an implicit agenda. Sigüenza's intervention means to inspire confidence and to fill in the gaps. But the agenda that remains below the surface means to gain authority by reclaiming the convent's history from Spain – i.e, from the chronicles and documents of the Conquest – with a baroque narrative history written in America. The undoing of the convent's surface history, its distortion into a tale of mystery and suspense, adds a layer of doubt and complication to what should be a straightforward account of the convent's foundation. The narrative voice of the author is the vehicle for that distortion.

Chapter 6 follows the political battle that ensues when Pedro Tomás finally returns from Spain in 1585. Finding the convent at a new site, housing wealthy women who have paid hefty dowries, he challenges the archbishop's approval of such changes, using the *cédula* as evidence to support the status quo. Ultimately, however, an *auto* is pronounced in 1587, affirming the convent's right to perpetuity in its second and more comfortable home under the royal protection and patronage of the king.

Chapters 7, 8, 9, and 10 are concerned with the building of a church for the convent, and list the names of its early benefactors and inhabitants. The theme of hard, factual evidence is carried out in these chapters, although not without frequent outbursts of opinion from Sigüenza. When the 1587 *auto* is quoted, for instance, he remarks that "quedando con esto desvaratada la temerosa tempestad, que por espacio de casi dos años havia horrorizado al desvalido Convento" [with this the frightening storm, which had terrified the crippled Convent for almost two years, was routed] (fol. 21r), an example of the way the narrative voice inserts subjective commentary without actually using the first-person "I."

The other reference to a haunting physical presence in Libro Primero is in Chapter 11. This chapter, "Del estado del Convento en lo que mira à lo espiritual" [On the state of the Convent in spiritual matters] (fol. 36v), offers perhaps the clearest, least encumbered example of Sigüenza y Góngora's prose in *Parayso Occidental*. It is a polished, worked piece of rhetoric, carefully structured in oratorial style, displaying all the typically baroque details and tropes of the time. Sentences that become paragraphs, twisted syntax, hyperbole, and strange metaphors form its passages, which address the contrast of the life of the spirit to worldly goods. The theme of *desengaño*, or disillusionment, emerges here as interior lives become "las espirituales fabricas, cimentadas en las piedras solidissimas de las virtudes" [spiritual constructions, cemented on the solid stones of virtue], and exterior things are those which "por materiales, y caducas finalmente sintieron la voracidad de la polilla del tiempo" [because they are material and hollow, in the end feel the voracity of the moths of time] (fol. 36v).

This exchange of qualities follows standard seventeenth-century conceits, but here there is an interesting twist. The convent's dedication to matters spiritual, after a century of existence, is lauded and placed in its historical context: "Y assi era fuerza que fuesse por no ignorarse en la amplitud grande de la Mexicana Republica, haver sido este Monasterio el que desde lo primitivo de su ereccion ha conservado sin diminucion los fervores en que se cimentò" [And so it had to be, so that it would be known throughout the entire Mexican Republic that it was this Monastery which, from the time of its initial erection, had preserved with no loss the fervor upon which it was cemented] (fol. 37v).

It is the last section of this chapter, though, that provides a complex and telling passage to end this discussion of body versus soul:

Puede ser el que muchos tengan por advertencia despreciable, lo que yo justo [sic] circunstancia muy misteriosa; y sin duda lo es, ser la mayor parte del sitio, que oy se ocupa con el Convento (como me consta por escrituras antiguas, y otras memorias) el que despues de la debelacion desta Ciudad se le dio para su vivienda al Capitan Juan de Xaramillo, y a su muger Doña Marina Tenepal, celebre en las Mexicanas historias con el nombre de Malintzin, y con razon, pues por haverle servido a D. Fernando Cortès de fidelissima interprete, no tanto se le facilito la conquista de tantos Reynos, quanto sirvio de medio para que se le aya agregado tan indefinito numero de almas à la Catholica Iglesia: Y si fabricarles casas fue el premio con que les pago Dios à las Gitanas haverles conservado la vida corporal à los Israelitas,

perpetuar para su habitacion la que fue de Doña Marina, seria levan-
tarle padron en ella a su agradable memoria, por el zelo con que
despues de haver professado la Religion Christiana la manifesto por
su lengua a los Mexicanos, para libertarlos de la muerte de la alma a
que los tenia condenados la idolatria. Si ya no es que haviendose
agradado Dios de que aquella huviese dado principio (materialmente)
a la justificacion de los habitadores desta tierra, con sus palabras
quiso que por otras mugeres se continuase esta accion, tanta mas me-
jorada, quanto va de las vozes à las obras, y de la persuasiva à los exemplos con que estas virtuosas Virgines estimulan a todos à no apartarse
de las veredas del Evangelio. (fol. 38v–39r)

Many may consider worthless something I judge without a doubt to
be a most mysterious circumstance; that is, that the greater part of the
location occupied today by the Convent (as is clear to me from old
documents and other writings) is the same as that which was given to
Captain Juan de Jaramillo after the siege of this City, and to his wife
doña Marina Tenepal, celebrated in Mexican history by the name Malintzin; and with good reason, since by serving don Fernando Cortés
as his most faithful interpreter, she not only facilitated the conquest of
many Kingdoms, but moreover served as the medium whereby an infinite number of souls have been joined to the Catholic Church. And
if God rewarded the Gypsy women who saved the bodily lives of the
Israelites by building houses for them, to perpetuate as His dwelling
that of doña Marina would be to raise a monument to her good memory, and to the zeal with which, after professing the Christian religion,
she made it known through her tongue to the Mexicans, in order to
liberate them from the death of the soul to which their idolatry had
condemned them. Or it may be that since God was pleased that this
woman had given a (material) beginning to the redemption of the inhabitants of this land, He wished for other women to continue this
action through His words, by the betterment of voices into works, and
persuasion into the examples with which these virtuous Virgins encourage all people not to stray from the path of the Gospels.

The second mysterious circumstance in *Parayso Occidental* has
much in common with the first, that of doña Michaela's paternity. Once again the vital evidence is missing and all that is offered to the reader as proof are uncited "escrituras antiguas, y
otras memorias." Whereas Michaela's illegitimacy enables the
convent's funding, the relationship of Marina to Cortés underlies its founding in the most literal sense, in the very ground on
which it stands. Marina's sexuality is left unmentioned in this
passage, as she becomes the legal wife of a conquistador and an
exemplary Christian. Her earlier enslavement to and relationship with Cortés (with whom she bore a child), her sexual in-

volvement with the Conquest, is absent. Although her life and her language are presented by Sigüenza as material signs of God's will through both the Conquest and the foundation of the convent, the violent, physical element underlying those two events is left out. We see here only Marina's spiritual self, an image glowing through one hundred and fifty years of colonial rule.

The Convento de Jesús María, symbol not only of divine Providence but also of Spanish Conquest, exists, then, through the agency of two female bodies. Michaela's body, which by its very presence brings fortune and royal status to what otherwise would have been a poor institution, is the fruit of Philip II's infidelity. Marina's body – bought and later given away by Cortés – is that of a woman involved in forced sexual liaisons before her conversion and marriage, but who is held here to be the reason for Mexico's religious salvation. In both instances there is a mystery that remains unsolved, since the sources that would decode it are unnamed. The real text, the body of the story, is not here, and, furthermore, it is written over a backdrop of sin. In this way, what ostensibly buttresses the convent's claims to history and permanence actually weakens those claims. The narrative voice of the criollo historian, attempting to assert his authority over the chronicles of the past, sets loose doubts and opens a Pandora's box of questions that point to the underlying contradictions of his colonial mentality, as he skips over the violent elements of the very Conquest that has brought New Spain into being.

In the case of this finale starring Marina, there are still more ramifications. Modern readers must resist the tendency to see her as *la Malinche* – a woman symbolic of the self-hatred of conquered peoples to postindependence Mexicans – and understand instead the way in which she is depicted in Sigüenza's criollo history: as a heroine. For the seventeenth-century writer, Marina embodies not only religious conversion, but the problematic of his own language as well. The emphasis is placed on the use of words and speech in Sigüenza's interpretation: it is through language that Marina both gains power and abets the conquest of her own people. Criollo writing, caught between the demands of classical, European discourse and that of baroque Spanish America, serves an analogous function in a text such as *Parayso Occidental*. As it shifts from one mode to the other, the battle for authority over the text is both won and lost. History and facts praise the Spaniards and their actions; baroque writing and excess undo those facts by asserting American complication and reality. Marina is a heroine for the criollo writer because she facilitates the Christian conquest and saves Indian souls, using the weapon of her own language.

In his book *The Conquest of America*, Tzvetan Todorov (1985) sees *la Malinche* as the earliest example of a cultural blending that embodies the semiological constraints of all language:

I myself see her . . . as the first example, and thereby the symbol, of the cross-breeding of cultures; she thereby heralds the modern state of Mexico and beyond that, the present state of us all, since if we are not invariable bilingual, we are inevitable bi- or tri-cultural. . . . She adopts the other's ideology and serves it in order to understand her own culture better, as is evidenced by the effectiveness of her conduct (even if "understanding" here means "destroying").

This is a perspective that reads the history of the colonial period through Todorov's own European lens. Marina's acculturation to the ways of the Spaniards surely was the result of a genius for adaptation that she had already exercised in Mayan society during her previous experience of bondage, and an exploitation of her linguistic talent as a tool for survival and personal gain. Todorov's position, equating her role as an accessory to destruction (which he acknowledges) with a subversive understanding of "her own culture" – a simplification in itself of her multicultural world – romanticizes the grim consequences of her actions, which were not unlike those of other Indians who chose the side of the victorious rather than that of the vanquished (such as the family of Sigüenza's admired reference, Alva Ixtlilxochitl). In fact, Sigüenza's criollo colonial ideology makes a similar equation: By using her language to help in the destruction of a heathen religion and save souls through Christian doctrine, Marina served her people via her own linguistic identity.[3]

As a final observation on this rich passage, I note that Marina, an indigenous woman, could not have entered as a full-fledged nun the convent Sigüenza would have her inspire with such pious example. Until the founding of the Convent of Corpus Christi in the eighteenth century, religious profession in colonial convents was reserved for white criollas (some of whom certainly may have had denied Indian ancestry) or peninsular-born Spanish women, although Indians and blacks did inhabit those sheltered precincts as slaves and servants.[4] To place Marina in the position of precursor to criollo nuns is yet another retelling of history, another way in which Sigüenza rewrites the chronicles of the Conquest. "Las vozes" become "las obras" when the words of the Old Testament are realized in the acts of the Gospels, when a classic chronicle is transformed into baroque history, and when West becomes East, even bettering it.

The last two chapters of Libro Primero introduce the thread that runs through the length of *Parayso Occidental*'s narrative and ties together its three separate books. That theme is the founding, not of the Convento de Jesús María, but of the Convento de San José de Carmelitas Descalzas (also known in Mexican history as Santa Teresa la Antigua). San José was the first discalced Carmelite convent to be founded in Mexico City, although a sister institution in Puebla predates it. It seems odd that a history dedicated to one convent would devote such space to another, and Sigüenza, the ever-conscious and omnipresent editor, once again intercedes in anticipation of this anomaly:

La mayor prueba de la bondad del arbol que los produce es la generosidad suavissima de sus frutos: y siendo no menos que el muy observante, y religioso Convento de San Joseph de Carmelitas Descalças de esta Ciudad, el que hasta aqui unicamente a producido el Convento Real de Jesus Maria, ociosas pareceràn las recomendaciones, quando esta, aunque singular, blazona de bastante para su abono. Advirtieronse en su fundacion todos los primores de que se vale la divina providencia en lo mas desesperado de los sucesos humanos; precisos motivos que me obligaran à redimir su noticia del aborrecible olvido, aun quando no me lo pidiera justicia la integridad del contexto desta mi Historia. (fol. 39r–v)

The greatest proof of the goodness of the tree that produces it is the mellow abundance of its fruit: and being that no less than the most religious and observant Convento de San Joseph de Carmelitas Descalzas of this City is the only fruit that the Convento Real de Jesús María has produced up to now, more reasons for praise would seem to be needless, when this one alone boasts enough to its credit. All the capacities upon which divine providence draws, amid the most desperate of human events, were at work in its foundation; motives that necessarily oblige me to redeem its memory from hateful oblivion, even though the integrity of the context of my history might not make such a demand.

When Sigüenza's voice appears in this way, it is like a red flag going up, a signal of an imminent encounter with something new and somewhat tangential to the narrative's flow. Such a signal has been noted already in the cases of chapter 1 (the Aztec virgins), chapter 5 (the story of Michaela), and chapter 11 (the presence of Marina). In each instance there is a protest, but rather than the standard rhetorical device of apology and affected modesty for what is lacking in the history, we find instead an abundance of available information. The following citation from chapter 10, part of a description of the first Mass celebrated in the church of Jesús María, makes this device stunningly evident:

Y si esto es algo de lo mucho, que se admirò la vispera de la fiesta, que pudiera (si la abundancia no me indeterminara la eleccion) dezir del dia! Y que no digera (aunque muchos lo tuvieran por increible) del resto del octavario! Pero mejor es encomendarlo al silencio, porque no se repute por chimerico lo que expresare. (fol. 27r)

And if this is but part of all that astounded one on the eve of the fiesta, what could I say (if abundance did not keep me from making a selection) about the day itself! And what would I say (although many would hold it to be incredible) about the rest of the week-long festival! But better to entrust that to silence, so that what I describe will not be reputed as chimerical.

The very wealth of available detail makes the history run the risk of appearing false and chimerical, and so is relegated to silence – but, of course, it has already been introduced into the narrative through the protest. This is a clever way to establish the author's competence and responsibility as a historian – his place in the classical tradition – while turning the book into a baroque chronicle.

The Renaissance historian was always on the lookout lest his work be taken for another kind of writing, the fantastic, chimerical prose of fictional literature.[5] Including the details of criollo society – its relationship to pre-Christian civilization, its elaborate and showy ceremonies – will make *Parayso Occidental* distinctly American, an outcome both desired and feared by creole historiography. On the one hand, an identity is established apart from the metropolis; on the other, that challenge to power risks the reprisal of further ostracism from European and Christian history. The push–pull effect of this tension shows up whenever Sigüenza's narrative voice explains his modus operandi, as it does throughout this first Libro and in the prologue as well. Establishing authority over his own history, and his own writing, the criollo historian tries to explain his difference through standard rhetorical forms, but cannot; baroque language and a history comprised of intricately layered levels are the result. The narrative voice, the voice of authority, always injects doubt back into the text by naming, and following, these unsteady tangents.

"La integridad del contexto desta mi Historia," as Sigüenza calls it, is history in the narrow, European, classical sense. Although such integrity does not ask that the story of the founding of San José be included, this is an example of the "enmienda" I discussed in Chapter 2. To retrieve San José's history from the "tribunal del olvido" is to commit it to perpetuity, to deem it worthy of endurance, and to correct the errors of the past. Yet, here too, there is a surplus, an excess of detail and evidence, an adding on to the classical narrative that transforms it into the heterogeneous text of a baroque history.

Chapter 12 traces the beginnings of the second convent, just as those of the first were described earlier. A group of nuns in Jesús María decide they would prefer the stricter rule of the Carmelites to their own vows as Concepcionistas, the reason being that "anhelaban à mayor perfeccion, y recogimiento" [they longed for greater perfection and seclusion] (fol. 39v). The Carmelite fathers serving as confessors to Jesús María find the nuns to be a willing audience for their sermons:

Consiguieronse con sus platicas domesticas, frequencia en el pulpito, y assistencia en el confessionario . . . mas vehementes impulsos en las Venerables Madres, para solicitar con todos los medios posibles su pretension; pero siendo unas pobres Religiosas destituidas por su encerramiento, y abstraccion de todo lo que se jusgaba necessario para esta empressa en solas ideas, y pensamiento se les pasaban los años. (fol. 39v–40r)

Through their personal conversations, frequency in the pulpit, and attendance in the confessional, they achieved . . . more vehement feelings in the Venerable Madres, to solicit by all possible means their objective; but, being poor nuns, destitute due to their enclosure and retirement away from everything judged necessary for this undertaking, the years passed in mere ideas and thought.

These years are full of political maneuvering, alliance building, and fund-raising, which move at a steady pace toward the realization of the sisters' goal. Finally, it seems the convent will be founded: "Se persuadieron las Religiosas del Convento Real de Jesus Maria, a que la fundacion de las Carmelitas iba de veras, y sintiendo privarse de las dos mas esenciales, y proficuas con que se hallaban, no omitieron quantos medios les parecian à proposito por detenerlas" [The nuns of the Convento Real de Jesús María became convinced that the Carmelite foundation was truly going to happen, and feeling the loss of the two most essential and useful nuns they had, they spared no effort to stop them from leaving] (fol. 41v). These two essential women are Inés de la Cruz and Mariana de la Encarnación, who feature prominently in Libros Segundo and Tercero. Another difficulty is posed by the Carmelite nuns of Puebla, who, sensing competition and feeling slighted, send a priest to Mexico City to

manifestarles à estas iban erradas, por no ser decente el que haviendo ya Religiosas Carmelitas en este Reyno, quisiesen fundar Convento de este instituto, las que por ser de la Concepcion tenian diferente habito, y otra regla, todo lo qual cedia en deshonor de las de la Puebla, supuesto que se atribuiria a falta de religion . . . el no valerse de ellas para esta empressa. (fol. 42r)

show them they were in error, because it was not decent that, when Carmelites were already in this Realm, sisters who as Concepcionistas wore different habits and followed another rule wanted to found a convent of the Carmelite institution, which would lead to dishonor for the nuns of Puebla, assuming that the fact that they were not called upon for this enterprise would be attributed to their lack of religion.

The reply of the Concepcionistas to this challenge is the first text written by a woman to be cited in *Parayso Occidental*. Mariana de la Encarnación's chronicle of the founding of San José is quoted here at length. It is a pointed, witty answer to the Pueblan nuns that reminds the reader of a more modestly intellectual Sor Juana. Mariana recalls, for example, how she dealt with her interrogator: "de mi le podia decir, que en el Convento a donde me havia criado me enseñaron a rezar bien el Padre nuestro, y Ave Maria" [regarding myself, I was able to inform her that in the Convent where I was brought up they taught me the right way to pray Our Fathers and Hail Marys] (fol. 43r).[6]

After this text, the last chapter of Libro Primero begins. Echoing the same troubles as those of the Convento de Jesús María in finding suitable quarters, this chapter tells the tale of the would-be Carmelites' search for shelter. A man named Juan Luis de Ribera, equal to Pedro Tomás de Denia in charity and piety, had willed to the hopeful founders houses and money for their cloister. However, the ensuing years of political intrigue and changing government officials placed Ribera's testament in the files of oblivion that characterized the colonial bureaucracy. By the time the Carmelite foundation finds new champions and begins in earnest, Ribera's nephew has taken possession of his uncle's property and must be sued in order to recover it. The hearing takes place in July 1615, and is decided in favor of the nuns. The archbishop is distressed, not knowing how he will actually be able to enter the already occupied houses. Luckily, among the tenants lives a close friend of one of the prelate's own pages, who agrees to help with an inside job, and in the middle of the night, with great stealth and silence, an altar is erected in his home. At dawn, bells are rung and all the inhabitants of the houses are awakened by pounding on their doors and calls to Mass. What follows is pandemonium:

Parecioles à algunos de los vezinos ser efecto de la fantasia del sueño lo que escuchaban, pero como no cesaba la campanilla, ni havia intermission en las vozes, y golpes, que les parecian formidables por no esperados, saltando de las camas, aun los que presumian de mas valientes, se comenzaron à apellidar los unos à los otros, para oponerse à la ignorada causa de tanto ruydo: aumentabase este por instantes en toda la casa con el horroroso estruendo de los domesticos, esforzado aun no tanto con las voceria de las mugeres, que pedian al Cielo misericordia, quanto con los ladridos de los perros, y los alaridos, y llantos de los muchachos: en unos quartos todo era pedir las llaves de las puertas, que por estar desatinados y medio dormidos los sirvientes no se hallaban: en otros por buscarlas tropezaban en las mesas, y sillas, que rodando por el suelo, y aun trayendose consigo los escritorios, persuadian a los menos turbados ser todo aquello originado de que temblaba la tierra. (fol. 44v)

Some of the neighbors thought what they were hearing was coming from the fantasy of their dreams, but since the bells did not cease ringing, nor was there a pause in the shouts and the pounding – which seemed to them tremendous because it was so unexpected –

even those who fancied themselves to be the bravest jumped out of bed, and started yelling at the others to go and stop the unknown cause of so much noise; the latter, growing by the minute all through the house with the horrendous clamor coming from inside it, grew in strength not so much from the yelling of the women as the howling of the dogs, and the crying and screaming of the children; in some rooms everyone was yelling for the keys to the door, which the half-asleep servants could not find in their confusion; in others, as they tried to find the keys they tripped over tables and chairs that rolled around on the floor, and they even took desks down with them too, convincing the less muddled that it was all the result of an earthquake.

It is interesting to consider Sigüenza's model for this episode. Certainly it is not Mariana de la Encarnación's *Relación* or, for that matter, the writing of any nun, for these women's stories are intensely spiritual and personal, and narrated in a more direct fashion. What we begin to see in this last chapter of Libro Primero are the narrative strategies Sigüenza y Góngora employs as history gives way to life stories, as the physical and the factual become spiritual and imaginative. These strategies are borrowed not so much from the classical rhetoric of history as from baroque literature. The dreamlike sequence just cited, for example, owes much to Cervantes: the archbishop acts the role of a clerical Don Quijote, a knight of the Holy Spirit. His Dulcineas are the Carmelite founders, as he informs the sleepy and shocked congregation that they must immediately vacate their homes to make way for the brides of Christ. Sigüenza plays the roles of both Cervantes and Cide Hamete in the narrative of *Parayso Occidental*, inventing for himself the narrative voice of the historian, the "I" that controls editorial and stylistic decisions and claims authority.[7]

In Chapter 4, I demonstrate more such strategies at work in the other two Libros, but the story of Libro Primero is not yet done. Although the houses are now empty and ready, and there is money to construct the new convent's sanctuary, day-to-day income is nil and must rely on charity. That is not good enough for the viceroy, who on orders from the king demands that the convent raise twenty thousand *pesos* as capital. Madre Inés de la Cruz appeals to her childless brother to provide the money. He refuses, saying such a sum is impossible, but Inés does not give up. She prays to God, and

pidiendoselo con aquella eficacia que le dictaba su espiritu consiguiò
el que al tercero dia volviese espontaneamente trayendole una escritura de diez y seis mil pesos, [que jamas se cobrò] y obligacion de
hazer lampara, y retablo para el altar mayor, y todo lo demas que
fuesse necessario para vestir la Iglesia: pero como quiera que fuesse
con el pretexto de aquel papel viejo, y que no servia, se obtuvo per-
fecta licencia para que esta, y el Convento se fabricase (fol. 45v–6r)

entreating Him with the effectiveness dictated to her by her spirit,
three days later she got her brother to return spontaneously, bringing
her a written pledge for sixteen thousand pesos (which was never collected) and a promise to furnish the lamps and the altarpiece, and everything else necessary to adorn the Church; and whether or not it
was with the pretext of that old paper, which was worth nothing, total
permission was granted for the building of the Church and the
Convent.

Here again are pretext and text, a contradiction between reality and appearance that hinges on a missing paper. Again,
too, there is the hint of a hidden sexual dimension: the childless brother whose written word, although useless and im-
potent, allows his sister the mystical union with Christ she
so fervently desires. Through these repeated instances involving the absent texts of incestuous or extramarital relationships, Sigüenza's own preoccupation with his book's paternity
emerges. How can his own voice, his own authority and po-
tency, be established as he constructs a history built around the
texts of women?

The answer is a narrative persona that assumes the mask of
historian to equate the fortunes of the convent with those of
the New World, the western Paradise that is New Spain. It is an
equation expressed in baroque terms, an excess, a decoration
on the plain backdrop of the chronicles. The final section of
Libro Primero explodes in a frenzy reminiscent of Balbuena's
La Grandeza Mexicana:

Hasta aqui me permitiò mi Historia acompañar, con notable gusto, à
tan heroycas Virgines; ni quizas pudiera pasar adelante, aunque lo in-
tentara, reconociendo debil mi pluma para tan grave asunto; como lo
es sin duda, haver de expresar todos los demas cariños de la divina
Providencia, que en la fundacion, y progressos deste religiosissimo
Convento se han advertido, y las virtudes, y prodigiosos exemplos,
con que se han hecho venerables, y generalmente aplaudidas por
ellos sus Religiosas: sirviendo todo ello de calificadissima executoria,
con que cada dia se ennoblece mas el Convento Real de Jesus Maria,

à cuyas hijas reconoce por Madres el del gloriosissimo Patriarcha San Joseph de Carmelitas Descalças de la Ciudad de Mexico: Ciudad verdaderamente gloriosa, y dignamente merecedora de que en los ecos de la Fama aya llegado su nombre a los mas retirados terminos del Universo, aun no tanto por la amenidad deleytosissima de su sitio; por la incomparable hermosura de sus espaciosas calles; por la opulencia, y valor de sus antiguos Reyes; por la copia, y circunspeccion de sus tribunales; por las prendas que benignamente les reparte el cielo, à sus ilustres hijos; por las mejoras con que en el tiempo de su christiandad ha conseguido ser la cabeça, y Metropoli de la America; quanto por que à beneficio de este, y de otros innumerables Templos, con que se hermosea su dilatado ambito se puede equivocar con el Cielo Empireo, quando desde ellos, sin intermission, se le embia a Dios Nuestro Señor el sacrificio, y holocausto de sus debidos elogios, y a donde viven los que los habitan con pureza Angelica. (fol. 47r–v)

Up to this point my history permitted me to accompany these heroic virgins with notable pleasure, and perhaps I could go no further even were I to try, for I recognize my pen is weak for such grave matters, as without a doubt would be the need to express all the other kindnesses of divine Providence that have been evident in the foundation and progress of this most religious Convent, and the virtues and prodigious examples for which its Nuns have become venerable and widely applauded. All of this serves as a most qualified pedigree by which the Convento Real de Jesús María becomes more noble each day, its daughters recognized as Madres by the most glorious convent of the Patriarch San Joseph of Discalced Carmelites of the City of Mexico: a truly glorious city, worthy and deserving of the way in which, through the echoes of Fame, its name has spread to the most remote corners of the Universe, not so much for the most delightful amenity of its location; for the incomparable beauty of its spacious streets; for the opulence, and valor of its ancient Kings; for the abundance and circumspection of its tribunals; for the gifts that heaven benignly bestows on its illustrious sons; for the betterment with which, in its Christian era, it has succeeded in becoming the head and the Metropolis of America, as much as because – thanks to this and other innumerable Temples with which its extensive area is made beautiful – it may be mistaken for the Heavenly Empire; for from those Temples, without pause, are sent to Our Lord God the sacrifice and holocaust of the praise owed to Him, and those that reside in them live in angelic purity.

Yet despite this eloquent tribute, the text comes back with a doubting question that undermines its own premise. If the Convento de Jesús María, symbol of the New World, is pure and perfect, why must its most saintly inhabitants leave to go elsewhere? Why do they endure such great hardship in order to found the Convento de San José when they already have Paradise on earth? Why is it that the subplot of the founding of the Carmelite institution is actually *Parayso Occidental*'s most constant theme, the glue that holds it all together?

The Convento de Jesús María was from its inception identified with the criollo group: founded to house the poor descendants of conquerors, it rapidly became a convent of choice for the American-born elite. This history is told in Sigüenza's narrative, which is based in large part on the testimony of the nuns themselves. Regarding the importance placed on material wealth, it is essentially the story of the majority of large convents founded in viceregal cities in the late sixteenth century, where purely spiritual impulses mattered much less than worldly prestige and local power. The small groups of privileged women who became nuns in these institutions held a limited amount of power within the convent through political alliances and in the outside world through economic and family influence. Inside the convent, all the divisions of colonial society had their expression in hierarchies based on class, race, and ethnicity. Among these was the criollo–Spanish conflict, which became especially heated during the last quarter of the sixteenth century and the first quarter of the seventeenth.[8]

The Convento de Jesús María, a Concepcionista bastion of criollo power, also admitted Spanish-born nuns to its community, and the result was identical to the struggle occurring in the larger world: a clash between the American and peninsular groups. That Jesús María was founded in the 1580s, when this social struggle was reaching a fever pitch, is especially important, for the conflict spilled over into the efforts of Inés de la Cruz and Mariana de la Encarnación to found a Carmelite convent. As the Mexican historian Manuel Ramos has convincingly shown, the weight of Spanish authority was placed solidly behind the Carmelite foundation, Inés de la Cruz herself being Spanish. The Carmelite convent would be a living symbol of Counter-Reformation orthodoxy and Spanish austerity (Ramos 1990, 45–73). Assessing the very positive picture that Sigüenza presents of the Carmelite convent as a "fruit" of the Concepcionista tree, Ramos notes a disparity between this picture and the resistance to the would-be Carmelites presented by the sisters of Jesús María themselves, as documented through the vidas (which I examine in my next two chapters). Ramos poses the question of whether or not the Convento de Jesús María desired the Carmelite foundation, leaving the query open to his reader's interpretation (60).

This question can be answered by separating Sigüenza's narrative history, written in 1684, from the nuns' testimonies, written fifty or sixty years earlier. Undoubtedly the nuns of the Convento de Jesús María were hostile to the future Carmelites, who, as we shall see, attempted to disrupt the convent's relaxed atmosphere of privilege in favor of austere religious reform. Moreover, the criolla sisters correctly identified the projected new convent as Spanish dominated and not in line with their own group interests. They were therefore not at all desirous of such an institution, and certainly were loath to see it emerge from their own ranks.

For Sigüenza y Góngora, criollo patriot and Jesuit follower, the issue was much more complicated. *Parayso Occidental* was written on the occasion of the centenary of the Convento de Jesús María, and one of its goals was to obtain continued funding for the convent from the king. Sigüenza centers his history on the premise of the convent's moral superiority as an American Paradise, a position very much in keeping with that of other criollos in the late seventeenth century whose patriotism crystallized around the figure of the Virgin of Guadalupe. He also stresses, as I have shown, the American character of the virgins of the New World Paradise, to the point of presenting Mexican priestesses as their forebears.

Yet as much as Sigüenza y Góngora insists on the criollo identity of his Paradise, he must also establish its Spanish roots for the royal benefactor. Thus Libro Primero takes pains to show the noble, peninsular "pedigree" of the convent, which traces its heritage back to doña Michaela, daughter of Philip II, as well as doña Marina, interpreter for Cortés. The Convento de Jesús María can thus claim a double lineage of kings and of conquerors, of service to both state and church.

For Sigüenza, however, the best way to praise the criollo convent was to praise its Carmelite offspring, a cloister fully identified with colonial authority and Spanish Catholicism. Moreover, the Carmelite foundation was supported by the

Jesuits, who participated prominently in the celebratory Mass and festival of San José's inauguration (Ramos 1990, 61–2). The Jesuits in New Spain – like the discalced Carmelite priests – were generally allied with the criollos in political disputes; they had built a power base for themselves among the latter through educational institutions like the one Sigüenza y Góngora attended. Yet the Jesuits, like the Carmelites, remained a predominantly peninsular order throughout the seventeenth century (Israel 1975, 84), with a puritanical and sometimes misogynist attitude toward women. It is not surprising that they would support the founding of a new convent for women that would follow strict Teresian rule.

Sigüenza, in *Parayso Occidental,* is caught between praise for the criollo world of his western Paradise, and praise for the more peninsular-oriented reformers who represent strict obedience to an orthodox rule. He tries to walk the line between them and praise both in order to satisfy the king, the Jesuits, the nuns of 1684, and his own patriotic criollo history. Thus the Convento de Jesús María becomes mother to the Convento de San José, the noble tree that bears a noble fruit. Through the tropes of baroque language, Sigüenza attempts to make the two institutions reflect one another, and to rewrite the very anti-criollo beginnings of the Carmelite foundation as a continuation of the New World Paradise begun within the walls of Jesús María. Much as Sigüenza overlooks the violence of the conquest that brought Christianity to Mexico when he places Aztec princes on his triumphal arch in *Theatro de virtudes políticas,* he reads in the saga of the Carmelite rebels glory for the convent that produced them, ignoring the contentious struggle of criollo against *española* (or disparagingly, *gachupina*) that characterized the history of the 1616 foundation.

Both the accounts of the Carmelite founders – the vidas I examine in my next two chapters – and Sigüenza's history tell the "truth" of events from different perspectives. Sigüenza's own objectives are in mutual conflict, not an unusual predicament for a criollo of his era; the result is a baroque history that looks to solve some of these difficulties through the complications of language. In Libro Primero the discourse, aimed at the king, is concerned with paternity, with who fathered the Conquest, the two convents, and the written history of the New World. Placing the vidas within his own criollo history in the second and third Libros, Sigüenza must manipulate them through another discourse – that of paternalism – to produce the kind of rewritten chronicle his narrative strives to be.

4

The discourse of paternalism

The second Libro of *Parayso Occidental* traces the life of Madre Marina de la Cruz from birth to death, and beyond. In the opening chapter of her story, Sigüenza's narrative voice returns to its overriding obsession with the question of authority. Here, though, the problems are different because the discourse has changed. Sigüenza is no longer writing history so much as biography: the spiritual biography of a woman who lived a long, full, and sometimes terrible life before entering the Convento de Jesús María at the age of fifty-one.

If in the first Libro the models were classical histories and the sixteenth-century chronicles of Conquest, and it was possible for Sigüenza to back up his work with legal documents signed by kings and archbishops, in Libro Segundo the requirements of language and truth have shifted. Moving from worldly to spiritual concerns, the narrative strategies for composing this story rely less on the tradition of history than on a mystical, ascetic doctrine adhering to religious, not rhetorical, laws. The line between truth and fiction grows ever more faint as acceptable language is measured by a standard that encompasses feeling and imagination. Instead of asking whether or not a history is true, here the question must be "Is this life good?" It is the same question that caused Teresa of Avila's *Vida* to be confiscated by the Inquisition in the sixteenth century, for the difference between a mystical vision and diabolic possession of the soul can be slight indeed. In Libro Primero, *historia* resists the poetic tropes and adornments of baroque literature; in Libro Segundo, vida must avoid blasphemy.

Sigüenza y Góngora was well aware that writing such a life story could lead him down a linguistic path full of pitfalls and traps. At the end of *Parayso Occidental* is a one-page text characteristic of the era, the "Protesta del autor" [Author's Disclaimer].[1] Here Sigüenza cites papal decrees ordering that

pious persons not be referred to as saints until formally canonized by the church "y que no se forme mas juyzio del progresso
de su vida, y milagros, que el que la Fè humana permite" [and
that no judgment, beyond that which human faith permits, be
made of the story of the life and its miracles] (fol. 206v).
Sigüenza vows his intention to follow such decrees, declaring,

esta historia no merece mas credito que el que se debe a la diligencia
cuydadosa de ajustar la verdad en lo que pide la gravedad de su materia; en que tambien puede haver falencia, como en las historias
humanas sucede a vezes. Y assi las palabras: *Santidad; Santa; Bienaven-*
turada; Gloriosa; Virtud heroyca; Revelacion; Vision; Profecia; Milagro, y
otras semejantes, que se hallaràn en la vida de la V.M. Marina de la
Cruz, y en las de otras personas que aqui se expresan, de ninguna
manera son para que se les dè culto, veneracion, ni opinion de Santidad. (fol. 206v)

this history merits no more credit than that owed the diligent care
taken to examine the truth, as required by the gravity of its subject; in
this too there may be error, as happens sometimes in human histories.
And therefore the words *Holiness, Saint, Blessed, Glorious, Heroic Virtue,*
Revelation, Vision, Prophecy, Miracle, and other similar ones that will
be found in the life of the Venerable Madre Marina de la Cruz and
in those of other people related here, in no manner are to be taken
as reason for their worship, veneration, or judgment regarding their
holiness.

The prologue to the reader states that the aim of history is to
"hazer presente lo pasado como fue entonces"; but officially, its
goal is to "ajustar la verdad en lo que pide la gravedad de su
materia." The difficulty for Sigüenza y Góngora in this part of
the history is how he will tell a life story both good and true,
while simultaneously asserting his own criollo narrative voice.
And complicating matters further, it is the life of a woman that
is to be told, a woman whose story must be couched in religious,
even miraculous terms.

What rules and models to follow, then? How to tell the story?
The classical, heroic mode of *Piedad heroyca de don Fernando*
Cortés does not apply to a female subject. Nor can Madre Ma-
rina become a heroine of the Conquest in the manner of her
namesake, doña Marina, for she served no such missionary or
acculturated role, and in fact was born in Spain, not America.
Neither was this nun a writer and intellectual such as Inés de la
Cruz, who left behind her own autobiographical account, which

is included in Libro Tercero. As she was unschooled and illiterate, Madre Marina's personal saga was written by others, and thus Sigüenza cannot simply absorb it as another first-person source. Finally, this is not the life of a consecrated saint, and to claim authority on grounds of holiness would border on heresy.

Sigüenza's role as historian, so effective in Libro Primero, will not serve the same purpose here. His models, as I demonstrated in my last chapter's reading of the dreamlike scene of the archbishop at dawn, are drawn from hagiography, from the moralizing examples of medieval and ascetic texts, and from literature, notably Cervantes. Madre Marina, her confessor Pedro de la Mota, and Inés de la Cruz become the characters of a story, and Sigüenza their inventor. Although his voice does still adopt a historian's "I" that makes substantive and stylistic judgments, and that "I" continues to be important, it is through the manipulation of others' voices that a structure is provided for Libro Segundo. The structure is sufficiently complex to satisfy the discourse of criollo historiography, laced through with a large dose of baroque language. And with the moral imperative of *escarmiento* – a chastisement or warning – highly evident, *Parayso Occidental* is guaranteed to pass the most orthodox scrutiny of church and state authorities, demonstrating an ideology regarding women that Sigüenza himself shared.

In the first chapter of Libro Segundo, the main threat to Sigüenza's authorial voice is neatly dispatched as the criollo marks off his territory and stakes his claim to this narration. Pedro de la Mota left an account of Madre Marina's life, composed after her death, and most of this first chapter is quoted directly from his writing. Sigüenza uses de la Mota's own, introductory, two-part preface – in which the latter's role as confessor and spiritual biographer is explained – and then critiques it. In this way he gains the religious credibility he desires for the narrative (de la Mota's preface being full of pious declarations) and at the same time asserts his own authority over matters rhetorical, and over the book itself.

For example, in between de la Mota's two prefaces (the first addressed to the sisters of the convent, the second to other readers), Sigüenza intervenes to say: "Hasta aqui la prefacion, ò carta con que à las Religiosas del Convento Real de Jesus Maria les remitiò el devoto Sacerdote la relacion de esta vida" [This is the end of the preface, or letter, with which the devout priest sent the account of this life to the nuns of the Convento Real de Jesús María] (fol. 51r). Clearly, Sigüenza is establishing a gap between his own writing and that of the confessor, by referring to the latter's work as a "carta" or "relación," legal forms of writing not in the same class as the learned *historia*.

De la Mota himself refers to his "relación" and "leyenda," enumerating his sources of information as oral ones, such as the testimonies of other nuns or Marina's own confessions. The priest knew himself to be uneducated in the particulars of elegant writing, as he disclosed frequently:

Me constituyeron en este cuydado, el qual acetè con arto temor, y verguenza de mi corta suficiencia, y espiritu [fol. 50v]; siento en mi una cobardia para empezar este escrito conociendo de mi ser cosa muy dificultosa à la facultad de mi pobre espiritu [51r]; excede esta materia que voy siguiendo à mis flacas fuerzas [51v]; como caresco de ingenio, pues no me es dado tal don, supla mi sana intencion [52v].

I was given this task, which I approached with much fear and shame for my lack of sufficiency and spirit; I feel in myself a cowardice to begin this writing, knowing that it will be very difficult for me and for the abilities of my poor spirit; this subject about which I am telling exceeds my scanty powers; as I am lacking in inventiveness, for I was not given that gift, may my good intentions make up for it.

It is also clear that de la Mota's sources are vague and doubtful. Protesting his limited relationship with Marina, he informs the nuns that "[la Madre] jamàs tratò conmigo casos particulares mas de aquellas que via ella ser necessarias para su espiritu" [she never discussed with me any issues other than those she believed to be necessary for her spirit] (fol. 50v), and that

razon verdadera es que las cosas acaecidas dentro de una casa los que viven dentro de ella sabràn la verdad de ellas, porque yo nunca vide à la Madre mas de solo oyrla en sus confessiones hasta la muerte, y como la noticia fue corta en espacio de dos años, seràn escasas mis razones, y las que ella me declarò eran tratar de sus exercicios, y modos de oracion, y no otra cosa. (fol. 51r)

it is a true statement that those who live in a house know the truth of the things that happen inside it, because I never saw the Madre other than to hear her confessions until she died, and since not much could be said in the space of two years, my own statements will be few, for what she declared to me had to do with her spiritual exercises, and ways of praying, and nothing else.

By citing de la Mota in this manner, Sigüenza fulfills the requirements of truthful history and manages at the same time to destroy his rival's claim of "fathering" the text of Marina's story. The criollo scholar then ends this chapter with a condescending nod to the priest's efforts:

No quise omitirlas, aunque prolixas, por servir una, y otra prefacion de admirable abono para lo que me queda de dezir en este Libro, que se compondrà de lo que el buen Licenciado Pedro de la Mota sin metodo, ni estilo escrivió en el suyo, añadiendo lo que . . . se conserva en la memorial . . . y lo que acerca de esta materia se halla en varios manuscritos de la Venerable Madre Ynes de la Cruz. (fol. 52v)

I did not wish to omit these prefaces, although they are prolix, since each one serves as admirable proof for that which remains for me to say in this Book, which will be composed of what the good Licenciate Pedro de la Mota, without method or style, wrote in his own book, adding that which . . . is preserved by memory . . . and that which is found in several manuscripts of the Venerable Madre Inés de la Cruz regarding this subject.

It is Sigüenza who will supply that absent style and method, the missing rhetorical expertise that will transform a mere account into history. Moreover, Sigüenza sees himself as the resident of the "house" – a symbol of the city of Mexico, or the American *patria* – who should know best about its internal things: the events of history.

Chapter 2 begins with a long, philosophical meditation on the relationship of material possessions to the divine will of God. Sigüenza echoes de la Mota when he states that the actions of Marina

pedian para que se manifestasen al mundo no solo una elegantissima pluma sino un espiritu ardiente, que supiese sentir lo que se pone a expressar . . . y atiendan todos, no à la imperfeccion, y rudeza de quien lo escrive, sino à la divina misericordia que con tan singulares privilegios honrò à su Sierva. (fol. 53v)

demanded for their manifestation to the world not only a most elegant pen, but also a burning spirit that would be able to feel what it tries to express . . . and may all heed not the imperfections and coarseness of he who writes it, but rather the divine mercy that honored its Servant with such singular privileges.

The "elegant pen" belongs of course to Sigüenza, who modestly excuses his own lack of moral perfection but clearly differentiates himself from the untutored de la Mota – he of the "prolix" pen – as does this learned preamble.

This scheme is carried out further as the details of Marina's life begin to unfold. She was born in 1536, Sigüenza writes, a famous year "porque en el le fue cortada la cabeza a la impia Ana Bolena muger de Henrico VIII Rey de Inglaterra, haviendola antes convencido de incestuosa con su proprio Hermano" [because in it the impious Anne Boleyn, wife of Henry VIII King of England, had her head cut off, having been convicted of incest with her own Brother] (fol. 53v), and also because the Protestant Reformation was gaining momentum. Sigüenza sets up a polar contrast between the death of Anne Boleyn and Marina's birth, an exchange of "una muger sacrilega" [a sacriligious woman] for "otra muger en cuyo zelo . . . tubiese el mismo mundo un nuevo modelo papa emmendar sus acciones" [another woman in whose zeal . . . the same would have had a new model for correcting its actions] (fol. 53v). The narrative of Libro Segundo is thus immediately thrust into the larger arena of world events, providing it with a historical, material context to complement the spiritual one.

At this point, when Marina's life story really begins, Sigüenza has already demolished de la Mota's claims to authority and asserted his own, pushing the confessor into a supporting background role where he will stay until again summoned. Sigüenza has set up the central theme of this vida (*lo terreno* versus *lo celestial*, or the worldly versus the heavenly), related it to European decadence through the person of an incestuous English queen, and declared Marina to be the "new model" for women and for the world, a New World model. Sigüenza's voice reaches the reader through his vigorous assertion of power over the language and sources of the text, and in the text's implicit Americanism.

With all the characters put into place, the action begins. Sigüenza's voice, as in Libro Primero, intervenes to speak of his research: "La falta de papeles, y de noticias me niega muchissimas circunstancias que pudieran ser, ya que no necessarias, por lo menos deleytables en la leyenda" [The lack of documents and information denies me many instances that could have been, if not necessary, at least delightful in their reading] (fol. 54r). This expresses a typical attitude of Renaissance historiography that intends to produce a fluid prose pleasing to the reader in its style; here, Sigüenza works that rhetoric into a nun's life story that is otherwise presented most solemnly.

Marina's life is told as a very human story with rich character development, put into a sternly moralistic framework. Chapters 2 through 8 describe her years "en el siglo" – in the world – before professing as a nun in 1587. In these chapters, narrated in the third person with occasional first-person authorial interventions, Marina marries and buries two husbands, leaves her native Spain for Mexico, has a child, makes and loses a fortune in the silver mines, and in between experiences numerous mystical visions. Such material might suggest a picaresque telling, and *Parayso Occidental* does not miss that opportunity.[2]

Although this narration is not an autobiographical account (a device present in Libro Tercero), many other elements commonly identified with the picaresque are present. The most notable is the fact that Marina's story, despite its spiritual premise, places great emphasis on the importance of money and social class. It is because of poverty that she marries her first husband, although her religious vocation is already apparent. The moment when Marina's parents betroth her is reminiscent of Lazarillo de Tormes's departure from home with his first master:

El primero que solicitò se la diesen por esposa fue un Luis de la Peña, hombre de cortissimo caudal, pero reputado por virtuoso, y con creditos de habil en el ministerio de escrivir, y contar, con que aseguraba su pasadia, y como esto era tan notorio, quanto era cierto que la dote de Marina era ninguna, determinaron sus Padres el darsela, sin reparar en la alcuña de Luis de la Peña muy inferior a la suya. (fol. 55r)

The first man who asked them to give her to him as his wife was one Luis de la Peña, a man of very little means, but reputed for his virtue, and with the assets of being able in writing and accounting, through which he was assured of a living; and since this was as well known as the fact that Marina's dowry was nil, her Parents decided to give her to him, without considering that the family background of Luis de la Peña was very inferior to their own.

Recalling the preface of Pedro de la Mota I cited earlier, as readers we can only wonder where these details of Marina's early, worldly life come from. She might have discussed them with her confessor, but considering his disavowal of such conversations, that source is doubtful. They may be included in the writing of Inés de la Cruz, or perhaps were confided to another nun whom Sigüenza had interviewed. The crucial point is that we do not know, for there are no citations. Without them, history, based on a "relación," slides into a biography that flirts with the picaresque. Sigüenza's narrative strategy of claiming authority through a mosaic of sources, then discounting their importance, again presents contradictory results.

In Marina's vida, because of the subject matter, what emerges is not just an undocumented history but one tending toward a fictional mode. In this same way, the manipulation of Pedro de la Mota's voice begins to recall the layering of narrators in *Don Quixote,* the difference being that Sigüenza always participates directly in the narration. Rather than hiding the strings of his puppets, this master flaunts them gleefully as evidence of his own superiority. De la Mota's sources and expertise are questioned, as are Cide Hamete's, but in Sigüenza's text this dismantling calls the historical truthfulness of his own text into doubt.

If the central opposition in *Don Quixote,* as Ruth El Saffar (1975) has expressed it, is that of distance and control of the author's and characters' time frames, in *Parayso Occidental* the conflict is a struggle between historical and fictional approaches to the control of the narration. The suggestion of false models undermines the truthful mandate of the narrative, turning a religious document into a heretical story. The female subjects and audience of *Parayso Occidental* have opened the door to this hybrid text by eliminating the need for documentation; thus, paradoxically, it is because the narrative treats the life of a nun that it can stretch into the realm of profane discourse.

Chapter 2 also marks the beginning of a topic central to the second and third Libros: that of *escarmiento,* or chastising examples set up to demonstrate good and bad to the female readers of the book. It is such a spirit of shame and scapegoating that underlies the moral asides of the narrator as he tells these life stories, constantly repeating the theme of physical/spiritual opposition. Marina does not want to marry and knows her husband to be her inferior, yet she goes through with the marriage because God wills it: "no atendiò en su desposorio à las leyes del mundo, sino à las disposiciones del cielo que deben ser el norte de las acciones humanas" [she did not follow the laws of the world in her marriage, but rather the orders of heaven, which should guide human actions] (fol. 55v).

Sigüenza is writing for women and his models are such ascetic tracts as Fray Martín de Córdoba's *El jardín de las nobles doncellas* and Luis Vives's *Instrucción de la mujer cristiana*.³ Although his concern with the male sources for his narrative – de la Mota, the *cronistas* – centers around the question of paternity and authority, it is paternalism that inspires his dealings with the nuns' writings and with his intended female audience. There is thus a double helix of narrative strategy present in the manipulation of texts in *Parayso Occidental:* the authority of other men must be defeated in a battle of style and erudition, whereas the writing of women, posing no direct threat, can be used to support an ideological program of orthodox, Counter-Reformation morality, as was associated with the Jesuit order during New Spain's seventeenth century.⁴

Both discursive strategies end up at odds with the stated goals of *Parayso Occidental*'s history. The derision of source material (such as de la Mota's text) casts a shadow on the narrative's reliability, while the criticism of the convent implicit in the orthodox agenda of *escarmiento* turns the western Paradise into one that is lost, rather than regained. This second point will become clearer as I trace the history-within-a-history of the founding of the Carmelite Convento de San José and the development of Marina's life story.

Chapter 3 finds Marina married, but with severe problems. She has continued her spiritual exercises in her married life and her husband is not pleased:

Ponderaba todo esto el bueno de su marido, y aunque muchas vezes se confundia, eran tambien muchas las vezes que se disgustaba, hasta llegar à dezirle: que para que se havia casado si havia de seguir en su vida tanta estrecheza, y que mejor estado le fuera el de religiosa. (fol. 56r–v)

Her good husband considered all this, and although many times he became confused, there were also many times he was annoyed, to the point of saying to her that if her life had to follow such strict rigor, why had she married at all, for a nun's status would be more fitting for her.

The underlying sexual conflict hinted at in this passage points to the problem Sigüenza has in narrating the vida, while fitting it into his cosmic scheme. It is virginity that represents the best of the New World, its very unspoiled quality, but Marina is a married woman and as such should engage in conjugal relations. Although Sigüenza does his best to portray the husband as a virtuous man, what emerges is an adversarial relationship akin to that of a *pícara* and her master. Marina's response to her husband's complaint is to comply with his wishes, but remain emotionally unmoved: "Callaba Marina, y sin faltar à las insinuaciones, y gusto de su marido no interrumpiò, ni cercenò en cosa alguna sus devociones" [Marina kept silent and, without failing her husband's wishes and insinuations, neither interrupted nor curtailed in any way her devotions] (fol. 56v).

Marina is transformed by Sigüenza into a *pícara a lo divino*, a holy outlaw, resisting the secular life into which poverty has forced her. If, as I noted in this chapter, the nonreligious *pícara* is a male-authored representation of the social control exerted on women in general and prostitutes in particular, this holy delinquent reveals the other possible script for women resisting the fetters of conventional marriage: a union with God. Marina's somewhat sullen approach to conjugal life becomes acceptable when framed in the context of a higher calling, for rather than asserting her own will, she is but an instrument of divinity. Sigüenza can thus make her the centerpiece of this roguish tale of adventure while preserving a tone of warning and chastisement for female readers.

The picaresque theme continues as Marina and her husband set sail for the New World. The narrative voice of the historian states with pride:

Era entonces el tiempo en que los Reynos de esta Nueva-España estaban en su primitiva opulencia, y como la fama de sus riquezas se havia esparcido por el resto del universo, eran innumerables los que de todo el concurrian à la America para conseguir en ella lo que les faltaba en sus patrias. (fol. 56v)

That was the time when this Realm of New Spain had its era of original opulence, and since the fame of its riches had spread throughout the rest of the universe, innumerable people from all over went to America to acquire there what they did not have in their own homelands.

Once again it is clear that Sigüenza's strategy for incorporating Marina's life story into his book is based on a criollo vision of the universe, with its center displaced from east to west. And again there is the combining of narratives, leaning toward both the picaresque (Marina as a roguish figure, at odds with the society around her) and the ascetic, as she resigns herself to fate and her husband's will, and leaves Spain behind for Mexico City.

Chapter 4 is one of the shortest episodes in *Parayso Occidental*, as Marina pleads with God for a mystical vision and is rewarded with a prophetic dream. The vidas written by religious women often described such experiences and trances; what is of special interest here is Sigüenza's manipulation of Marina's dream and the way he makes it part of his own narrative. Neither Marina nor Pedro de la Mota is quoted directly, as the nun is "llevada en espiritu à un lugar dilatadamente grande, y en que havia innumerables exercitos de escorpiones, serpientes, basiliscos, y quantos otros animales son temidos de los hombres por su veneno mortifero" [taken in spirit to a spacious and large place, in which there were innumerable armies of scorpions, serpents, basilisks, and many other animals that are feared by men for their deadly venom] (fol. 58r). These fearful reptilian armies try to swallow Marina, who prays to God for help. The Lord descends to her in a resplendent light and gives her a rod with which to beat off the creatures. Triumphant, she awakens and gives thanks for such a vision, equating the threatening serpents with a sinful world to be resisted with God's help and salvation.

The exaggerated detail of this horror is a baroque trope, using hyperbole to surprise and evoke a response to the sheer weight of words. To that description, Sigüenza adds on another layer of interpretation as he tells how Marina continues her fight against evil in her later life as a nun, where she encounters "la actividad del fuego de la detraccion que contra la pureza de su vida, y la candidez de su alma excitaron algunas personas, en quienes se hallò la astucia de las serpientes, la lengua del aspid, y el veneno del escorpion" [the workings of the fires of detraction with which some people, whom she found to have the astuteness of serpents, the tongues of asps, and the venom of scorpions, worked against the pureness of her life and the candidness of her soul] (fol. 59r). To Marina and her con-

fessor, the symbolic relationship of serpent to sin and temptation was a direct one, but to Sigüenza the representation is
mediated: it is the poison that stands for the scorpion, a tongue
that means an asp, and cleverness that suggests the snake. The
nun's dream has been made baroque through the tropes and
conceits of excess, through the layering of language.

The trials of secular life go on through chapter 5. Marina's
husband, following her virtuous example, is rewarded with
riches. He decides to exploit the opportunities of the northern
settlement of Zacatecas, where silver mines had recently been
discovered in the latter part of the mid-sixteenth century. Marina says a tearful goodbye to her confessor, Diego de Aguilar,
who tells her to pray for a better day when she will reach a state
of grace and mercy. Zacatecas lives up to its promise, yet Marina, surrounded by worldly goods, retires more and more
from exterior life.

Suddenly at this point she is left a widow, far from home and
family. The historian's narrative voice intervenes to inform the
reader of the source for his information: Marina's 1572 will, in
which she left the bulk of her estate to religious institutions.
Sigüenza avers: "Debole à este testamento, hallado casi milagrosamente en parte donde solo de esta maners podia hallarse,
la noticia verdadera de muchas cosas, cuya omission fuera muy
notable en aquesta historia" [To this will, found almost miraculously in a place where it could only be found in that way, I
owe the true information about many things whose omission
from this history would be very notable] (fol. 61r–v).

Another mysterious text: What was the miraculous circumstance that enabled this discovery? How and where did
Sigüenza come upon it? The enigma continues as a group of
people, "que a lo noble de su sangre añadian lo Christiano de
sus procederes" [who to the nobility of their blood added the
Christianity of their conduct] (fol. 61v), decide to arrange a second marriage for Marina. Her new husband, Benito de Vitoria,
is a pious and observant scribe, a man who recognizes himself
to be unworthy of Marina and considers marriage to her an
honor. The widow prays to God for guidance, and once again
submits to divine will.

This second matrimony differs from the first. Marina's de-
ceased husband was a man of action and ambition, whereas

Benito de Vitoria – a scribe by profession – is quiet and supportive of her religious vocation. But before describing their domestic life, Sigüenza inserts another chapter (6) on Marina's increasing number of visions. Although we may assume that the content of the visions comes directly from Marina's confessions – her visions are consistent with those ubiquitous in other vidas, notably that of Saint Teresa – the manner in which Sigüenza absorbs them into his own book of history is literary in nature.

These visions – "representaciones intelectuales" [intellectual representations] (fol. 62r) – serve as textual decoration and Sigüenza cannot get enough of them, as he writes in another criticism of Pedro de la Mota:

> y aunque la noticia que ay de ellas es en estremo corta, assi por no haver escrito su Confessor las que de este tiempo se le comunicaron, que fueron muchas, y lo que es mas por el decurso prolixo de tantos años, con todo no falta tan absolutamente su memoria, que no aya quedado una, ù otra que deba ponderarse aqui como en lugar oportuno. (fol. 62r)

> and although there is very little information about them, because her Confessor did not write down the ones communicated to him at that time, which were many, and even more so because of the course of so many years gone by, despite all this, memories of her are not so totally absent that one or another has not been left to be considered here in its proper place.

Again the voice of the historian-narrator intervenes in the story to cast doubt on the worthiness of his rival, to overtake and control de la Mota's voice and incorporate it into his own. And once again the mention of problems with source material undermines Sigüenza's "veridical" narration.

The visions, which will become more important to the narrative as Marina leaves secular life for the convent, function on several levels. Superficially, they give a religious, spiritual tone to the worldly story line of Marina's life. These flights of the imagination also give Sigüenza an opportunity to speak through Marina's voice and pull her character into his own narration, for it is through her visions that the mystic is most directly visible to the reader. Sigüenza thus takes over another's writing, another's history, to claim authority over what becomes his book. On a textual level, the insertion of such short stories or memories – timeless tales – in an otherwise chronological biography is a baroque conceit, a twist on the plain thread of chronicle-type history.

Chapter 7 picks up anew the story of Marina's second marriage. Although Benito de Vitoria supports her religious vocation, and she regularly leaves their bed at night to have "coloquios suavissimos con su amado" [the gentlest of conversations with her beloved] (fol. 65r), which consist of self-torture and mortification of the flesh, a daughter, Juana, is born to the couple. This child is destined from birth to become the nun her mother always longed to be.

The years go by and finally Juana is mature enough to enter the convent. Marina is greatly distressed that she cannot accompany her daughter, and prays to God that he fulfill her own desire for a religious life. God hears this plea and takes action: "Acceptò la divina Magestad el amoroso sacrificio de tan ardientes afectos, y para facilitarle los medios de conseguirlos, quitandole el necessario inconveniente que lo estorvaba, le embiò à su esposo Benito de Vitoria una gravissima enfermedad, con que haviendose purificado de sus defectos pasò à la eterna bienaventuranza" [His divine Majesty accepted the loving sacrifice of such burning desires, and to facilitate for her the steps to attain them, taking away the compelling obstacle that blocked them, he sent her husband Benito de Vitoria a very grave illness, from which having purified himself of fault, he passed on to eternal blessedness] (fol. 65v).

Reading on the next page that Marina is to inherit all of Vitoria's estate, the suggestion of an absent text in this family romance emerges. There is more than a hint of black magic here, of congress with the Devil rather than with God, of a hidden text we cannot see. A healthy and virtuous man is struck down, and his death is a cause for rejoicing rather than a tragedy. It is an inversion of the expected text, a surprise as we read it, and as readers we wonder here whose voice is speaking: Sigüenza's, de la Mota's, or Marina's.

And so Marina joyfully enters the novitiate of the Convento de Jesús María. Chapters 8 through 20 narrate the days she spends as a mystical reformer in the cloister, imitating in her life that of Teresa of Avila. Chapter 21 is concerned with Marina's death and passage to heaven; the remaining chapters (22–28) are dedicated to the examination, one by one, of the nun's many virtues, and of the miracles she performs after death. Such was the standard organization of saints' lives, proceeding from religious convictions gained in the secular world, to profession in a religious institution, to death and the works carried out from heaven.

The rest of my discussion of Libro Segundo will center on the earlier chapters, which complete Marina's biography and tell the story of her life within convent walls, first as a novice and later as a nun of the black veil, the highest station in the convent hierarchy. It is in these chapters that the picaresque theme emerges with renewed force and the literary strategy of *Parayso Occidental*'s narration crystallizes.

As Marina prepares to enter the convent in chapter 8, Sigüenza cites her directly for the first time. She lacks the entire sum normally required for a dowry and must plead for special consideration from her sisters. Recording the novice's humble beseechment of charity, the historian introduces Marina's quotation with an intervention of his own: "Quiso el que esto se perpetuase en la escritura con las siguientes clausulas, que si no mueven à devocion, y lagrimas à quien las lee, arguyrà no ser imposible encerrarse corazones de marmol en el pecho humano" [she wished for this to be perpetuated in writing with the following phrases; and if they do not move the reader to tears and devotion, one could argue that it is not impossible for the human breast to enclose hearts of marble] (fol. 67v).

The tone is set for a story that will pull at the reader's heartstrings and inspire pious sentiments; Sigüenza manipulates his audience by incorporating Marina's own voice at an emotional moment in the narrative. Despite his assurance that this voice is truthful by virtue of its written character, nowhere is the textual source noted. This lack of reference allows Marina to become Sigüenza's own heroine, whose story will be told within the framework of his own narration.

Mother and daughter then enter the convent as novices, and misfortune befalls them almost immediately. Marina dotes on her pretty twelve-year-old to an extreme degree. In a horribly graphic scene, Juana is struck with a sudden and fatal fever: "Atronando todo el Convento con desentonadissimos alaridos comenzò à desvaratarse à bocados las tiernas carnes, y à herirse con las uñas su hermoso rostro. . . . En breves instantes, sin podersele administrar Sacramento alguno, entre espumarajos, y borbozadas de sangre le faltò el alma" [Making the entire Convent thunder with the most inharmonious shouts and howls, she began to tear away at her tender flesh by the mouthful, and to wound her lovely face with her fingernails.... In a few short moments, foaming at the mouth and gushing with blood, before she could be administered any Sacrament at all, her soul expired] (fol. 69r). In the ascetic tradition, Juana's death is considered a punishment from God meted out to correct her mother's worldly attachment to beauty.

Sigüenza uses the occasion to put forward another scolding example for wayward nuns:

Es cierto no haver cometido Marina en este descuydo culpa mortal, y mucho mas cierto es cometerla gravissima quantas Religiosas olvidandose de la fidelidad prometida à su Esposo en su profession ocupan sus potencias, y sentidos en la inquietud de los devanèos, que aun entre las que habitan en el siglo son execrables. (fol. 69v)

It is true that with this lapse Marina committed no mortal sin, and even more true that such a sin is committed in the most serious degree by all those Nuns who, forgetting the fidelity promised to the Bridegroom upon their profession, occupy their energies and senses with the restlessness of idle pursuits that even for those who live in the world are execrable.

An authorial intervention then follows: "Punto es este que no me permite pasar adelante sin ponderar el que si es irracionalidad despreciar una belleza por amar à un monstruo" [This point will not permit me to go further without considering whether it is irrational to scorn beauty and love a monster] (fol. 69v). In a clever and surprising conceit, beauty becomes that of Christ and the beast becomes worldly attachment, "el monstruo de la devocion mundana" [the monster of worldly devotion] (fol. 69v), a baroque trope used in the service of a moralizing example and directed at seventeenth-century female readers.

Chapter 10 introduces Inés de la Cruz, an educated nun who will be of great importance in Libro Tercero. Marina's relationship to Inés is a fiercely passionate, sublime love expressed in mystical terms as the older woman becomes enamored of the younger one's pure soul:

Lo mesmo fue mirarla, que suspenderse ... se la disolvieron sus tinieblas, y se le cayeron de los ojos las cataratas que hasta alli la havian

tenido ciega, para no ver la diferencia que ay de lo terreno, y perecedero que ella aplaudia, a la grandeza de bienes de que es capaz
nuestra alma. (fol. 71r)

At the same moment she saw her she became suspended . . . her darkness disappeared, and from her eyes fell the cararacts that had
blinded her until then to the difference between the earthly, perishable things she had extolled, and the great good of which our souls
are capable.

Their beds side by side in the novitiate, the two nuns speak,
when allowed, of the profession they so fervently desire.
Sigüenza first quotes Inés at this point, introducing her autobiographical writing: "Assi nos lo dexò escrito esta insigne Vir-
gen en la relacion de su vida, de la cual como en lugar oportuno
es necessario trasladar aqui las siguientes clausulas" [Thus the
remarkable Virgin left this written down for us in the account
of her life, from which it is necessary here to transfer the following phrases] (fol. 71v). Inés now becomes yet another member of Sigüenza's cast of characters, her authorship controlled
by Sigüenza's narrative and his omnipresent voice.

The tortures of Marina begin in earnest in chapter 11. She
has taken the vows of a nun of the black veil, the highest level
of profession, yet is assigned the menial household tasks of the
legas, lay sisters of a much lower rank. The reason for this
demotion is Marina's advanced age, judged unsuitable for full-
time study and meditation. Paradoxically, the work she performs is heavy construction: "Constituyendose por jornalera,
como uno de ellos los ayudaba en todo lo que hazian con fervor
grande: ella misma daba las piedras, ripiaba las paredes, batia
la mezcla, disponia los andamios" [Appointing herself a laborer,
just like one of them she assisted in everything they did with
great fervor: she herself lifted rocks, patched the stone walls,
mixed the mortar, built the scaffolding] (fol. 73r). And she soon
falls ill: "dentro de pocos meses le llegò à faltar la salud con
achaques graves" [within a few months her health was failing,
with chronic and serious sickness] (fol. 73r). Blindness is her
worst torment, but Marina's power of sight is restored through
the miraculous intervention of the Virgin Mary.

In chapter 12, however, the longed-for cloister becomes a
scene of bitter confrontation. God tells Marina that she is to
serve as the guardian of His honor in the convent. Her first ac-

tion is to inform the abbess of Jesús María of God's wishes, and here the story takes a sharp turn toward the picaresque. Sigüenza, finding himself once again with a missing text, invents one for Marina: "y si no fue con las siguientes seria sin duda con mejoradas razones" [and if not with the following argument, without a doubt it would have been with better ones] (fol. 75r).

What follows is a citation that literally puts Sigüenza's words into Marina's mouth, absorbing her voice into his. It is clear that this is Sigüenza's writing when Marina tells her superior:

> Aunque es verdad que a los que hasta aqui me comunicaron con estrecheza les puede parecer en lo que pretendo practicar en lo de adelante, no hago otra cosa sino continuar los dictamenes de mi genio. . . . Necessariamente se ha de atribuir à muy superior impulso el que esta vilissima, y despreciable criatura desde oy aya de corregir en esta comunidad lo que fuere malo. (fol. 75r)

> Although it is true that to those who have known me intimately up to now what I pretend to do may seem like work far beyond me, I am only following the dictates of my inspiration. . . . That this most vile and despicable creature from today on should be the one to correct whatever is bad in this community must of course be attributed to a far superior impulse.

This is a transcription of the simple, direct language of an uneducated nun into the baroque rhetoric of the seventeenth century, and Sigüenza follows it with yet another absent response: "Aunque no se sabe con certidumbre lo que responderia la Abadesa à proposicion tan extraodinaria lo que no se ignora es haverse transformado desde este punto en un Elias la Venerable M." [Although it cannot be known with certainty how the Abbess would have responded to such an extraordinary proposition, what is known is that from this point the Venerable Madre became transformed into an Elijah] (fol. 75v).

Sigüenza y Góngora has supplied the missing dialogue and filled in the blanks with his own interpretation, letting the reader know that the text is not strictly substantiated with facts. Since the basis of those facts is a divine vision, by definition an unwritten script, Sigüenza can manipulate and invent this *vida* to a degree impossible with the documented history of *Libro Primero*. Through his invention of a first-person narration for Marina, her role as the convent's divine outlaw continues to unfold. As the mystic's attempts at reform begin to affect other sisters, her martyrdom to God's cause becomes ever more apparent and her physical suffering all the more intense.

As in a picaresque novel, the themes of class and wealth emerge when Marina interferes with the relaxed atmosphere of her convent's locutory: "No faltò quien respirando colera, y sentimiento le propusiese à la Abadesa ser indecentissimo el que una Lega . . . tubiese avilantes de corregir tan imprudentemente a las que si estubieran en el siglo quizas no la recibieran en su familia, ni aun por criada" [Those were not lacking who, breathing anger and resentment, told the Abbess that it was most indecent that a lay sister . . . should have the boldness to so imprudently correct others whose families in the outer world would not receive her even as a servant] (fol. 75v). The offended nuns also complain that Marina, as a twice-married woman of older years, steps beyond her station by dictating behavior to lifelong cloistered virgins. Faced with numerous and vocal protests, the abbess treats Marina "con excesivos rigores" [with excessive rigor] (fol. 76r) and indicates openly her profound displeasure with this attempted reform of convent life.

Heartened by the removal of the abbess's administrative sanction, Marina's enemies plot against her, and her work load is increased:

Como si su officio de obrera no fuese incomportable à sus fuerzas, se le mandò que por su mano, y sin ayuda alguna matase, desollase, y desquartizase los carneros que se traian de provission cada semana, y aun cada dia, y pareciendo juguete esta ocupacion se le añidiò el que barriese los corrales, limpiase los gallineros, y aun que purgarse los lugares comunes, y los immundos vasos. (fol. 76r)

As if her work as a laborer were not already incompatible with her strength, she was ordered to kill, gut, and quarter, with her own hands and no help whatsoever, the lambs that were brought in as provisions every week, and even every day; and this occupation seeming like play, they also gave her those of sweeping out the corrals, cleaning the chicken coops, and even purging the public places and the filthy chamber pots.

The symbolic identification of Marina with the innocent lambs she is compelled to slaughter is evident: as God's Christlike emissary, the nun must suffer a purging of sin during her earthly residence. But the fact that her terrestrial trials are

played out against the background of a convent, rather than
the secular "siglo" she had so joyously left behind, twists this
routine exemplary plot into another kind of tale. The combination of an ironic inversion of Paradise into hell with graphic,
excessive descriptions of the most base detail suggests a picaresque reading. It is as if the Convento de Jesús María were yet
another one of the stops on Marina's unhappy route, with the
abbess and her sisters cruel masters, and the priests paragons
of faith: "Exortandola à la paciencia, y sufrimiento la obligò su
Confessor à que no dexase de hazer lo que Dios mandaba"
[Urging her to have patience and to suffer, her confessor obligated her not to stop doing what God had commanded] (fol.
77r).

As a comparison, Teresa of Avila writes in *Libro de su vida*
([1562] 1979) about being mistreated for her work as a reformer:

Estaba muy malquista en todo mi monasterio, porque quería hacer
monasterio más encerrado: decían que las afrentaba, que allí podía
también servir a Dios, pues había otras mijores que yo. . . . Unas decían que me echasen en la cárcel, otras, bien pocas, tornaban algo
para mí: yo bien veía, que en muchas cosas tenían razón, y algunas
veces dábales discuento aunque como no había de decir lo principal,
que era mandármelo el señor, no sabía qué hacer, y así callaba. (258)

I was very disliked by my entire convent because I wanted to make it
a more cloistered convent. They said that I insulted them, that God
could be served there also, since there were others better than I. . . .
Some said I should be thrown in jail; others, very few, defended me
somewhat. I could see that in many things they were right, and sometimes I lessened up on them, although since I couldn't say the most
important thing, which was that God had given me an order, I didn't
know what to do and kept silent.

Although Teresa sees doubt and opposition to her plan as a
test of spirit and faith, the kind of tortures to which Marina is
subjected are not found in the *Vida*. Their inclusion in *Parayso
Occidental* is a narrative device of Sigüenza's that combines the
piety of an ascetic tract with the layering of baroque excess in
order to create a criollo history of the New World and the convent. It is here that the issue of textual authority (paternity) and
the ideological program of *escarmiento* (paternalism) emerge
most plainly. Both are at the root of this picaresque narration,
which at the same time provides the format to tell a life story,

gain control of the text, and put unobservant seventeenth-century nuns in their place.

In chapters 13 to 17 the question of mysticism versus diabolical possession becomes a main theme. As Marina's tortures at the hands of her sisters escalate, she is accused of witchcraft: "La zaherian de bruxa, de nigromantica, y de hechizera, evitando su presencia con ceremonias, y con melindres como de quien tenia pacto con el demonio" [They reproached her as a witch, a conjurer, and a sorceress, avoiding her presence with ceremonies and fastidiousness as if she had a pact with the devil] (fol. 78r). At this point Sigüenza begins to quote Marina more frequently, as she martyrs herself to the cause of convent reform.

As before, it is not clear where these citations come from, or how much they have been polished by Sigüenza's pen. Without noted references, they become part of his text, the words of a character in his narration; here again are the disclaimers that invalidate the truth of the life Sigüenza tells and the history into which he tries to incorporate it. For example, following a passage in which Marina's visions of Teresa speaking from beyond the grave are held up as glorious instances of piety, Sigüenza observes: "Pero como fueron circunstanciadas estas visiones, ni la tradicion nos lo dize, ni su confessor nos lo expressa" [But how these visions were circumstantiated, neither does tradition tell us, nor does her confessor express] (fol. 8lr). The conflict between the discourses of historical tradition and American authority fragments the criollo text into confusing disarray.

Chapter 14 contains a moral tale of *escarmiento* with an unusual detail. A "diabolic" nun of Jesús María had forgotten her vows and spent all her time being courted by suitors in the convent locutory. She is struck with a sudden illness, then cured by Marina's constant prayer and vigilance. However, her friends visit the infirmary to tell of her suitors' distraught state, and plead with her to write one of them in particular to thank him for his ardor. The recently reformed nun hesitates, but ultimately gives in, and Sigüenza dramatically reports what follows: "Ah pobre Monja! . . . Aparta de ti esse papel; dexa essa pluma. . . . Assi se lo gritaria su alborotada conciencia, quando descargando Dios el azote temerosissimo de su ira, sin que aca-base de escrivir el primer ringlon le quitò la vida" [Ah, poor Nun! . . . Push away that paper; put down that pen. . . . This is what her agitated conscience must have been shouting at her, when God, cracking the most fearsome whip of his rage, took her life before she could finish writing the first line] (fol. 82v).

This is an exemplary story with a distinct message: writing is dangerous. For a woman, writing signifies power that should be put to use only in the service of God; any deviation from that humble position merits the strictest punishment. For a criollo writer like Sigüenza y Góngora, subject to censorship and his own conflicting discourses, the contrasts of Paradise/hell and mystic vision/diabolic possession that surface constantly in these pages echo his own uneasiness with the text. Words must be carefully chosen so as to shepherd Marina's life story through the dangers of too much sanctity on one hand, or too little on the other. Moreover, her story, which condemns the sisters of Jesús María as obstreperous and even immoral, must be interpreted to praise this same problematic convent. Sigüenza juggles many balls in this attempted balancing act that is not consistently successful.

In a moment of ecstatic vision, Marina wonders:

Que es aquesto! Quien a mi me ha hecho Poeta? Quien es quien me ilustra mi entendimiento rudo, y le sugiere semejantes palabras a mi torpe lengua? Quien puede ser sino vos, ciencia infinita, elegancia infinita, sabiduria infinita, Dios immenso, de donde sale, y a donde se refunde como en su origen, y principio quanto se admira bueno. (fol. 88r)

What is this! Who has made me a Poet? Who is it that illuminates my base intelligence and suggests this sort of words to my clumsy tongue? Who could it be but you, infinite science, infinite elegance, infinite knowledge, immense God, from whom all things good come and are recast to be as they were in their original beginnings.

Who, indeed, has made this simple woman's direct language into poetry? Who has made the story of her pious life part of a book, part of a New World history? Who "originates" these words? This passage is a comment on the power of the written word. The nun's inspired speech is a gift from God; transcribed by the criollo writer's pen, it becomes part of his narration, his own creation, and finally praise for the American Paradise. The preoccupation of a colonial writer with written power, with authority over his own history, emerges repeatedly as the text itself dwells on this same concern.

I end my discussion of Libro Segundo with a look at some references to history and its writing that Sigüenza makes in chapter 18 and also in chapter 28, the book's final chapter. The theme of the New World history developed by Sigüenza in Libro Primero returns in another guise as he laments his lack of reliable sources:

Quexome quando aqui llego del Confessor de la V.M. por que pudiendo darnos materia para muchos capitulos en este asunto, ocupandose en digressiones impertinentes, escrive no querer referir lo mucho que de esto sabe, por que no le pusiesen en el catalogo de los Autores prolixos. Quexome de las Religiosas del convento Real de Jesus Maria, que no anotaron lo que vieron, ni conservan con tenaz memoria lo que oyrian à cerca de esta à sus mayores, y antiguas. Quexome del tiempo que lo borra todo, y quexome de mi misma nacion de lo mismo. (fol. 91v)

Upon reaching this point, I blame the Venerable Madre's Confessor, who could have given us material for many chapters on this topic, but occupying himself with impertinent digressions, writes that he does not want to report the many things he knows so that he will not be placed in a catalogue of prolix authors. I blame the Nuns of the Convento Real de Jesús María, who did not record what they saw and do not preserve with tenacious memory what they must have heard their older sisters say about this. I blame time, which erases everything, and I blame my own nation for doing the same.

In other words, the written tradition of the convent, along with that of New Spain – the "nation" Sigüenza refers to[5] – does not provide sufficient material for a truly baroque history, and Sigüenza takes his sources to task for omitting the very excess that would make such an account possible. Quoting de la Mota's desire to "evitar prolixidad" [avoid prolixity] (fol. 95r), Sigüenza's retort is fierce: "Y como si todo esto no bastase para acreditarse de no prolixo, al fin de su relacion volviò à molestar à sus Letores con repetir lo proprio. . . . Pero yo digo que nada sobra en esta materia de que siempre le resulta a la divina Magestad alabanza, y gloria" [And as if all this were not enough to establish himself as not prolix, at the end of his account he bothers his readers again by repeating the same things. . . . But I say that nothing is too much for this subject, which always results in the praise and glory of the divine Majesty] (fol. 95r–v).

In light of my discussion of a picaresque strategy in the telling of Marina's life story, this demand for more takes on another dimension. Marina's visions serve history as proof of its truth, proof that the story is being told just as it happened. They also prove the will of God in the foundation of the Convento de Jesús María through the presence there of a divinely inspired mystic, conveniently ignoring her own challenge to the convent's character. For these reasons, Sigüenza declares there can never be too much material related to a holy life; it provides the excess of detail required by baroque historiography.

Yet these same visions, which should bear witness to *Parayso Occidental*'s historical accuracy, undermine it through their imaginative, poetic language. Divine visions have no written tradition, no classic form from which to develop a baroque history.[6] Thus Sigüenza the historian wants to distance his own erudition from their lack of traditional learning and knowledge, from that same absence of learned reference that his "Prologo al letor" declared to be the proper style for a history by and for women. This distance is accomplished by questioning the judgment of sources, especially Pedro de la Mota, and by asserting Sigüenza's own preparation as superior.

The criollo historian paints himself into a rhetorical corner. Visionary episodes are necessary to historical truth, but are built on dangerously shaky foundations, so shaky, in fact, that they can be considered heretical if wrongly presented. How, then, to include a nontraditional form of writing within what purports to be the one and only history of an occidental Paradise? How to declare paternal control over an unruly female text?

The way in which Sigüenza y Góngora presents the life of Marina de la Cruz is yet another baroque retelling of the sixteenth-century American classics. The sober rhetoric of de la Mota's *relación* (as Sigüenza himself calls it) is imaginatively expanded by Sigüenza – who invents speeches for Marina in the classical historiographical tradition – until it becomes a picaresque history. It is in dialogue with de la Mota the chronicler that Sigüenza writes Libro Segundo and incorporates the authority of others' voices into his own narrative. The picaresque strategy in *Parayso Occidental* is a direct descendent of de la Mota's *relación*.

In the final pages of Libro Segundo, Sigüenza once again takes up the theme of American history, declaring that if more of the miracles performed by Marina had been written down in the past, more would be in his 1684 text. The miracles undoubtedly occurred, he avows, since Inés de la Cruz witnessed them; if they had been preserved, "pudiera haverse estendido este libro à mayor volumen" [this book could have been enlarged into a greater volume] (fol. 127v). Just as Marina's miracles were lost to posterity until Sigüenza stepped in to rectify the situation, so were her bones "promiscuamente" [promiscuously] (fol. 127v) buried in the convent church along with those of other nuns. The mystic's skull, however, was saved by an anonymous follower of her reforms. Sigüenza mentions that he has provided the skull with a suitable resting place: "una caxa aforrada de brocado con cubierta de terciopelo carmesi, y tachonada curiosissimamente con clavazon dorada, la qual hize yo de los bienes de D. Juan de Alva Cortes su pariente, de quien fuy Albacea" [a box, lined with brocade, with a cover of crimson velvet, and very carefully garnished with a set of golden nails, which I had made using funds from the estate of her relative don Juan de Alva Cortés, for whom I was executor] (fol. 128r).

This is Sigüenza's material reason for writing Marina's life story. Alva Cortés was Marina's great-nephew and the son of Fernando de Alva Ixtlilxochitl, descendant of caciques, poet, and chronicler of indigenous history. Sigüenza writes his Libro Segundo to repay a debt to Alva Cortés:

Esta circunstancia acompañada de la gratitud por los cariños, y beneficios de que le soy deudor, à que se añade haver sido esta su voluntad, me obliga à perpetuar su memoria en aqueste libro, y para ello me parece el mejor de todos el siguiente modo, por que puede ser que en los tiempos venideros les sirva à algunos. (fol. 128r)

This circumstance, along with gratitude for the affection and favors I owe him, to which I add that his own will was that it be so, obliges me to perpetuate his memory in this book, and to that end I believe the following to be the best manner of all, because it may be that in future times it will serve others.

As Irving Leonard (1959) notes, Sigüenza helped to save Alva Cortés's estate from a takeover by the colonial authorities – it was said Alva was not an Indian and had no title to the land – and in return was given a small plot, plus the collected papers of Alva Ixtlilxochitl (200 – 1). Alva Cortés is described by Sigüenza as an "Interprete que fue de la Real Audiencia, y Jusgado de Indios, Cacique del Pueblo de S. Juan Teotihuacan, hombre muy ajustado en sus procedures, y devotissimo de los Santos" [Interpreter of the Royal Court of Appeals and the Indian Tribunal, Cacique of the Town of San Juan Teotihuacán, a man very correct in his conduct, and extremely devoted to the Saints] (fol. 128v). Alva's father, too, was an interpreter who had served Fray García Guerra, archbishop and later viceroy of New Spain at the beginning of the seventeenth century. As Leonard puts it, the mestizo poet was "a descendant of the only Texcocan chieftain who remained loyal to Cortés during the siege of Mexico City, and for this fidelity his heirs had enjoyed aristocratic privileges in the viceregal community" (78).

Thus the text of Libro Segundo concludes with the same order of inversion demonstrated in the first book. By blurring the forensic rhetoric of a *relación* into an inventive picaresque tale, by absorbing the life story of an uneducated nun into the complicated patterns of a baroque New World history, Sigüenza asserts American authority and makes those texts his own. Dedicating the entire second book to a family of caciques who were instrumental in the success of the Conquest adds on a final narrative layer of inversion. The betrayal of their own people by the Alva clan, their use of language and interpretation to collaborate with the Spaniards, are in turn interpreted by the criollo writer as a triumphant contribution to the establishment of a better, western Paradise. That Sigüenza y Góngora's own rhetoric is fluid and fundamentally contradictory is evident in its internal pattern of inversion, culminating in a picaresque hell made from a Paradise.

As Carlos de Sigüenza y Góngora composes his baroque narrative through the prism of criollo historiography, his sources and references are steadily absorbed into the book called *Parayso Occidental*. In examining the first two Libros of *Parayso,* I have mapped out a narrative voice moving between the discourses of paternity and paternalism. The concern of the first is to gain authority over the text of Spanish American history; to that end Sigüenza establishes his domain of expertise as a Mexican historian. The second discourse demonstrates an ideological program aimed at female readers that offers moralistic examples of good and bad conduct for women, especially religious women. Through these two strategies, Sigüenza y Góngora draws the texts of others into his book and enhances his own stature as a historian and seeker of truth.

Libro Primero gathers materials pertaining to the foundation of the Convento de Jesús María in the late sixteenth century. In this Libro Sigüenza displays his talent for archival research and his thorough knowledge of documentary evidence. Libro Segundo, treating the life of Marina de la Cruz, presents a vida originally oral in nature but written down by the nun's confessor, Pedro de la Mota, and by another nun, Inés de la Cruz. The challenge for Sigüenza is to absorb the nun's mystical life story into his historical narration and in the process discount the authority of de la Mota as a complete source. As I have shown, there are instances where Sigüenza invents text for Marina. He can do this because she did not write her own story; those who wrote about her did so after her death.

Thus in the first two parts of this baroque New World history Sigüenza y Góngora manipulates documents and biography, sometimes transforming the latter into an imagined first-person account. I have looked at the manipulative schemes he employs to cut and paste his narrative sources into a book, according to precepts of the baroque era. In the drama of that composition lies part of the story of the development of narrative in Spanish America, the blending of history with the baroque language of hyperbole and exaggeration that today we call the chronicle of America.

In the third section of the narrative a change takes place, for the criollo historian is now dealing with autobiography as well as biography, with first-person stories written by the nuns themselves about their own lives. The absorption of these women's autobiographies into a learned history is a different exercise from that of the previous two Libros because greater manipulation is required on the part of the historian to contain the many voices within his overall plan. In this final section of *Parayso Occidental* Sigüenza builds a wall of discourse around the vidas he uses as examples in a text destined for two different audiences: the king and other women.

Libro Tercero, the last book of *Parayso Occidental,* combines all the narrative strategies of its two predecessors. It is a heterogeneous mixture of numerous vidas and historical narrative, pertaining to convent life in the Convento de Jesús María and to the 1616 founding of the Convento de San José. In this book Sigüenza's narrative voice reaches an apogee of personal expression and his own writing process becomes most apparent; the picaresque material and examples of *escarmiento* become pronounced and their reasons for incorporation into the history readily evident. This third Libro's blended nature and polyphonic voice thus exemplify the entire text of *Parayso Occidental*.

Of the book's twenty-five chapters, the first nine are dedicated to the two principal Carmelite founders, Inés de la Cruz and Mariana de la Encarnación, who appeared first as actors in Marina's story. One of their followers, dead before she could leave one convent for the other, is the subject of chapter 10. These ten chapters taken together constitute a unified segment of Libro Tercero, built around the theme of the Carmelite foundation.

In chapters 1 through 6 Sigüenza's first-person "I" intervenes only once, in the first two pages. For the balance of these chapters he ceded center stage to Inés de la Cruz's account of her early life and experiences as a convent reformer. Inés's vida is introduced by Sigüenza, who notes the special circumstances that have led to his decision to quote her directly: "Occupa en este libro el lugar primero quien pide de justicia para grandes hechos, y virtudes heroycas especial historia: Estorvame el emprenderla no ser licito meter la hoz en agena mies; ni quizás pudiera perficionarla aunque lo intentase por la incomparable grandeza de su noble asunto" [The first position in this book is held by one who claims a special history because of her great deeds and heroic virtues; I am kept from undertaking it, since reaping what others have sown is unjust. And perhaps I would not be able to perfect it even were I to try, due to the incomparable grandness of its noble topic] (fol. 129r).

If Sigüenza is ready to abdicate modestly the role of narrator, he reserves authorial power as discoverer of the text. Moreover, God stands behind him in this effort,

poniendo en mis manos una brevissima relacion en que la misma V.M. Ynes de la Cruz le diò cuenta de su conciencia à su Confessor, que es la que ya se sigue . . . con advertencia de ser mias algunas palabras, que se añadieron, ò por que se necessitaban en el contexto; ò por que, para necessarias noticias las jusguè precisas, omitiendose tambien algunas en otras partes, por ser inescusablemente necessario el que assi se hiziese. (fol. 129v)

placing in my hands a very brief report in which the Venerable Madre Inés de la Cruz herself gives an account of her conscience to her Confessor, which is the one that now follows . . . with the advisement that some words added are mine, either because they were necessary for the context, or because I judged them indispensable for necessary information, some words in other places also being omitted when it was inexcusably necessary for me to do so.

This is Sigüenza y Góngora's clearest statement of his editorial policy in *Parayso Occidental*. But as no documentation in the printed vida informs the reader which words have been added or deleted, we are left with a text that has become part of a larger design, a version both abridged and enlarged. A similar narrative device of a miraculously discovered text had been widely adopted by novelists in the seventeenth century to make their fictions more like histories. Although there is no doubt that Sigüenza actually did quote from a real vida – other writings of Inés de la Cruz are still in existence – in the absence of more detailed annotation, his historical narrative suggests fictional devices.

Inés's life is told in a flowing narrative, which, although somewhat polished, is certainly her own and not Sigüenza's. The story is simple and direct, moving in a chronological manner through the nun's childhood, profession in the convent, and career as a reformer. Owing much to Teresa of Avila's *Vida*, it is a text I explore in detail in Chapter 5. Considering here the way in which it fits into Sigüenza's history, various elements make a picaresque discourse reemerge more strongly now than before. Among these elements are the first-person narrative voice, an unfortunate young life, and later troubles in the Concepcionista convent told in a spare and realistic manner without the extreme detail of Marina's story in Libro Segundo.

However, as soon as Inés reaches the end of her account, Sigüenza rapidly takes over with a typically baroque flourish: "Si de la expression de un solo artejo se induce legitimamente la descollada estatura de algun gigante, que serà lo que se debe inferir de la relacion pasada" [If from one sole joint the surpassing stature of some giant may legitimately be assumed by induction, what might we infer from the previous account] (fol. 150v). The metonymic part represents the whole, and a small portion of the many things that could be said about Inés must stand in for the entire life. Sigüenza fills in the missing details, the nun's death figuring most prominently among them. Comparing her to Teresa, he coyly denies any personal opinion: "Tocale al Historiador referir los sucesos desnudamente, vistalos el Letor de ponderaciones si de ello gusta" [It is up to the Historian to present the events naked, the Reader may dress them with pondered thoughts if desired] (fol. 152v).

According to this division of labor, the historian's text must be devoid of all unnecessary detail, denuded of lyricism or poetry. Yet the next paragraph describes Inés's physical appearance in terms borrowed from the courtly love tradition:

La estatura de su cuerpo fue delgada, derecha, y gallardamente proporcionada: el rostro aguileño de color sonroseado tirante à blanco, la boca aunque no pequeña muy agraciada por tener los labios encendidissimos, y el de abaxo belfo, los ojos tenia en buena proporcion, y de colores varios, la nariz larga sin demasia, y derecha con hermosura. (fol. 152v)

Her bodily stature was slender, straight, and gracefully proportioned: the aquiline face of a rosy color tending toward white; the mouth, though not small, very nice with its extremely red lips, the lower one protruding; the eyes well proportioned and of a variegated color; the nose long but not too long, and beautifully straight.

This is a Renaissance portrait, measured and balanced, everything in proportion: the portrait of a lady.

But this lady is a nun and a mystic, and the historian a baroque writer, so the tranquil peace of this picture is interrupted with a twist:

En el aspecto se le alternaba la gravedad venerable con el agrado apacible, pero despues que le fueron frequentes los extasis, y arrobamientos se la mudò el rostro de hermoso en penitente, pero sin fealdad, faltandole tambien la viveza de sus colores; pero en vez de ellos arrojaba un resplandor admirable. (f. 152v)

In her expression a venerable seriousness alternated with a mild pleasantness, but after she began to have frequent ecstasies and seizures her face changed from beautiful to penitent, but without ugliness, and also without lively colors; in their place glowed a marvelous splendor.

The baroque description celebrates the shift from color to light and shadow, the effects of ecstasy and emotional seizures. This final paragraph closes the seven chapters of *Parayso Occidental* devoted to Inés's life, and although the bulk of the story is told in the nun's own words, Sigüenza begins and ends it. Thus the rough, slightly smoothed-over canvas of Inés's text is framed by the criollo's ornamentation, his own text, which never completely relinquishes authority.

In chapters 8 to 10 Sigüenza's narrative control grows because his editorial role is not so openly stated as before (although a comparison is made with Inés's autobiography). Mariana de la Encarnación has also written her own life story and Sigüenza considers it a reliable source: "Fuera querer meterme en igual empeño al antecedente escrivir la vida de la religiosissima M. Mariana de la Encarnacion con difuso estilo" [I would be getting myself involved in the same type of effort as the preceding one were I to write the life of the most religious Madre Mariana de la Encarnación with exuberant style] (Fol. 153r). Therefore, he will make no attempt to write a new vida, preferring instead to rewrite the old one, "lo que ella propria escrivió (que procurarè reducir à compendio breve)" [what she herself wrote (which I will attempt to reduce to a brief summary)] (fol. 153v). Given Sigüenza's complaints about a lack of source material, it is worth asking why he condenses such a solidly authentic document, as chapter 9 begins: "No quiero empeñarme en sucesos particulares en que pudiera sin duda estenderme mucho" [I do not wish to dwell on particular events about which, without a doubt, I could elaborate] (fol. 155v).

Having given up a measure of authority for Inés, Sigüenza declines to do the same for Mariana. Here the pattern set down in Libro Segundo returns, with Sigüenza directing the action as the quotes from others' writings become details in his own text. However, it is now autobiography being reduced to fit the space allotted to it within the history; Mariana's story as she herself told it is selectively excerpted. The authenticity of this eyewitness information is beyond question and Sigüenza cannot fault it on grounds of what is missing, as in the case of Pedro de la Mota's account of Marina. Instead there is an overabundance that needs pruning and polishing performed – with assurances of the greatest of respect – by the historian's pen.

In these three chapters devoted to Mariana are citations from Inés's work, from Mariana's, and from that of another sister, Catalina de Christo. These women are all introduced by Sigüenza in much the same way a character in a story would be: "Ella propria nos ha de referir el caso de aqueste modo" [she herself will describe the case in this way] or "Dexo varios sucesos de su vida para su propria historia" [I leave various events of her life to her own history] (fol. 156v). In Chapter 3 I offered the example of narration in Cervantes, where various levels of discourse are manipulated by the author to create an illusion of verisimilitude. But whereas Cervantes's sophisticated narration plays with and parodies the concept of authority, Sigüenza's embraces it with a deadly seriousness befitting a writer steeped in a tradition of orthodoxy and neoscholasticism. His presence as moralizing historian is always exposed, even insisted on, either through overt declarations of narrative intervention or the absence of citations to the contrary.

The life of Ana de la Concepción, which is the subject of chapter 10, continues to advance the dominance of the criollo's narrative voice. The primary sources of information are the vidas of Inés and Mariana. The two sisters had wanted Ana to join them in the Carmelite foundation. Unfortunately, she died before the new convent was established, but the circumstances and details of her later years at the Convento de Jesús María were dutifully recorded by her sisters. Her early life there, however, constitutes another absent text about which Sigüenza may speculate:

Aunque es cierto ignorarse lo especial de sus exercicios, y ocupaciones en sus primeros años, debemonos persuadir haver sido todo ello perfectissimo en subido grado. . . . Assi lo escrivió la V.M. Ynes de la Cruz en lo que queda referido en lo antecedente que volverè aqui à referir con alguna difusion como en lugar proprio. (fol. 158v)

Although it is true we know nothing about the special nature of the exercises and concerns of her early years, we must be persuaded that they were all extremely perfect in the highest degree. . . . Thus wrote the Venerable Madre Inés de la Cruz in what was related before, which I will relate here again at some length, this being the appropriate place.

Ana becomes a reformer whose campaign in the convent is expressed in terms of a holy war waged against the Devil's work. Like a good soldier – or more accurately, a guerrilla fighter – she risks her life for the cause:

Publicò guerra contra los vicios con singular esfuerzo. . . . Lo mismo fue esto que comenzarsela a hazer el infierno horrorosamente, valiendose para ello assi de algunas de sus subditas à quienes de ninguna manera agradaba tanta reforma, como de seculares que intentaron quitarle la vida por esta causa, y que lo huvieran conseguido sin duda alguna si no lo estorvara Dios milagrosamente. (fol. 159r)

She waged a war against vice with a singular effort. . . . At the same time, hell began a most horrendous war against her, relying for this on some of her inferiors who in no way cared for such reforms, and also on some lay sisters who tried to take her life for this cause, and who would have done so with no doubt whatsoever if God had not miraculously stopped them.

A typhoid fever kills Ana before the Carmelite Convento de San José is built, but her spiritual legacy lives on in the person of her sister Elena, who outlives Ana by ten years. Elena, occupying Marina de la Cruz's former cell, is given to frequent levitation, so powerful is her faith: "Continuamente se arrobaba, suspendiendose hasta llegar con la cabeza al techo de la celda" [She repeatedly went into raptures, levitating until her head reached the ceiling of her cell] (fol. 161v). With Elena's death in 1620, chapter 10 ends.

Considering Libro Segundo – Marina's life story – and these first ten chapters of Libro Tercero together, some notable themes emerge. The lives of these mystical reformers and disciples of Teresa comprise a story-within-a-story: that of the founding of the Convento de San José. Sigüenza presents them as such, building a narrative in which the characters are closely involved with one another and form a dynasty extending from Marina through Inés, Mariana, and Ana, and finally completing the cycle with Elena's trances in the same holy place where it all began.

From this perspective the collective vidas chronicle yet another holy war and another conquest, that of asceticism over laxity and worldly temptation in the convent itself. The parallel with Libro Primero and its history of a New World Paradise is inescapable; where the first Libro presents a rewriting of the sixteenth-century chronicles, the Carmelite cycle is its baroque, Counter-Reformation complement. The first supplies the material foundation, the second a spiritual fulfillment of promise.

However, the retelling of the vidas, which to Sigüenza y Góngora means transforming others' accounts into his own history, is carried out by the author in such a way as to undo the original premise of Libro Primero, the establishment of an occidental Paradise in the Convento de Jesús María. The revised narration takes place on two levels as it simultaneously retells both the old documents (of de la Mota and the nuns) and the new (Sigüenza's own Libro Primero). In the portrayal of the Convento de Jesús María as an "infierno" of resistance to Carmelite reforms, its identity as a western Paradise becomes that of a Paradise lost. Despite Sigüenza's attempt to interpret the vidas to his own ends by making Jesús María the originator of San José – an effort to manipulate the vidas through an always-present narrative voice that imposes the rhetoric of history – the contradiction is unresolvable in the text.

Again, the presence of women in this text has forced a rhetorical crisis. A female audience inspires the paternalism seen in tales of *escarmiento* and asceticism; women writers, a heterogeneous, sporadically documented narration of visions and lives bordering on the picaresque and fictional. As Sigüenza struggles to assert paternal authority over the women's texts while denying association with their more imaginative aspects, his history shifts rhetorical camps and boundaries at a dizzying pace. Ultimately, the shifting text of the criollo historian is what is left for us as readers.

In the final sections of *Parayso Occidental,* autobiographical sources give way to oral history and new narative strategies emerge. Chapters 11 through 18 string together the lives of various nuns, an abbess, and three servants (two of whom are Indian and one black). Their lives are narrated by Sigüenza as a series of *casos,* or short tales that usually end on a didactic or miraculous note. Together these stories make up a mosaic that effectively represents the social spectrum of the convent. Convent society mirrored the racial and class stratification of the colonial city that surrounded it, and in these chapters Sigüenza provides just such a panoramic view of New Spain.

An evident comparison exists here with another colonial text of the seventeenth century: Juan Rodríguez Freyle's *El carnero*

(1638), a composite narration of the same type of *pétites histoires*. Although this work chronicling the society of New Granada (colonial Colombia) is a secular account, and *Parayso Occidental* is a religious one, here they share a similar structure, with one tale leading easily into the next. More important, they are based on similar types of sources, for these eight chapters of *Parayso Occidental* are not rewritings of autobiographical texts, as was the case with the Carmelite founders' *vidas*, but rather sketches drawn from oral history and the recollections of living nuns.

Some factual details, such as dates of profession in the order, are taken from the *Libro de profesiones* kept in the convent archive, but Sigüenza openly states that written sources for these *casos* do not exist: "Ya que no todo, porque me faltan noticias para emprenderlo, por lo menos dirè de la M. Maria de S. Nicolas lo poco que se conserva, à pesar del olvido, en la comun memoria" [Although I cannot be complete because I lack the information for that undertaking, I will at least say what little is preserved in the common memory, in spite of oblivion, about Madre María de San Nicolás] (fol. 161v). The "common memory" of convent folklore provides the stuff of these *casos*, as do gossip and rumor in *El carnero*.

Rodríguez Freyle's work, however, aspires to none of the pretensions to rhetoric that *Parayso Occidental* claims for itself. Freyle ([1638] 1973) declares in his *Prólogo al lector* that "aunque en tosco estilo, será la relación sucinta y verdadera, sin el ornato retórico que piden las historias, ni tampoco lleva raciocinaciones poéticas, porque sólo se hallará en ella desnuda la verdad" [although written in a rough style, the account will be succinct and truthful, without the ornate rhetoric the histories demand, nor will it have poetic ratiocinations, so that in it will be found only the naked truth] (50).[7] Sigüenza, on the other hand, avers that his text conforms to the "estrechas leyes" of history, and scoffs at the rudeness of style he finds in de la Mota's account.

Whereas Freyle intends to flesh out the sixteenth-century chronicles of New Granada with entertaining, moralistic, and sometimes ribald stories, Sigüenza's ambition is to rewrite history, a desire more akin to that of Inca Garcilaso in his *Comentarios reales*. The pretension is not only rhetorical but patriotic as well, for to write a true criollo history will give New Spain a past equal to Europe's. Although both Sigüenza and Freyle equate less ornate style with truth, Sigüenza equates truth with history; nothing less will satisfy the requirements of this baroque revision of classic history.

The oral history of these small tales is a marked detour from the narrative framework of Libros Primero and Segundo and that of the Carmelite vidas. Sigüenza's sources remain unnamed for the most part, although a few are mentioned. It is the fate of the American historian, he says, to be forced into reliance on such materials because the New World's written tradition is scanty and held in contempt by the Old. María de San Nicolás, for example, had her life recorded by a confessor only to have it disappear with him somewhere in Spain:

Alcanzòle tambien à ella la infelicidad con que procura nuestra desgracia el que no se propague por el mundo lo que por ser Americano, aunque en si sea muy grande, lo tienen en el resto del universo por despreciable cosa, pues no quedando ni aun el primer borrador de su vida en la Nueva-España, pereciò el original de ella en la antigua donde muriò su Autor. (fol. 161v)

She, too, was affected by the unhappiness procured by our misfortune that American things are not promoted around the world, although they may be great, but thought of in the rest of the universe as worthless; for not even the first draft of her vida was left in New Spain, and the original perished in the Old [Spain] where its author died.

This lament for the one that got away serves as an excuse for a lack of documented sources and is also a convenient device through which Sigüenza may finally claim his own narrative authority without reservation. This group of chapters flows smoothly, without interference from any other author's narration. In fact, Sigüenza's control over his narration has become so emboldened that his text begins to cite itself as a source. Mentioning María de San Nicolás's uncle, Francisco Losa, he writes: "Algo queda dicho de este excelentissimo Varon desde el numero 366 de aqueste libro" [Something was said about this most excellent Man in paragraph 366 of this book] (fol. 162r). Similar references are scattered throughout the text of Libro Tercero. This internal folding of the text back over itself is yet another baroque trope, a mirror imaging that causes characters to exist in more than one place at a time and gives a layered structure to the story as each self-reference leads to another that went before it.

The *casos* related in these chapters of *Parayso Occidental* deal with varied events in the lives of María de San Nicolás and the other nuns portrayed, and provide an excuse for Sigüenza both to tell a good story and put forward examples of piety. For example, the tale of a reformed woman of the world who enters the convent novitiate is incorporated into Madre María's biography to demonstrate the nun's special gift of faith. A Mexican lady, "aplaudida de todos . . . inspirada del cielo dando de mano à las vanidades del mundo quiso reformar en la religion su pasada vida" [who was celebrated by all . . . with inspiration from heaven and despising all worldly vanities, wanted to reform her past life through religion] (fol. 163v).

María is staying in the infirmary, recovering from one of her perpetual illnesses, as the lady takes her vows. The Devil appears to María and tells her: "Me han quitado a essa picara de Juanilla, pues yo aseguro el que me lo paguen en la misma moneda las infames Monjas" [They've taken that picara Juanilla away from me, but I swear those damnable Nuns will pay me back in kind for her] (fol. 164r). He then sets to work on another novice whose vocation is weak and whose capital is slim, falling short of what is needed for a full dowry. Easily persuaded to leave the cloister, the novice steals away under cover of nightfall to escape. But Madre María, "ocupada entonces en contemplar à su Amado, pidiendole para sus Esposas de aquel Convento muchas mercedes" [occupied at that time in contemplation of her Beloved, requesting many mercies for His Brides in the Convent] (fol. 164r), sees the would-be escapee, informs the abbess, and saves a potential sinner by providing the needed cash for the dowry from her own funds.

Although short, this story has the basic elements of a Golden Age play: a virtuous maiden, a villain, a case of interchangeable identities, and a *barba,* or patriarchal authority figure – here, Madre María – jealously guarding the family's honor. Told in the context of a convent, the father becomes a mother, but the scheme remains familiar. The imaginative element in these *casos* is strong and Sigüenza's role of editor has grown to total authorship of this vida. He closes it with a nod to the written source he lacks: "el libro que tanta falta me ha hecho para no dilatarme en esta vida quanto yo quisiera" [the book whose lack has caused me not to dwell on this life as much as I would have liked to] (fol. 167r]. But clearly he has had no trouble providing the embroidery to ornament the bare facts.

So on go these stories, some with truly supernatural or humorous detail. After the custom of midnight prayers is discontinued, a nun begins to show up, dressed entirely in white, for the same services at the male monastery of la Merced. Questioned by a shocked friar, she claims to be a dead soul from Purgatory who can no longer perform her required penance at the convent. In another case, a nun is so wrapped up in thoughts of God that "se ponia el habito al revez con que causaba rise" [she put her habit on backwards, making people laugh] (fol. 170r). These sight gags or instances of transvestism fall within a range of commonly used baroque tropes, devices that mislead or complicate reality. They are part of the fabric of Sigüenza's tales that together form another illusion: that of an integrated narrative told by one (and only one) author.

The inclusion of three Indian and black subjects in chapters 15 and 16 distinguishes Sigüenza's convent history from other chronicles of convent foundations. It again underscores the differences of a history written by a scholar with an American perspective as compared with a strictly religious document penned by a priest. Neither does Sigüenza treat the non-European convent residents as unusual, since the number of servants in a large convent such as Jesús María was much greater than that of the elite group of nuns of the black veil. Sigüenza's treatment of Jesús María as an institution with the same racial and class composition as the society surrounding it follows his general scheme for *Parayso Occidental:* the presentation of the convent's founding in a universal historical context. Alongside the nuns, who represent purity and virginity in the western Paradise, the women of color who serve them stand for the success of the Conquest in converting indigenous (or imported) groups or *naciones.*

Still, Sigüenza, mindful of classic histories that view Indians and blacks as species of animals to be catalogued, feels compelled to explain why they are deemed worthy of their own chapters in *Parayso Occidental.* All three of these servants were especially religious, devout Christians; the same types of miracles and visions attributed to their mistresses occur here also. Chapter 15, which follows the story of an Indian girl named Petronila, begins:

Hecha ya mencion de la buena de Petronila, no ay razon para no ha-
zerla de otras humildes, y pequeñitas, que oy en la corte del supremo
Rey de los Reyes seràn muy grandes, y à quienes para que sea una
sola la digresion, me parece muy conveniente el ponerlas juntas.
(fol. 174r)

Since the good Petronila has already been mentioned, there is no reason not to do the same with other humble, little women, who today in
the court of the supreme King of Kings must be very great, and who,
I think, it will be very convenient to group together so that there will
be but one digression.

These lives are a divergence from the normal order of things in
a learned history, and their inclusion must be justified.

Francisca de San Miguel, India – an Indian woman – more
than proves her Christian piety: she foretells (and mourns) the
Mexico City insurrection of 1624 in which a largely Indian
crowd ransacked the viceregal palace and overthrew the viceroy
Marqués de Gelves (Israel 1975, 135–60). Sigüenza takes advantage of this anecdote to pronounce a moral aside: "Proloquio antiguo es, 'pagar el pueblo lo que los Reyes delinquen,'
y no proloquio, sino verdad infalible es, el que siente Dios
gravissimamente lo que estos pecan. Pero quien me mete a mi
en querer referir lo que aqui no toca" [It is an ancient maxim
that "the people pay for the Kings' transgressions," and it is not
a maxim, but an infallible truth, that God feels the sins of the
latter to be of the utmost gravity. But how is it that I have gotten
involved in relating things that have no place here] (fol. 174v).
The voice of the historian intervenes, as in Libro Primero, to
comment on a subject Sigüenza will return to in later years: the
rebellion of the Indians, treated in his 1692 *Alboroto y motín de
los indios de México*.[8] But the mask of historian is just as quickly
shed, for it does not appropriately belong in the context of the
narration of a vida. Nevertheless, this political and moral topic
has been mentioned, and in the narative it stays, a reminder of
Sigüenza's authorial presence.

Chapter 18, the last in this succession of *memorias*, offers a
medley of half a dozen short lives, introduced in this way: "Quisiera dezir mucho de muchas, pero no puedo sino dezir poco de
pocas, porque no se alargan à mas las noticias que se me han
dado; ni pide lo contrario la integridad de la historia, y mas
siendo el asunto de la presente publicar sucesos admirables, y
ponderar virtudes" [I would like to say much about many, but I

can only say little about a few because the information that has
been given to me amounts to no more. Neither does the integrity of history demand the contrary, and all the more so since
the business of the present history is to publish amazing events,
and to ponder virtues] (fol. 183r). The amazing events and
meditations on morality that are the stuff of this history require
no more than the truth, the documented evidence. Yet that evidence bears witness to events that have no text, visions and
miracles that have become memories caught in the web of time.
When Sigüenza attempts to present those events critically, he
writes the missing text, authoring a history cast in an American
context, a history of the virtuous Conquest that resulted in a
superior western Paradise.

It is appropriate, then, that chapter 18 end with notice of Isabel de San Pedro, the illegitimate daughter of Don Pedro Cortés, Marqués del Valle, who takes her vows some one hundred
years after the Conquest of Mexico. Isabel is an example of
"la abnegacion propria" [abnegation itself] (186r), sobbing
when she is addressed by her noble title, even by her own relatives. The latter include, according to Sigüenza, "D. Pedro
Nuño Colon Duque de Veragua, y Almirante de las Indias"
[don Pedro Nuño Colón, the duke of Veragua, and admiral of
the Indies] (186r).

This daughter of discovery and Conquest – of Columbus and
Cortés – felt herself unworthy of any special treatment and
thought that "no ero [sic] justo sino que todas la pisasen, y
ultrajasen como à quien merecia estar en el infierno por sus
enormes culpas" [it was only just that all would step on her, and
abuse her, as one who deserved to go to hell for her enormous
sins] (fol. 186r). Remembering the maxim "pagar el pueblo lo
que los Reyes delinquen," the text has completed another circle
with this penitent nun who turns Paradise into her own private
hell. Through Isabel the text settles its score with European history, her humiliation bringing glory to the New World. Once
again, the players have been recast and the chronicles rewritten
as Sigüenza lays claim to authority with a baroque finish.

Sigüenza y Góngora's control over his text reaches its zenith
in the final seven chapters of Libro Tercero. Two are devoted to
Tomasina de San Francisco, four to María Antonia de Santo
Domingo, and the very last to Matías de Gámez, chaplain of

the convent. Tomasina's story is a passionate one about a roguish sinner who finally heeds God's call late in life. A beautiful girl, she is jealously guarded and shut up at home by a cruel mother who tries to force the unwilling daughter into the cloister. Instead Tomasina marries a gentleman of the viceregal court, but her life only becomes worse:

Y si mala vida tubo con la Madre cuando muchacha, no fue digna de compararse con ella la que le diò el marido. Al segundo dia tapiò las ventanas de la casa, y quando salia de ella la dexaba encerrada en el ultimo aposento con muchas llaves, y aunque con tan nimia diligencia le quitaba las ocasiones, nunca le faltaron motivos al zeloso hombre para andar à pleytos. (fol. 187v – 88r)

And if her unmarried life with her mother was bad, it was nothing compared with the one her husband gave her. The day after they were married he boarded shut the windows of the house, and when he went out, he left her in the back room, locked up with many keys, and although owing to such excessive diligence he had no occasion for complaint, the jealous man never lacked for reasons to do so.

Within a month the jealous husband dies, leaving his widow enough money for a dowry with which to enter the convent. Tomasina, however, wants to enjoy her newfound freedom and looks upon the religious life as one more type of incarceration. Eventually, however, she sees the light and becomes an exceptionally devout example of piety and self-mortification.

Sigüenza's role has further shifted in this chapter, for now he is a witness to the events as well as their editor. Describing Tomasina's years as a widow, he notes, "gustosamente especificara yo singulares sucesos à cerca de esto por haver vivido entonces junto mi casa, si no tuviera que dezir de ella mayores cosas" [with great pleasure I would tell of specific, singular events regarding this, since I was living then in a house nearby, if I did not need to tell of greater things about her] (fol. 188r). Later, during the nun's period as a novice, she is miraculously burned on the arm by the fingers of a dead priest who suffers in purgatory. Sigüenza recalls viewing the evidence as a young man:

O por vezino, ò por curioso, dos dias despues consegui ver esto proprio en la porteria, y aunque como mosuelo estudiante no puse todo aquel cuydado que se debia, acuerdome muy bien el que no se estendian las quemaduras, sino à lo que con las yemas, y parte de los segundos artejos de los dedos se havia oprimido ... quedaron alli

estampadas las rayas y mayores poros de los dedos del difunto distin-
tamente. (fol. 190v)

Perhaps because I was a neighbor, or just curious, two days later I was
able to see this myself at the entryway to the convent, and although
being a young student I did not pay as much careful attention as I
should have, I remember very well that the burns only showed where
the fingertips and parts of the second joints had pressed . . . leaving
the lines and large interstices of the fingers of the dead man clearly
stamped there.

No longer relying on the memories of others, the narrative
has been advanced to a higher level of truth with Sigüenza's
first-person testimony. At the same time, it is transformed into
a vida belonging not only to Tomasina but to the criollo writer
as well, for the story relates part of his own early life. Sigüenza's
text has shifted from biography to autobiography, calling on
the authority of the eyewitness historian.

The four chapters regarding María Antonia de Santo Domingo extend Sigüenza's narrative authority even further.
Their subject was a personal friend of Sigüenza's and, as he
tells it, the muse who inspired the writing of *Parayso Occidental,*

quien queriendo yo escrivir la vida de la V.M. Marina de la Cruz por
mi espontaneo gusto, me estimulò con ruegos, y con noticias à la com-
posicion del primero, y segundo libro de este volumen en que quiso se
comprehendiesen las grandezas materiales, y formales de su convento
Real de Jesus Maria. (fol. 193v-4r)

who, when I wanted to write the life of the Venerable Madre Marina
de la Cruz for my own spontaneous pleasure, urged me with pleas
and information to compose the first and second books of this volume, which she wanted to cover the material and formal grandeur of
her Convento Real de Jesús María.

María Antonia died before the book's publication. Thus her
vida serves as an epitaph for both the nun and the text: "Con su
vida pues para terminarlo con buen fin se cerrarà este libro"
[Therefore, with her life story to finish it, this book will close
with a good ending] (fol. 194r). Sigüenza, with a sense of drama
for the ending of his history, affirms that the termination of the
narrative is his unilateral decision.

María Antonia's life was devoted to prayer from her earliest
years. When her parents tried to betroth her at the age of four-
teen, she refused to receive the potential suitor, "escondiendose

en un desvan de la casa por todo el dia" [hiding in the garret of the house all day long] (fol. 196v). Upon finally entering the convent, her piety causes no small consternation among the community, "pesadumbres originadas de quienes por sus tibiezas no gustaban del fervor con que havia comenzado su noviciado" [worries instigated by those who, because of their weaknesses, did not care for the fervor with which she had begun her novitiate] (fol. 196r). Nonetheless, she is later elected abbess by her sisters.

When María Antonia takes her vows in 1655, the convent's religious observance is at an all-time low level. The future abbess becomes a reformer, leading a reinstitution of daily communion and inspiring her own group of allies in the cause: "Comenzaron a establezer las penitencias publicas que ya no estaban en uso; à recogerse à los exercicios Carmelitanos, y Jesuitas, y à quitarse los tocados curiosos, las pulseras, los anillos, y semejantes adornos fantasticos con que se afean las almas" [They began to reestablish the public penitences no longer in use; to withdraw for the practice of Carmelite and Jesuit spiritual exercises, and to remove the unusual headdresses, bracelets, rings, and other fantastic adornments with which souls are defaced] (fol. 198v). The same superfluous ornamentation, according to Sigüenza's prologue, destroys a history. María Antonia's reform of the cloister is paralleled in Sigüenza's goal of reforming the writing of baroque history.

Ultimately, however, the baroque discourse of criollo culture pervades Sigüenza's text, not only in its convoluted language but in its structure as well. The death of this nun is a drawn-out agony of fever and pain, lasting from the eve of the Assumption (August 14) to the twelfth day of September. Her suffering is described in detail, especially the last three hours of death throes that imitate Christ's final hours on the Cross. María Antonia's death closes a life, a book, and a cycle of convent history. She dies on September 12, 1682,

en que cien años antes se havian trasladado las Monjas del antiguo Convento . . . al que oy poseen como lugar mas commodo; y haviendole yo advertido anticipadamente esta circunstancia tenia dispuesto regocijarla con grande fiesta . . . siendo ella el fruto centissimo que cogiò Dios de este Parayso, ò el casual portento con que los siglos suelen cerrarse, solo el docto sabe. (fol. 202r)

the day that one hundred years before the Nuns had been transferred from the old Convent . . . to the more comfortable one they have to-day. And since I had realized this circumstance beforehand, I had planned for a celebration with a great fiesta . . . she being the one-hundredth fruit that God picked from this Paradise, or perhaps the accidental portent with which centuries often close, only the learned may know.

Again, a parallel is drawn between events in the sixteenth and the seventeenth centuries; again, the convent's history is expanded into the larger arena of cosmic and world events, representing a significance extending far beyond the walls of its garden.

One hundred years of history, of American history, truly show the hand of God in the Conquest and the foundation of a New World Paradise. This centennial commemoration is followed by what Sigüenza considers an even more wondrous occurrence. María Antonia's face retains its lifelike beauty even after death, and the sisters hire a portrait painter to record forever their abbess's memory. As the painter lifts his brush, the face of the corpse begins to swell monstrously, but only on the side he tries to portray; the other side, which he cannot fully see, remains perfect. Turning the body around does no good: "Volvieron el cadaver del otro lado, y al mismo instante sucedio lo proprio" [They turned the cadaver around, and the identical thing occurred in that very instant] (fol. 202v).

The nuns cover María Antonia's horrible mask. After a few hours, a curious viewer finds it changed back again to its former perfection. Sigüenza concludes from this that God means for each one of the sisters of Jesús María to be "en sus procederes el retrato de las virtudes que la M. Maria Antonia de Santo Domingo exercitò viviendo; y que este es, sin duda, el que quiere la divina Magestad se perpetùe entre ellas para eterna memoria de su fiel Sierva, y alabanza suya" [in their conduct an image of the virtue that Madre María Antonia de Santo Domingo practiced during her life; and this is without a doubt what the divine Majesty wishes to be perpetuated among the sisters, in eternal memory of his faithful Servant and praise to Him] (fol. 202v).

An image of the body in death, then, is impossible to achieve. The representation must be alive and active, not flat and cold.

So, too, must the baroque text change a dead rhetorical form – the classic chronicle, the European history – into a representation, rather than a resemblance. The criollo writer uses baroque form to put American reality into action, to make the chronicles of Conquest come alive, to claim authority and assert narrative control over the historical text. As each one of María Antonia's disciples re-creates the martyr's example with her own actions, so too does Sigüenza's book rewrite both the nun's life and the story of the convent's founding, making them his own through a complicated baroque narrative strategy. A mere resemblance of the truth will not suffice; it must be complicated through trope and artifice, layered in form and concept as well as language, to make it bear witness to the American patrimony.

For it is ultimately a patrimony that Sigüenza sets out to create. Writing a narrative for and about women that will reflect his paternal role as author and father of a new history is the primary goal of *Parayso Occidental,* as is evidenced by chapter 25 of Libro Tercero. Although María Antonia de Santo Domingo's life closes the story of the convent, that of a man, Matías de Gámez, actually ends *Parayso Occidental.*

Gámez, chaplain of the convent, lived from 1600 to 1641, dying four years before Sigüenza was born. His pious, ascetic life of fasting, discipline, and penitence is told exactly as were those of the sisters, following the standard form of saints' lives with an emphasis placed on the virtues of charity, humility, and chastity. The chaplain is popular in the confessional, "en que le ganò a Dios infinitas almas, por ser muchas las que atraydas de su virginal modestia, penitente rostro, y afabilissimo trato lo buscaban de todas partes" [where he won infinite souls for God, for many were those who, drawn by his virginal modesty, penitent face, and most affable manner, sought him out from all over] (fol. 206r). Even after death the purity of his body remains uncorrupted, and violence breaks out among those who desire relics of this saintly man.

Gámez is interred by the Jesuits in the vaults of their main sanctuary. Thirty-one years later, in 1673, as the bones of these members of the Society of Jesus are moved to a new resting place, a miracle occurs: "Se hallò el cuerpo de nuestro exemplarissimo, y penitente clerigo absolutamente incorrupto, y como estaba en el dia que lo enterraron" [The body of our most exemplary and penitent cleric was found to be absolutely un-corrupted and as it was on the day he was buried] (fol. 206r). This is the final line of Libro Tercero, followed by the only di-rect citation of the Bible in the entire narrative: "Non nobis Domine, non nobis: sed nomini tuo da gloriam" [Not to us, O Lord, not to us, but to Thy name give glory].[9]

Thus does the baroque history of a convent close with the life story of a man whose saintly qualities are indistinguishable from those of the sisters, but who possesses the male authority of the confessional. Since Sigüenza considers María Antonia's vida to be an appropriate end for his book, Matías de Gámez's story appears as a coda, a reprisal of familiar themes. To go over territory already covered – the saintly life, the self-sacrifice, and the miracle of uncorrupted flesh – is redundant and breaks the circular symmetry the historian finds so attrac-tive as a narrative trope. Making the subject a Jesuit priest, however, pays homage to the order with which Sigüenza was as-sociated since adolescence, and which he unsuccessfully tried to join during his adult life. It also furthers the ideological agenda of *Parayso Occidental* – a Jesuit abhorence of women who trans-gress strict boundaries – by reasserting the authority of reli-gious men over the female residents of the convent.

Carlos de Sigüenza y Góngora's book attempts to rewrite the classic chronicles with baroque narrative strategies in order to claim authority over the text of American history. Since the chronicle in question comprises texts written or narrated by women, these strategies are pervaded by a desire to assert the male roles of father and moral adviser, the duties of paternity and paternalism, over the narrative voice of the vidas. These strategies are exposed as the author grapples with the para-doxes that a learned history by, for, and about women implies.

5
Reading the vidas

Up to this point I have been examining the ways in which Carlos de Sigüenza y Góngora uses the vidas written by nuns to further his own ideological, rhetorical, and patriotic programs. Now I turn to the vidas themselves to see what the nuns had to say about women's lives in the convent and the outside world, and what narrative vehicles they used to tell about those lives. In this gesture, I join an ongoing discussion taking place among feminist literary and cultural critics who read the vidas as women's texts. My interest, in the context of this study of Sigüenza y Góngora, is to address the relationships of discursive power and subversion that have been noted as characteristic of the vidas. Were the vidas a vehicle through which women could gain power by using written discourse? Do they describe a movement toward greater autonomy in convents that nurtured a separate space for women's culture? How did the nuns participate in the politics of the outer world from inside their cloistered space? What is the relationship of an eternalized, mystical discourse to written forms of history and chronological time? Some general background pertaining to this discussion will be useful before beginning my readings.

Interest in the women of colonial Latin America has become more and more widespread since the beginning of the 1980s. This can be attributed to several factors, among them a general interest in women subsequent to International Women's Year in 1975; a new generation of historians interested in social history and everyday life; the rise of women's studies in the Americas and in Europe; and the vogue in things colonial with the advent of the commemorative year 1992. Both the fields of literature and history, just to name two areas of study, have seen a great increase in publications related to the status of women. Works of history have dealt with education, marriage, sexuality, and the even more unexplored zones of witchcraft and popular culture.[1] Books about literature by women of the sixteenth and seventeenth centuries generally deal with the institution of the convent, where most women writers were located.

The work of pioneer historians such as Josefina Muriel and Asunción Lavrin has been crucial as scholars attempt to reconstruct the world in which these women lived and wrote. Shared by historians and literary critics alike is the painstaking labor of archival scholarship needed to unearth the texts of writing nuns, very few of which have been published. In this regard the work is largely that of finding and editing manuscripts. Electa Arenal was a trailblazer in this area, searching out the works of nuns in the archives, libraries, and convents of Europe and both North and Latin America. *Untold Sisters*, the book she and Stacey Schlau published in 1989, has contributed to the field excerpts of several important writings, making them accessible for the first time to a wider audience in both Spanish and English. In a like manner the work of Kathleen Myers and other scholars is bringing entire texts by nun writers into print in critical editions and English translations, a crucial step forward for a literature that has usually included only Sor Juana, and perhaps Madre Castillo, among its female voices.

Now that there are texts to read, they can be approached from various critical angles. Stephanie Merrim (1991) maps out some of these possibilities in her introduction to the volume of essays on Sor Juana that she has recently edited. What this brings to the surface is a hotly debated topic among scholars taking a feminist approach to women's texts, namely, the question of a separate sphere in women's culture. One tendency thus far has been to read the narrative life stories of nuns – the vidas – in the context of the work of other women writers and thinkers, placing the texts in a separate intellectual tradition much like the famous one set out by Sor Juana in her *Respuesta*. I am thinking here, for instance, of the genealogy put forth in *Untold Sisters* that posits "a woman's religious and literary tradition that grew largely separated from, although partly parallel to, the culture of men" (Arenal and Schlau 1989, 2). The idea of a separate literary space for women fits intriguingly with the separate physical space afforded by the convent itself; it is, indeed, almost irresistible not to picture a separate culture being forged by nuns writing behind the walls and grilles of their cloisters.

The delineation of a tradition of women's texts across geographical and chronological boundaries is thus one path toward a reading of the life stories of Hispanic nuns. It is equally crucial to consider the vidas of Spanish American nuns in the context of other colonial narrative forms. Therefore, in this chapter I venture out of the separate space of the vida as a link in the chain of female tradition and into the rather murkier waters of the juxtaposition of these life stories with other colonial narratives written by men. I do this not to erase gender differences, which I believe are present in the vidas, but to demonstrate how texts by men and women must be taken together in order to reconstruct the broader colonial discourse of Spanish America. My project is to work toward the location of colonial women's writing within colonial discourse, rather than a within a separate tradition or textual lineage. Instead of positing an autonomous sphere for the vidas, I situate them in a region of semiautonomy, where I think they can be most fruitfully understood.[2]

The vidas have been classified most often under the heading of hagiography. Lavrin (1991) has called hagiography a historical-literary genre – already a hybrid designation – and Muriel's difficulty in classifying the vidas in her *Cultura feminina novohispana* (1982), where they appear in sections devoted to biography, chronicle, and mysticism, also demonstrates how slippery they are to categorize. Muriel's view is comprehensive and the information invaluable; she has unearthed dozens of manuscripts and first editions that offer great possibilities for future research. It soon becomes clear, however, that a generic approach to this literature is only partially satisfactory because the categories run over and into one another. Muriel categorizes Sigüenza's *Parayso Occidental* as a chronicle, as she does the *relaciones* of Inés de la Cruz and Mariana de la Encarnación; the life of Marina de la Cruz, by Pedro de la Mota, is a biography. None of these texts is included under the rubric of mysticism, which Muriel reserves for a very small, select group of works written for purely spiritual purposes. The exemplary stories of nuns, published precisely for their didactic value, fall outside this wholly religious set of texts.

The vida, then, is not included as a genre, but it appears consistently as a flexible structure molded into the shape of its surrounding text. Marina's biography is certainly a vida, as are

some of the texts considered mystical, and some of the chronicles. The cross-pollenization of life and chronicle is noted
by Muriel (1982) as central to the latter form, when written
by nuns:

Tras la declaración que hace la cronista de los motivos que mueven su
pluma, sin indicación previa se pasa de inmediato a la crónica. Allí
encontramos un segundo elemento, que es la autobiografía, si la que
escribe es la fundadora o biografía, si la crónica la hace otra persona. . . . Las crónicas femeninas cobran mayor importancia como ex-
ponentes del pensamiento femenino del momento histórico que
reflejan, pues en la mayoría de ellas la cronista es, al mismo tiempo,
sujeto que escribe y objeto mismo de la historia. (96 – 7)

Following the chronicler's declaration of the motives inspiring her
pen, with no advance notice she passes directly into the chronicle.
There we find a second element, which is autobiography if the writer
is a founder, or biography if the chronicle is written by someone
else. . . . The female chronicles are most important as exponents of
feminine thought during the historical moment they reflect, for in
the majority of them the chronicler is at the same time the writing
subject and the very object of the history.

Muriel then continues the discussion of the link between the
two narrative discourses: "Al lado de la relación biográfica que
es medular en estas obras, se va haciendo la historia de las in-
stituciones. Es el subjetivismo una de las características de las
crónicas femeninas" [Alongside the biographical account that is
central to these works, the institutional histories are constructed. Subjectivism is one of the characteristics of the female
chronicle] (98).

The vida emerges as a kind of specter throughout all this; ev-
erywhere and nowhere, adapting itself to whatever the intentions of its author may be, it has no definite form. However, the
vidas, especially those written by Carmelites, do follow a tradition with certain requirements. To a certain extent, they remain
outside the formal categories of rhetoric, taking instead as their
model Teresa's works and other saints' lives. Thus the mixture
of biography with chronicle; as in the *Vida* of the Carmelite reformer, heaven and earth blend in the narrative. Visions and
miracles become part of everyday life, and the founding of the
convent is identical to the story of the nun's life if she was involved in that founding. The precise genres of biography and
chronicle do not apply entirely in the case of the vidas; they are

straitjackets forced onto texts that cannot be measured by such standard categorizations.

We know that many of the prose forms imported from Europe changed in America, as shown in Walter Mignolo's 1982 discussion of *carta* [letters], *relación* [accounts], and *historia* [history] in his extensive treatment of colonial discursive types, or Roberto González Echevarría's theory of the legal model for narration found in the *relación*. Such formulations have led me to speculate where the vidas might fall in the array of types and, moreover, how they might radically alter the configuration. Would the generic categories change with regard to a less exclusively male canon of texts? Many vidas, after all, were called *relaciones* by their authors, especially those texts that narrate the foundations of convents. What would happen if we were to examine those nuns' *relaciones* alongside their better-known brothers, the texts by men that accounted for discovery, conquest, and colonization occurring outside the convent's walls?

Both the vida and the *relación* existed in counterpoint to the learned *historia*, which, as I have described in the case of *Parayso Occidental,* was a form steeped in tradition and exclusion that presented rhetorical challenges to colonial subjects writing down their vision of history in the New World. The vidas, however, often blurred into subjective life stories, blending public and private spheres of experience and attributing events to mystical forces outside the scope of conventional religious doctrine. They could be placed discursively between *relación* and *historia*, between the discourse of legalistic accounts and that of a Western, Christian tradition that saw itself as universal. The vidas were infused with the universal language of religion, as were the natural histories of the New World, like *Parayso,* in their providential dogma. At the same time, the vidas are personal accounts, based on subjective, eyewitness presentations of series of chronological events.

What differentiates the vidas from other colonial prose and from male-authored *relaciones,* however, is their condition of mediated authorship. The figure of the confessor or superior officer was ever-present, whether he was a benign supporter or a stern taskmaster, for the nun was prohibited from carrying out such an individualistic act as the writing of her life story unless sanctioned or obligated to do so by male religious authority. Be-

sides enforcing obedience and humility, this control was considered necessary because of the danger that a nun's writing could
veer off into the heretical areas of sensuality, imagination, or at
worst, demonic inspiration. Thus the vidas constantly make reference to the act of writing as a burdensome task, undertaken
for the love of God and obedience to His earthly representative, the confessor; the nun absolves herself of responsibility
as she records not only mundane events, but mystical trances
and visions.

This is the area where recent feminist criticism has dealt with
the question of autonomy and the woman writer, stressing the
subversive quality of the female-authored text, its resistance to
domination, and the ways in which the confessional mode can
be used in the service of woman's empowerment. Arenal and
Schlau (1989) emphasize this, stating categorically: "Especially
after the Council of Trent, the prose of women in the convent
was always an act of defiance although it purported to be an act
of obedience" (16). In her 1989 study *Plotting Women,* Jean
Franco takes another position when she discusses mystical discourse in the context of transgression, locating resistance in the
speech act based on a subjective experience that was expressed
in writing only at the cost of great anxiety and torment:

It was only by disappearing as authors and becoming mediums for the
voice of God that these women were able to speak of their experiences
at all. . . . More important, this self-effacement and their constant
professions of obedience whenever they appeared to be trespassing
on alien territory were the preconditions for their flights of the imagination. (15)

In this way, according to Franco, knowledge that "bypassed the
authority of the confessor" (15) could be authorized, a private,
irrational knowledge that acted both as a space for the empowerment of women as feeling beings and as a vehicle for their
exclusion from rational, public discourse. The feelings made
women mystics powerful, but the writing down of those feelings
only enforced their subjugation.

The paradigm of these feminist readings of the vidas is the
palimpsest, for the writing of the nuns is often hidden from
view by the words of the confessor, who is responsible for the
public life of the text. The defiance declared by Arenal and

Schlau or Franco's private transgressive act contribute to a revisionist reading of the life stories that looks to reveal the creation of a space without male domination, productive or destructive to a greater or lesser degree. According to this model the vidas, engaged in the narration of historical events through personal experience, subvert (or attempt to subvert) the dominant male authority of the confessor by asserting a female voice that manipulates the religious discourse of humility and obedience to its own ends. Yet as Franco observes, this is a transgression fraught with ambiguity, "caught up in the dominant discourse" of the system of church and state (21).

Within its cloistering space, the convent really was a female realm. But how empowering was that space for the women who shared it? Were the strategies employed for writing the vidas always subversive elements of women's discourse? And, is a defiant palimpsest always to be found, either in the mystical speech act or the writing down of the nun's life experience?

It is important when thinking about the possibly subversive aspects of the vidas to place them in the context of the values of their era. For many of the men who worked closely with religious women as biographers or as facilitators of autobiography, the work inspired occasion for increased prestige in the confessor's larger community.[3] This was certainly the case for *Parayso Occidental,* where Sigüenza uses the vidas as proof of an American Paradise in order to gain fame for the convent. In colonial Spanish America of the late sixteenth and seventeenth centuries – the period when vidas began to be written in the Indies – these texts were regarded as examples of piety, although the mystical aspect was repressed when it crossed the line into possible heresy.

But the vidas were not marginalized from their surrounding culture in the manner that we see them today. As modern critics we need to resist the temptation to identify them with the model of subversive palimpsest proposed, for example, in Sandra Gilbert and Susan Gubar's influential study of nineteenth-century writers, *The Madwoman in the Attic* (1979). The religious cell was not equivalent to an attic room, hidden away, secret and shameful. In many cases women entered the convent because of a religious conviction entirely attuned to their era, although today we may recognize that era as misogynist and repressive.

In my reading of the vidas as semiautonomous narratives, I propose a model different from that of the individualistic, defiant palimpsest. I read these biographical or autobiographical life stories in concert with the narration or presence of the confessor who served as mentor, publisher, editor, and perhaps tormentor, demanding obedience and a written text when the writer may have preferred other activities less solitary in nature and more attached to her community. Undoubtedly some women derived pleasure from their writing and intellectual solitude; certainly Sor Juana did. But the expression of individuality, a struggle to find oneself, was not a general goal for religious women or men of the early colonial period.

When nun writers describe their willingness to write as a service to God and a sacrifice, I believe that their words and their desire to be obedient should be considered as an expression of the cultural values by which some wished to live. As Franco (1989) points out in her discussion of Sor Juana, "[she] was not a lone sniper resisting the state, but was, at times, the very voice of that state" (49). To posit an individual struggle in each and every case overlooks the ways in which the Spanish American vidas, in particular, participated in the discourse of colonial society, semiautonomous in their dependency on the authority of male superiors and embedded in hierarchical structures of power.

The life stories of Hispanic nuns in the sixteenth and seventeenth centuries are a heterogeneous group of texts, although they share some general formal and rhetorical conventions. They exist within the confines of the male power structure that surrounded them. Some resisted that power, others did not. The act of writing in and of itself was not a subversive gesture, if we are to understand subversion as a challenge to the discursive structures of authority in an absolutist society. The lives that emerge in these texts are embedded in the history of their time. If the vidas are placed back in the larger cultural surroundings of their era and set together with, rather than separate from, the writing of men, we can get back to the questions I raised earlier in this chapter. How do the vidas bring to bear an influence on the histories and accounts of male writers?

How did the life stories of nuns in the New World contribute to a colonial discourse that was radically changing the writing of history? Could the vida in America, like the *relación* that developed alongside it, be an important source for studying the heterogeneity of the evolving colonial narrative and for expanding rigid generic categories?

I have shown how Sigüenza y Góngora approached the writing of the nuns of the Mexican Convento de Jesús María: as exemplary stories of the spiritual fortitude of a New World subject, inscribed within a book destined for the royal or viceregal court. That these vidas exhibit qualities we identify now as picaresque only makes more evident their heritage in a colonial discourse that tried to locate itself within a world where definitions of caste and nationality were rapidly changing. Along with those definitions went the generic categories that separated subjective life stories from universal history, as is abundantly clear in Sigüenza's text. The vidas of Spanish American nuns participated in that redefinition of written history, as I illustrate through examples taken from *Parayso Occidental*.

Parayso Occidental, read in such a way as to concentrate on the place of women in the text, emerges quite a different book from the one read by Irving Leonard, José Rojas Garcidueñas, or Elías Trabulse. In developing theoretical insights related to the *barroco de Indias* and to issues of colonial authority in writing, my focus has been made from a new angle, enabling me to revise traditional literary history, and, in so doing, to recover lost chapters of women's experience.

However, my task of reading the vidas making up most of *Parayso* is complicated by the lack of extant archival material from the Convento de Jesús María. So thoroughly has Sigüenza's book absorbed the life stories of these nuns, that it has become the primary reference for the study of the convent's foundation. This situation was created, in part, by the expropriation of private convent libraries in nineteenth century Mexico, which was carried out by Benito Juárez's soldiers during the anticlerical period of government reform. Juárez's actions, according to Josefina Muriel's *Conventos de monjas en la Nueva España* (1946), resulted in the loss of many valuable documents; however, it must be added that many also found their way to libraries and public archives where today they can be accessed more readily by scholars.[4]

But the convent archive that Sigüenza consulted was lost, and because of this *Parayso* has taken its place. Muriel (1982), for instance, lists Pedro de la Mota's *Vida de la Ven. Mariana* [sic] *de la Cruz* as a manuscript cited by Sigüenza y Góngora in *Parayso Occidental*, although the original has disappeared (520). Given the dispersion or disappearance of Sigüenza's own library, neither is there any documentation of the oral sources for the *casos* of Libro Tercero. However, the Carmelite founders Inés de la Cruz and Mariana de la Encarnación, following the example of Teresa of Avila, did write *relaciones* that have been preserved. The present-day Convento de San José in Mexico City retains a manuscript by Inés that, although not the same one cited by Sigüenza, includes a similar narrative pattern and subject material.[5] Mariana de la Encarnación's *Relación*, as I indicate in Chapter 3, exists in a nineteenth-century manuscript copy made by another nun, who dates it 1641. With these exceptions, it is difficult to discuss women's writing outside the context of Sigüenza's work, for the vidas are intricately entwined with the book of the criollo author.

Therefore, I focus now on the Carmelite founders' narratives. In *Parayso Occidental*, as I have noted, the selection of nuns in the text is weighted heavily to those who eventually became the founders of the Carmelite convent. Mariana de la Encarnación and Inés de la Cruz stand out as the standard-bearers for the founding of a strictly contemplative cloister, organized according to the rules set out by Teresa in her writing. Both Mariana and Inés wrote extensively after the Carmelite foundation was achieved, narrating their own vocation and the work they had carried out in Mexico City.

As I explain in Chapter 2, issues of national loyalty are rife in these accounts. Arenal and Schlau (1989) have explained the cultural issues involved in the actions of Inés and Mariana toward the Carmelite foundation (343 – 6), an aspect of Mariana's text noted previously by Muriel 1982 (66 – 70). Inés was a peninsular-born Spanish woman who had emigrated to America as a child; Mariana was a criolla, as were the majority of the sisters of the Convento de Jesús María. The viceregal establishment at the highest levels – the viceroy and the archbishop – enthusiastically supported the foundation of the Carmelite cloister, working to obtain the licenses, permission, and funding for a convent that would represent the austerity and strictness of Spanish Teresian rule in the colony of New Spain. Such reform was seen as particularly desirable in Mexico City, where convents such as Jesús María had abandoned religious vows of poverty and contemplation in favor of an institution that participated fully in the political and cultural affairs of the outside world (Ramos 1990, 46 – 7).

Thus the vida of Mariana de la Encarnación, for example, tells of two nuns who found their own community wanting and desired to leave it. Arenal and Schlau have called this vida a document of Mexican manners, demonstrating the ability of the nuns to work the system to their own advantage in order to achieve their goal. Yet to what ends was that ability put, and what went into the writing of this story? Is it an act of defiance to write about a project officially sanctioned by all male authorities concerned? The Carmelite founders participated in a movement that desired the repression of certain freedoms found in the more lax Mexican convents of the time, where whole families of women lived and participated in the surrounding culture. This was the kind of convent where Sor Juana resided later in the seventeenth century, a convent where a small, elite group of women did find a room of their own. Sor Juana herself had initially entered a Carmelite convent, but had found its rule too rigorous.

Sigüenza y Góngora writes over the texts of these reformers with his own words, shuffling the papers on his table and using the words of women to redefine New World history in the occidental Paradise. Yet the palimpsest that results in this case does not mute the voices of defiant women; rather, it locates them in the structure of power that the women themselves manipulated to the detriment of other women, and glorifies their role as the willing instruments of colonial authority. Alison Weber's 1990 reading of Teresa's *Book of Foundations*, which identifies the double strand of one narration of picaresque, antiinstitutional reformism juxtaposed with a second story of authoritarian punishment for rebel nuns, is useful in this context (123). The Carmelite reformers of Mexico City likewise displayed both characteristics in these accounts of their own lives and works.

Alongside this political aspect – the public side of the vidas – the life stories often recount intensely private mystical experiences and visions. Such episodes of revelation and transport go beyond earthly categories and find much of what they would tell to be ineffable and impossible to explain in rational terms. These characteristics are shared by the narratives of both male and female mystics as they strive to erase the body (and physical desire) in order to replace it with a holy union with God. The vidas, as Muriel (1982) indicates, have no structured plots; their narratives modulate between chronicle and spiritual transport, between the public and the private, as in this excerpt from Inés de la Cruz;

Otra vez me pareciò me llevaban al cielo, y entendi havia de estar allà junto a Santa Escolastica su hermana de S. Benito. Pregunté: y la M. Mariana donde ha de estar? Dixeronme: su lugar se tiene guardado. No vide nada, ni oi palabra, ni la hablè, porque todo pasò en el entendimiento. . . . Esto ha mas de veinte y cinco años. (fol. 142r)

Again it seemed to me they were taking me to heaven, and I understood I was going to be there with Saint Scholastica, the sister of Saint Benito. I asked: and where is Madre Mariana going to be? They told me: a place is reserved for her. I saw nothing, and neither heard nor spoke a word, because everything took place in my understanding. . . . This happened more than twenty-five years ago.

It is in this shifting between the eternal time of mystical union and the linear, historical time of the chronicle that the stamp of the nuns' vidas on *Parayso Occidental* is marked. Although Sigüenza's rhetorical model for history would set the sisters of Jesús María firmly within the strictly limited space of the cloister, and would describe the foundation of their institution and its universal importance using the measure of historical time, the nuns' texts continuously elude these boundaries. Through the blending of public and private spheres, history itself is modified.

In Chapter 4 I discuss the lack of rhetorical tradition that makes the vidas problematic for Sigüenza's book; in this case, there is another dynamic, as the inclusion of mystical visions in the narrative actually transforms it. These visions effect a decentering away from the rhetorical model of history, causing a breakdown of that discourse into one more akin to literature. The criollo history, baroque and American, would never come to be without such a temporal shift. Thus the baroque narrative of *Parayso Occidental* can be read as a response not only to the challenge of authority – i.e., the narrative role of the American historian – but to that of temporality as well.

Clearly, the two are intimately related, for the narration of history is constructed on a chronological progression of past and present time. Although Sigüenza y Góngora shared the Jesuit postulation of syncretic culture that identified different figures of the past with one another – Quetzalcóatl with Thomas the Apostle, for example – he still ordered his history in terms of a progressive chronology moving toward Christian redemption. The vidas represent other kinds of religious time, those of the mystic and the cloister. In *Parayso Occidental* the modalities meet and combine. Moreover, they are marked by the difference of gender, always present both in Sigüenza's strategy for authority, and in the vidas' mediated narrative.

What kind of time, then, represents the reality of a New World convent? How can the story be told to present the past just as it was in the present, when much of that tale is based on ineffable visions? Where is the space related to that American history to be found, both within the text and the walls of the convent? These questions, on a local level, investigate the role of the vidas in the dominant discourse of written history. On a larger scale they are part of a feminist rethinking of the field of history itself that would change standard methodological assumptions so as to take into account the subjective experience of women.[6] We must make that kind of radical leap to see how the vidas of colonial nuns themselves narrated history and made its traditional forms change in America through their effect on writers such as Sigüenza y Góngora.

Julia Kristeva, in her 1981 essay "Women's Time," notes the classical identification of woman with space. According to this traditional formulation, time is considered a masculine element, definite and limited, whereas space is open, receptive, and feminine. Reviewing the penchant of the modern human sciences, including psychoanalysis, to make such an identification, Kristeva (1981) states:

But they all converge on the problematic of space, which innumerable religions of matriarchal (re)appearance attribute to "woman," and which Plato, recapitulating in his own system the atomists of antiquity, designated by the aporia of the *chora,* matrix space, nourishing, unnameable, anterior to the One, to God and, consequently, defying metaphysics. (1981, 16)

In this important essay, Kristeva wishes to place women in history with respect to time, rather than space. She reminds her readers that the cyclical or monumental concepts of time associated with women are those attributed to mystics of all genders, and to certain civilizations as well: "This repetition and eternity are found to be the fundamental, if not the sole, conceptions of time in numerous civilizations and experiences, particularly mystical ones" (17). In such a temporality, then, unnameable pleasure (the French *jouissance*) results from the union of time with space, from a perception of time that originates in the rhythms of the body. Both women and mystics may experience this pleasure because they remain outside the linear time of history: "In return, female subjectivity as it gives itself up to intuition becomes a problem with respect to a certain conception of time: time as project, teleology, linear and prospective unfolding; time as departure, progression, and arrival – in other words, the time of history" (17). It is time measured out in doses, with a beginning and an end, that can never know that unlimited pleasure; the two concepts of time remain separate.

Kristeva's effort to place European women in modern historical time while respecting their difference from it is useful for my discussion of the vidas and their situation in colonial culture. I wish to avoid the fetishism of Woman and women's culture as a separate, idealized category, something Kristeva mentions as a clear danger for feminist practice. As I observed before, this is particularly important when discussing nuns and their cloistered convents, by definition spaces reserved for women. Although Kristeva refers to modern narrative history – itself something of a fetishized institution in France – the idea of a female (or a feminized mystical) subjectivity that poses problems for linear time is also fruitful for my reading of the vidas and the way they affect the premodern history of *Parayso Occidental.*

The power of intuitive time as a challenge to historical discourse is amply demonstrated by the vertigo accompanying a reading of *Parayso Occidental.* As I have shown, Sigüenza y Góngora must resort to many strategies in order to contain the vidas within his history; he does so based on a recognition of gender differences as one of many hierarchies. By writing or telling about their lives and visions, the sisters of Jesús María alter the history that *Parayso Occidental* would claim to be. The notion of historical narrative time, a European model for discourse, is challenged here by mystical time as experienced by women.

Since this an American text, the circumstances of the challenge are not so clearly demarcated as would be the case with a European history. Sigüenza y Góngora would claim for the Convento de Jesús María a significance extending far beyond its walls: after all, it is a Paradise. The convent's cosmic importance as a metaphor for the Conquest of the New World and as a symbol of divine will in the colonization of America are of prime consideration to this history. Linear time in the European sense, then, is already skewed from the start because its origin is American, new and off-center. The vidas are a mixed blessing, for although they attest to the divinity of the enterprise of Conquest, they detract from the progress through time that Sigüenza wants his history to show. And so the effort to enclose them firmly within rhetorical limits, which I call *encerramiento:* keeping the nuns and their life stories in the proper place. It is the physical equivalent of the moral *escarmiento* of Chapter 4, a textual attempt to limit the overflow of a writing with no limits, with no definite points of departure or arrival. Although these women's stories, in their very cosmic character, are necessary to the chronicle of a western Paradise, they must be controlled. And so Sigüenza sets limits, reining in the texts of eternal time and setting them in a closely watched space.

Sigüenza's history, then, would use the vidas to further its own discursive cause, enlisting them in the struggle for authority over Old World models. But instead, the text of mystical time unravels that carefully laid plan, changing the progression of events that Sigüenza uses to bring his history into line with European rhetoric. The women's texts make *Parayso* into a more complicated kind of history, that of the criollo, a baroque narrative that follows twists and turns instead of that straight line. Closed in behind cloistered walls, the women's stories nevertheless seep through, giving pause to those readers who expect a history on the order of *Piedad heroyca.* Such personal testimonies detour the narrative away from the facts, and away from a consistent chronology as well. They introduce a different notion of time, and thus upset an essential element of narrative history.

Relating the events as they actually happened entails putting them in order and straightening them out. This Sigüenza means to do with his larger framework for the convent and the vidas. Placing Marina's birth in the same year as that of Anne Boleyn sets up the New World as superior to the Old, gives an American identity to the convent, and creates a baroque kind of complication that sets this history apart from others. We can see now how such complication comes to be: the time of the vidas twists that of narrative history.

Sigüenza's history would change the women's writing he presents not so much in the text (the words used by the nuns) as in its context. When the vida of Inés de la Cruz is both introduced and concluded by Sigüenza's voice of historian, such a change is effected by converting that text's sense of eternal time into a more worldly chronology. For Madre Marina's long story the process is accelerated. Rather than quoting de la Mota's account verbatim, as he does with that of Inés de la Cruz, Sigüenza tells the tale himself in the hope that mystical visions and miracles, in the context of a learned history, will somehow retain their religious fervor while losing their irrational temporality. This must be accomplished through language, through the extra layer of third-person narration and the polishing of rough prose into baroque conceits.

Sigüenza deals with the Carmelite vidas by manipulating their sense of time. Josefina Muriel (1982) describes Mariana de la Encarnación's *Relación* in this way:

Su sentido de la historia está manifiesto a lo largo de la obra. Dios providente interviene en toda acción humana. La obra está concebida como la exposición de una vivencia de la autora. No hay separación de capítulos, pero sí un orden cronológico. Tiene un estilo claro, sencillo, en el que sólo se usan las palabras necesarias para exponer sinceramente la verdad vivida. (56)

Her sense of history manifests itself throughout the work. A providential God intervenes in all human action. The work is conceived as a setting down of the life experience of the author. There is no separation into chapters, but there is a chronological order. It has a clear, simple style, in which only the words necessary to sincerely set down the lived truth are used.

The chronological order of the account, as Muriel states, does indeed exist, but the clock that measures time for Mariana de la Encarnación is different from that of narrative history. It is not so much as a progression of events, but as a process spanning many cycles, that the foundation of the Convento de San José is described in this narrative of Mariana's. The passing of days and years is kept track of according to the cyclical events of the church calendar, daily prayers, and personal visions, as I will show through several examples.

Much of the *Relación* is concerned with the political intrigue surrounding the establishment of a new convent, which required an extraordinarily complex set of bureaucratic mechanisms to be put into motion. Both the colonial and Spanish hierarchies of church and state were involved; the entire operation took years to realize, and at many points the nuns all but abandoned hope that their project would ever reach fruition. They constantly looked to God and to earthy representatives of the divinity such as the archbishop for encouragement, and also sought counsel from Quesada, an official instrumental to the foundation. About halfway through the *Relación*, Mariana (1641 [1823]) tells of a vision received by Inés de la Cruz:[7]

Estabamos a este tiempo con mucho cuidado de la tardanza del Breve que esperabamos de S. Santidad, y encomendandolo a nuestro Sr. salio un dia de su oracion la Madre Ynes de la Cruz muy alegre, y dixome ya concedio hoi el Breve, y apuntando con curiosidad el dia, mes y año, en que nuestro Sr. le havia dado a sentir esto, hallamos despues que vino el Breve, ser puntualmente como ella me lo havia dicho y escrito en un quaderno que yo vide muchas veses. [78 – 9).

At that time we were very worried about the delay of the Brief we awaited from His Holiness, and entrusted this to our Lord one day Madre Inés de la Cruz emerged from her prayers very happy, and she told me, today the Brief has been granted, and noting with care the day, month, and year in which our Lord had given her to feel this, later we found that the Brief had come to be precisely as she had told me and had written in her notebook, which I saw on many occasions.

Mariana mentions the annotation of the day, month, and year of Inés's vision, but nowhere does she record what they were. Such corroboration is important to the chronicle only for its miraculous value; the facts do not matter so much as their outcome. I contrast this with Sigüenza's concluding remarks in *Parayso* on the life of Mariana:

Conmuto esta vida calamitosa, y perecedera por la que siempre dura, el dia seis de Diziembre de mil seiscientos y cinquenta y siete en que cumplia ochenta y seis años, ocho meses, y diez y seis dias, de los quales assi secular, como Religiosa gasto los treinta y seis, un mes, y diez y nueve dias en el Convento Real de Jesus Maria, y en el de S. Joseph de Carmelitas Descalzas quarenta y un años, nueve meses, y seis dias. (fol. 158r)

She exchanged this calamitous and perishable life for the one ever-lasting on the sixth of December, 1657, when her age was eighty-six years, eight months, and sixteen days, out of which, both as a student and a Nun, she had spent thirty-six years, one month, and nineteen days in the Convento Real de Jesús María, and forty-one years, nine months, and six days in that of San Joseph de Carmelitas Descalzas.

The precision of this counting up of the years, months, and days spent as a nun is standard in hagiographical writing, but in the context of Sigüenza's history it takes on another importance. Particularly in this passage, the criollo's delight in excess detail is readily apparent, as is the need for authenticity. It is no accident that this pinpointing of a certain moment in time ends the two chapters devoted in Mariana's vida. It serves as a reassertion of the history that is *Parayso Occidental*, as a resurfacing of the factual data that must temporarily cede way to a religious woman's text with another time frame.

Mariana recounts how the settlement of Juan Luis de Rivera's will, awarding the building he left to the Carmelites, drags on and on without resolution to the point where other sites for the convent are suggested. However, the archbishop and the *oidor*, Quesada, decide one day that only the originally designated houses will do. The archbishop vows to use his money and influence with the viceroy to obtain a hearing for the case before the *Audiencia*, and, writes the nun, "con esto se dieron tan buena maña, que puesta esta determinacion un dia de Pasqua de Resurrecion el año antes de la fundacion, por el mes de Abril, y el [línea ilegible] . . . del mismo año, vispera de nuestra Señora de la Visitacion, y parecio obra suya" [they were so adept and artful, that this decision made on Easter Sunday of the year before the foundation, in the month of April, and the [illegible line] . . . in the same year on the eve of Our Lady of the Visitation, it seemed to be her doing] (Mariana de la Encarnación, 82; the illegible line must refer to the hearing on the *Breve*).

Mariana does state at the beginning of her text that the Convento de San José was founded in 1616, thus the year to which she alludes is not entirely unclear. What is of interest is the way in which she thinks of time and its passing. The days go by in an eternal cycle of observances and prayers; time takes on a different rhythm for the nuns, cloistered away from the outside world although very much a part of its politics. Sigüenza narrates somewhat differently the same scene that Mariana describes:

Era entonces el Licenciado D. Pedro de Otalora el que por Oydor mas antiguo presidia a sus compañeros en la Real Audiencia, y haviase reconocido hallarse prendado de D. Alonso de Ribera a quien descubiertamente patrocinaba, a este pues se determino hablar con resolucion el Oydor Quesada, y fue en tan buen sazon, y con tanto espiritu, que respondiendo no solo el que no permitiera Dios hiziese el yerro que pretendia, sino el que tambien (como lo hizo) reduciria a sus compañeros a su dictamen, se destino el dia primero de Julio de mil seiscientos y quince para ver el pleyto. (fol. 44r)

At that time the Licenciado don Pedro de Otalora was the one who, as senior Oidor, presided over his fellows in the Royal Audiencia, and having recognized him as partisan to don Alonso de Ribera whom he openly patronized, Quesada decided with resolution to speak to him; and Quesada did so with so much spirit, and in such a good manner, that answering not only that God would not permit such an error to be made, but also that he would (as he did) bring his fellows into line with his opinion, the first of July of 1615 was fixed for the hearing of the case.

In Sigüenza's version the exact date, according to historical time, is established. Along with the rhetorical shift from *relación* to *historia*, from religious to secular writing, from cyclical to chronological record keeping, the gender of the author also changes. My argument is not an essentialist one; not solely because a woman writes the *Relación* are events narrated with a perspective implying a different progression of years, months, and days from that of Sigüenza y Góngora. However, the fusion of gender-marked women's texts with a religious temporality is so complete in *Parayso* that it is not possible to speak of one without the other. I do not believe that a mystical sense of time is essentially feminine, but it is clear that Sigüenza brings an awareness of the presence of women and the nonprogressive temporality of their vidas into his writing, along with a knowledge of the effect that presence will have on his history. The nuns write, fully cognizant of their position as women within a religious hierarchy that frowns on any motive other than the strictly orthodox. Gender difference in the narrative of *Parayso Occidental* pervades the text, implicitly and explicitly.

The episode immediately following this last quote cited from *Parayso* is that of the archbishop's occupation of Ribera's building, the same scene I quoted in Chapter 3. It is the story of a plot carried out under cover of night, and of a Mass said at dawn to a group of incredulous, sleepy tenants who wonder at how an altar came to be set up in their courtyard. This is the last chapter of Libro Primero, capping off the story of the founding of the two convents (Jesús María and San José). Once again, Sigüenza changes Mariana's text to give an exact date rather than a liturgical one, as he writes: "En el mayor silencio de la noche del dia tres de Julio se dispusiese en aquella sala un Altar muy decente en que dezirse Missa" [In the greatest silence of night on the third of July, a most proper altar was set up in that room where Mass could be said] (fol. 44v). Mariana tells it in this way:

Encargole al paja que en anocheciendo llevase todo aquel aderezo a la casa, y se fuese a dormir con su amigo, y le pusiese el altar, y todo aderezo para decir Misa, que en amaneciendo estava alla su Illustrisima pareseme seria esto dos dias despues de la visitacion de nuestra Señora. (85)

The page was ordered to take that whole apparatus to the house at nightfall, and to sleep at his friend's place, and to set up the altar and all the apparatus for saying Mass there, because his Illustriousness would be there at dawn it seems to me this must have been two days after our Lady's Visitation.

This is not the only change that Sigüenza makes in his source, which is never cited. Mariana, however, does say where her material comes from: her source is the archbishop's eyewitness account. This is how Mariana describes the scene at dawn, after bells are rung all over the house to call the people to Mass:

Fue tanto el alboroto, sobresalto y ruido conque se levantaban que parecia dia de juicio, por ser mucha la gente que vivia alli ocupando las tiendas, y demas oficinas de la casa donde vivian muy de asiento con sus hijos y mugeres y demas familia; que le sirvio de recreacion al S. Arsobispo, que fue quien personalmente nos conto esta relacion que boi escribiendo, que le causaba risa, ver salir a unos medio desnudos, a otros cubiertos con solo las frazadas. (86)

They woke up with so much noise, uproar, and shock that it seemed like judgment day because there were so many people living there in the shops and the offices of the house, where they lived all settled in with their children and wives and other relatives; this amused the Archbishop, who was the one who personally told us the account I am writing, it made him laugh to see some of them come out half naked, and others covered only with blankets.

Recalling Sigüenza's fantastically exaggerated version of this event, complete with barking dogs, lazy servants, crying children, and the fear of an earthquake, it is evident he has embroidered on Mariana's simple account of the facts with his own baroque imagination, fueled by literature and its narrative strategies. It is a paradoxical outcome: Sigüenza, wanting to write a history, adds on detail to a rather spare narrative, and instead makes something more akin to literature. It is a historical vision that sees excess as reality, that needs a complicated language to make vivid the world of the criollo, that aspires, above all, to retell the story and claim it.

Here Sigüenza's choices, made as editor of the text, become more visible. He quotes Mariana's words as she writes of the letter sent to the would-be Carmelites of the capital by their sisters in Puebla (Libro Primero, chapter 12), and the answer sent by Mariana in reply. Sigüenza takes care to attribute credit to the original author, introducing Mariana's text by stating:

Lo que contenia la carta de la M. Maria del Costado, y su respuesta, no se podra relatar con mejores palabras, que con las mismas con que la Venerable Madre Mariana de la Encarnacion en la noticia que nos dexo de esta fundacion, lo encomendo a memoria: las quales copiadas fidelissimamente del original en que se contienen estos sucesos, dizen assi. (fol. 42v)

What the letter of Madre Maria del Costado and her reply contained cannot be told in better words than the same ones in which the Venerable Madre Mariana de la Encarnación, in the account she left us of the foundation, entrusted it to memory: which words, faithfully copied from the original where these events are contained, say the following.

After the citation from the nun's text, the historian intervenes again: "Hasta aqui la Venerable Madre Mariana de la Encarnacion, cuya relacion original se halla en el archivo del Convento de S. Joseph de Carmelitas Descalzas" [Up to here is quoted the Venerable Madre Mariana de la Encarnación, whose original account is found in the archive of the Convento de San Joseph de Carmelitas Descalzas] (fol. 43v). But the very next chapter, telling of the early morning near riot caused by the archbishop, nowhere mentions that Mariana's *Relación* is the original source for Sigüenza's text.

Why are such choices made in the composition of *Parayso Occidental*? This is a question I explore in the last section of this chapter. First, however, I wish to examine the writing of Inés de la Cruz, Mariana's cofounder. As I indicate in Chapter 4, Sigüenza's intervention in the first six chapters of Inés's vida is limited to that of an editor, providing opening remarks and chapter titles. In the seventh chapter, Sigüenza's narrative voice is heard once again, supplying the requisite account of the nun's death and miraculous afterlife, and ending with the description of her face and body inspired by the conventions of courtly love poetry. Although chapters 1 through 6 are presented in the first person, directly from Inés's own writing, it seems clear that Sigüenza has performed his editorial duties with an eye toward the construction of a cohesive narrative based on devices drawn once again from literature, and especially from the picaresque. The very division of the life story into seven parts immediately suggests the model of *Lazarillo de Tormes*, as do many of the incidents Inés recounts.[8]

Inés's extant manuscript (called the *Relación*), located in the present Convento de San José and dated 1625 by Josefina Muriel, is not the same one quoted by Sigüenza; in fact, it narrates the same basic story from a completely different angle. Nuns did write more than one account of their lives if requested to do so by more than one confessor, so it is entirely possible that Inés wrote both these texts. It is also possible that Sigüenza used the *Relación* we have today, expanding some parts and leaving out others, to a much more extensive degree than he indicates. Without another manuscript we cannot know for certain. In either case, how he organized and presented the material, and how *Parayso* contrasts with the *Relación* are of great interest to me here.

In both *Parayso Occidental* and the *Relación*, Inés's story begins in the standard legalistic mode with a declaration of her parents' names and her own date and place of birth in Spain; the *Relación* includes as well the names of her confessors, the men who asked her to write. In *Parayso* there is immediately a portent of the life she will go on to lead, for her great-grandmother (who is also her godmother), about to profess the religious vows of a nun, puts off entry into the convent just to attend the baby's baptism: "Buen pronostico de que el Señor me prevenia de misericordias para ser suya" [A good sign that the Lord was mercifully preparing me to be his] (fol. 130r).

From the beginning, the factual parts of this account are tempered with spiritual and mystical ones. Inés's precocious childhood is rife with episodes of religious transport and the desire for self-mortification. She secretly fasts on bread and dried foods, and rises after her sisters have fallen asleep to commune with God: "Era estar en una suspension la voluntad embebida en Dios, sin discurso, que no podia tenerle, ni rezar vocalmente. . . . Parece se me volaba el alma a Dios, solo mirando al cielo, y considerando estaba alla su Magestad" [It was like being suspended, my will drinking God in, without the discourse that I could not have, nor pray vocally. . . . It seemed like my soul was flying up to God just by looking at the heavens, and thinking that his Majesty was there] (fol. 130v). The child's propensity to martyrdom is mixed with more than a little arrogance: "Pareciame me havia Dios criado parar Santa, y que en siendo Monja le serviria, y como si yo sola huviera de serlo me tenia por mas dichosa que la Reyna" [It seemed to me that God had made me to be a Saint, and that by being a Nun I would serve him, and as if I were the only one who had ever done so, I felt more blessed than the Queen] (fol. 131r). Already, the destiny of a life dedicated to Christ is linked with the inadequacy of words to express that inner certainty, to describe a colloquium with no words and no discourse.

The picaresque touch of a father in trouble with the law occasions the family's immigration to the New World from Spain. Inés is the first to discover the permission to leave granted her father by the King, and it is for her a moment of joy:

Di yo por hecho el viage, y alegreme tanto como si me truxeran para Reyna, porque con mis ignorancias, y boberias se me figuro havia pocos Christianos aca, y muchos Gentiles, y que en llegando me huyria, y me iria a padecer martyrio, y con esto estaba tan alegre dando cada dia traza de los martyrios que me havian de dar, que no via la hora que se pusiese por obra la venida. (fol. 131v)

I assumed the voyage was definite, and I was as happy as if they had made me a Queen, because in my ignorance and foolishness I thought there were few Christians here, and many Heathens, and that when I arrived I would run away and go become a suffering martyr; and I was so happy thinking every day about the martyrdom they were going to give me, that I couldn't wait for the time when I would arrive there.

This is a view of the New World from a young Spanish girl of the late sixteenth century, which continues on in a description of the passage from Seville in the convoy. The journey gives Inés's story in *Parayso* an added historical dimension, as was also the case in Marina de la Cruz's vida. But here the Conquest of America is seen from an entirely subjective, intensely religious perspective, patterned on Teresa's own wish to convert the Moors in her *Vida*. Evidently, what matters to Inés is becoming a nun and dedicating her life to God.

Part of this decision involves a strictly puritanical attitude toward anything to do with sex or sexuality, an attitude pervading the length of this account. At the same time, there is a fascination with the idea of being taken for a "bad" woman, humiliated unjustly, and therefore martyred for God. As a child in Toledo, Inés tries to run away from home to become a hermit, but loses her way in city streets. As an adolescent in Mexico, the fantasy returns:

Supe que las Monjas tenian mosas, y estube haziendo grandes trazas para sin ser conocida entrar por criada de alguna, y mudarme el nombre, y no dezir de donde era, porque mis Padres no me hallasen, y assi podria estar sin jamas ver a nadie, y estaria humillada, y me tratarian muy mal pensando que era alguna mala muger. Deseaba mucho me tubiesen en poco por tener que ofrecer a Dios, no halle traza para cumplir esto, porque no me fiaba de nadie, ni yo podia yrme, porque no sabia las calles. (fol. 132v)

I learned that the Nuns had servant girls, and I was making plans to enter the convent as someone's servant without anyone recognizing me, and to change my name there and not say where I was from, so that my Parents wouldn't find me, and that way I could live without ever seeing anyone and I would be humiliated, and they would treat me badly thinking that I was a bad woman. I greatly desired for them to regard me with contempt so I would have something to offer God; I couldn't come up with a plan to carry this out, because I didn't trust anyone else, nor could I leave by myself, since I wasn't familiar with the streets.

The image is of a woman who has taken to such extremes the opposition of good/bad female behavior that the two roles have merged in her mind. By being "bad," she is actually "good," a contradictory situation reflected in the confusion of unknown streets. This obsessive theme of antieroticism continues with Inés's attitude toward the Carnival season: "los tres dias de car-nestolendas . . . cerraba las ventanas por no oyr el tropel de effe mundo: lloraba, y afligiame mucho de ver la locura, y desatino de los hombres en estos dias" [the three days of Carnival . . . I closed the windows so as not to hear the tumult of that world; I cried, and was tormented upon seeing the craziness and wild-ness of men during those days] (fol. 133r). It was the girl's cus-tom to stay at home praying in solitude on holidays.

At one point her father allows an unmarried man to stay in their house; Inés discovers he has a reputation as a seducer and watches zealously over her sisters. Indeed, she is a self-appointed guardian of morality outside her home as well: "Teniase por muy sabido, por los que me conocian, que donde yo quedaba se descuydaban las Madres de sus hijas, y las tenian por muy seguras" [Among those who were acquainted with me, it was well known that wherever I stayed mothers had no need to worry about their daughters, and felt them to be very safe] (fol. 133v). When the houseguest tries to make overtures, she is impervious: "Diome Dios buen natural, que ni por primer movimiento he tenido amor por mal a ningun hombre" [God gave me the natural good fortune never to have felt even the beginnings of a wicked love for any man] (fol. 133v). This role as her sisters' keeper will return with greater force later on in the convent.

Thus chapter 1 of Inés's story as told in *Parayso* establishes the legal, religious, and moral precepts that will guide the entire vida, and sets them in a New World historical context. In contrast, in the *Relación* all these details of Inés's early life are treated quickly in the first paragraphs of the document, which concentrates on the story of the Carmelite foundation.[9] There are two possible narrative strategies at work: that Sigüenza embellished Inés's text to make it fit perfectly the themes and aesthetics of *Parayso Occidental;* or, that the nun's story contains those themes and thus it has been included with no change in the 1684 history.

Without the original documents it is, of course, impossible to know the answer to this question. This predicament limits what we can read in *Parayso* as women's writing authored by a woman's pen, but not what I maintain is the gendered "feminine text" that is the product of the difference brought to bear on Sigüenza's history by the presence of women in the narrative. Such difference affects the criollo's choices as editor as surely as his cuts or additions change Inés's words. The juxtaposition of historical and literary models making up criollo historiography is akin to the mixture of subjectivity and objectivity readily apparent in the nuns' texts, and is most certainly affected by their inclusion.

Chapter 2 of Inés's story in *Parayso* finds her ready to enter the convent, but distressed that no Carmelite institution exists in Mexico. The other American cloisters are far too lax for her tastes: "Un dia, que una señora me llevo a ver a una sobrina suya Monja (y era tenida por muy religiosa) videla muy conversable con Frayles, y me afligi mucho, y estube toda la noche llorando" [One day when a lady took me to see a niece of hers who was a Nun (and she was considered very religious) I saw her readily conversing with Friars, and it tormented me, and I cried all night long] (fol. 134r). Finally, she settles on Jesús María and quickly enters on 2 April 1588. The second precise date to appear in Sigüenza's account, it is the date of her profession, the equivalent of marriage to Christ and the beginning of a new life, and is also included in the *Relación*.

Again the desire for self-abasement is evident, as the nuns of the convent suspect Inés's haste to be due to a moral mishap. This pleases the novice: "Siempre me he alegrado mas en que dixesen males, que no bienes de mi, quando no era verdad, que si lo era me pesaba mucho y procuraba no lo supiesen" [I have always been happier to have bad things, rather than good things said about me, as long as they weren't true, for if they were I would be very upset and would make sure no one found out] (fol. 134v). For Inés, subjective feelings have little to do with objective facts: to be considered bad, when she is not really bad, is good.

Talented with numbers, the new nun becomes the convent's accountant, a task she considers base and therefore a martyrdom. As treasurer, Inés works intimately with the abbess, and thus each change of officers marks a different three-year regime with new problems. These shiftings are Inés's equivalent of Lazarillo's movement from master to master; indeed, one particular episode would have suggested such a reading to Sigüenza:

A poco mas del año cego tan del todo la Prelada, que no via sino los vultos de las personas: dexaronla en el cargo hasta que cumpliese los tres años, porque era muy buena, y prudente, y mandaronme no me apartase de ella para escrivirle, y registrar cartas, y todas lo llevaban bien, porque me vian como si fuera muda, poco entremetida, y pacifica, aunque dezian era yo Abadesa, y dezian verdad, porque ella no era mas que sombra para todos los negocios. (fol. 136v)

After a little more than a year the Abbess became so completely blind that she could only see people's shapes. They had her stay in her position until the three years were up, because she was very good and prudent, and they ordered me not to leave her side in order to write for her, and to inspect letters, and everyone took it well because they saw it was as if I were mute, and peaceful, and not nosy; although they did say I was the Abbess, and they were right, because she was no more than a shadow in all business dealings.

This guide for the blind abbess, however, does not remain peaceful for long. Taking advantage of her position, Inés begins to enforce a strict morality on her sisters. Some of the letters coming in, she discovers, are from male admirers ("algunos devotos" [fol. 136v]); she promptly undertakes a campaign to expunge such behavior. Inés is an anti-Celestina, declaring: "Me pedian les escriviese a sus devotos, y nunca lo hize, si no era pactando, el que la respuesta havia de ser a mi modo, y siempre que era assi al instante se despedian" [They would ask me to write to their admirers, and I never did so unless they agreed that the answer would be done my way, and every time that happened they left on the spot] (fol. 136v). Naturally, this harsh attitude wins her the contempt of her sisters and furthers her martyred position. Sigüenza's text emphasizes that martyrdom and the conservative moral position that causes it; such details are not a feature of the *Relación*.

At this point, the descriptions of visions and mystical ecstasy begin again on a more intense level. Chapter 3 in Libro Tercero offers an especially vivid, horrific image with mystical overtones:

Pareciome estaba una niebla muy obscura, y espesa que me cercaba sin poder ver otra cosa, y ponianme en una puente tan angosta que solo me cabian los pies, y estaba esta puente sobre un cenegal que parecia hondo, con muchas sabandijas, y mal olor, y la puente era tan larga que no se hallaba termino, y quien me puso en ella (que no vide quien era) me dezia que llevase con migo algo que comer, porque en todo aquel largo camino no hallaria quien me diesse nada, porque le havia de andar sola, y me dezia, que si no queria perderme no mirase atràs, ni arriba, ni a los lados, sino solo adelante donde estaba una muy pequeña luz muy lexissimos. (fol. 138r)

It seemed like a very dark and thick mist surrounded me so I couldn't see anything else, and they were putting me on a bridge so narrow that it only had room for my feet, and this bridge was over a swamp that looked deep, with many disgusting reptiles and a foul smell, and the bridge was so long that it had no end, and the person who put me on it (I couldn't see who it was) told me that I should take something to eat along with me, because on that whole long path I wouldn't find anyone to give me anything, because I had to walk alone; and the person was telling me that if I didn't want to get lost I shouldn't look behind, or up, or sideways, but only forward where there was a little light very far away.

Once again arises the theme of being lost, of not finding the right road. Inés, although totally single-minded in her zeal for reformation, consistently writes of confusion and powerlessness. Her strength in the convent's business and political matters is thus tempered, in Sigüenza's narrative, with inner doubt and weakness. This two-layered complexity further contributes to the blurring of public and private concerns characteristic of the nuns' chronicles.

Inés describes the routine of daily life in the cloister and her own demanding, self-sacrificing schedule of work with convent books. Nowhere are to be found dates or a specific time reference. It is the ritual of prayers performed at specified times each day that provides a time frame for Inés's life and life story in both *Parayso* and the *Relación*. The cycle of prayers connects her to the eternal, infinite power beyond linear time: "A cada verso parece se me volaba el alma, y me hallaba toda en Dios, y mientras mas largos eran los maytines mas me alegraba, despues de acabados tenia disciplina, y me quedaba alla hasta las cinco que iban a prima" [With each line of prayer I felt my soul fly, and I found myself entirely in God, and the longer matins were the happier I was; after they were over I had discipline, and I stayed there until five o'clock when everyone went to prime] (fol. 138v). In this linkage of the mystical experience with the cyclical time of the canonical hours, the effects of the nuns' sense of time on the narrative are clearest. Although the vida ensconced in *Parayso* follows a chronology, it is not the same as that of Sigüenza's history; not words and facts, but a more cosmic subjectivity is Inés's vehicle for explaining her experience.

After an illness that leaves her unable to read for eight months without entering into ecstatic transport and unconsciousness, the nun resigns her position as accountant and begins plans for the foundation of the Convento de San José. From here on, the visions in *Parayso* are fast and furious. Inés stresses their nonvisual quality: "Pareciome un dia via a la Santissima Trinidad (digo entendilo, porque no vide nada) en una gloria como globo" [One day it appeared to me that I saw the Holy Trinity (I mean I understood it, because I didn't see anything) in a glory like an orb] (fol. 142r). Words are of limited use when describing such episodes. Never are they introduced as occurring at specific times; rather, they are begun with phrases such as "otra vez" [another time], "en otra ocasion" [on another occasion], or "a pocos años que entre Monja" [A few years after I became a Nun]. This last date of profession in particular – 1588, as Inés has said – serves as the guidepost for all events happening after it. Thus these visions are included as part of the totality of religious life, not as isolated instances along a linear time line.

Nevertheless, Inés does have what could be termed a historical perspective on the past when relating the founding of her
new cloister, the chronicle part of the narration. Speaking of
the work to be done in a convent – she is, at this point, trying to
rid herself of all duties in order to place her total energy in the
Carmelite foundation – she writes: "Aora que lo miro de lexos
me espantan los trabajos que ay en los rincones de los Conventos" [Looking back on it now from afar, the work in every corner of the Convents shocks me] (fol. 144r). Her attitude causes
more trouble with her sisters, and Inés becomes a hermit within
Jesús María:

Recatabanse mucho de mi, y yo escusaba el andar por la casa, tanto
que si no era del aposento donde estaba al coro, o refectorio, no
andaba mas: passaronse una vez muchos años sin passar del primero
al segundo patio, y quando me vine dexe sin ver muchas celdas, ni se
hazia reparo en ello, porque en Conventos grandes como el de Jesus
Maria se passan años sin que se hablen unas o otras. (fol. 144r)

They stayed away from me, and I stopped walking around the house,
to the extent that if it wasn't to go from my room to the choir, or the
refectory, I didn't walk anywhere; at one point many years passed
without my going from the first courtyard to the second, and when
that happened I stopped going past many cells, and no one noticed,
because in the large Convents like Jesús María years go by without
some nuns talking to others.

This interesting commentary on convent life continues with
a remark about this microcosm of the complex outside society:

Siempre me han parecido los Conventos grandes como un pueblo de
muchas naciones, con la multitud de mosas, y criadas que han encon-
trado de tantos generos de metales; y lo malo es que cada Monja tiene
dos, y tres ... tienen mas inquietudes, y pleytos por ellas, que tuvieran en sus casas con la familia. (fol. 145v)

The large Convents have always seemed to me like a town of many
peoples, with the multitude of servant girls they have found of so
many types of tones; the bad part is that every nun has two or
three ... and they have more problems and arguments about the servants than they had with their families at home.

Inés thus supplies implicit and explicit criticism of unreformed
institutions and their moral laxity. In contrast, this follower of
Teresa of Avila knew, from the earliest age, what God was expecting from her: "La oracion que Dios me dio desde muy niña

fue sobrenatural sin trabajo, ni cuydado mio, sino con una sua-
vidad del cielo" [The prayer given to me by God since I was a
little girl was supernatural, without any effort or worry on my
part, but rather with a heavenly ease] (fol. 146r).

Sigüenza's chapter 6 of the vida finds Inés at last in the Carmelite Convento de San José. In this version, all the political
problems and high drama accompanying the actual foundation
are skipped over; however, in the extant *Relación* (as in Mariana's text) it is the story of the foundation itself that makes up
the bulk of the narration. We cannot know if Sigüenza eliminated this from the vida he used for *Parayso*. In any case, what
ends the story in both *Parayso* and the *Relación* is a section on
Padre Francisco Losa, his date of death (1624) being the third
definite year mentioned in Inés's account. Losa was the first
chaplain of San José, and the nuns have kept his body as a relic.
As she nears the end of her story, Inés begins to address her
confessor (V.P., or *vuestra Paternidad*).

Attributing her understanding of God's grace to the confessor's superior wisdom and guidance, Inés again remarks on her
difficulty in writing about divine gifts:

Assi lo he visto . . . en el conocimiento de la grandeza incomprehensible de su Magestad . . . y tal que me faltan palabras para dezirlo: y
tengo tan clara luz en los ojos del alma, que me parece no creo las
cosas de la Fè, sino que las miro, y en las palabras, y promesas de Nuestro Señor, y en lo que obro tengo mas certidumbre que si los viera, y
este mundo visible, y todo lo que perciben los sentidos me parece
sombra. (fol. 150r)

I have seen in this way . . . in the knowledge of the incomprehensible
greatness of his Majesty . . . such that I lack words to describe it; and
I have such a clear light in the eyes of my soul, that it seems to me I
do not believe in matters of faith, but rather see them, and in the
words and vows of our Lord, and in my works, I have more certainty
than if I saw them, and this visible world and everything the senses
perceive seem like a shadow.

The nun attempts to put the ineffable into written words, and
within her own model of discourse succeeds admirably. But
mindful of the other time frame, that of the outside world, she
admits the formal limits of her narration: "Todo va sin pies, ni
cabeza, y algo repetido dos vezes, y segun el mal orden de mi
poco entendimiento, y el ser cosas de ninguna importancia ha

de obligar a V.P. a romperlo luego" [It is all without end or beginning, and some things repeated twice, and according to the bad order of my own slight knowledge, and it being a thing of no importance will obligate your Paternalness to rip it up right away] (fol. 150r).

Thus Inés's vida ends on a typical note of humbleness and servitude, denying any function for her writing beyond the exemplary and didactic. The last sentence includes this text's fourth, and final precise date: "Y esto acabo oy tres de Henero de mil seiscientos y veinte y nuevo años" [And I finish this today, 3 January 1629] (fol. 151r). The *Relación* is dated, according to Muriel, 16 September 1625.

The history that *Parayso Occidental* strives to be must absorb and contain the vida-*relación* of the nuns for several reasons: (1) to categorize and regulate them, changing their cyclical, mystical quality into a chronology; (2) to use them as factual evidence, enhancing the truthfulness of the historical test; and (3) to claim for the New World, and for New Spain, a place in the Christian universe equal to, or better than, that of Europe. Each motive builds on the next, for written history indicates a past worth recording and truth requires evidence that must be believable to be useful. The presentation of events in chronological sequence is key to such credibility. As Sigüenza sorts through the convent archive, discarding some materials and retaining others, he makes editorial decisions based on these criteria because some of the nuns' texts are more easily incorporated than others. Some need to be rewritten or tinkered with to bring them up to his standard, some can be accepted as is, and some are useless.

The texts accepted into the narrative with little or no editing are those that follow a more linear order of chronology, like Inés de la Cruz's account as presented by Sigüenza, and certain episodes of Mariana's tract. These texts by women are the ones more similar to those by secular male writers and, in particular, to the chronicles of discovery and colonization. In the same way that the latter chronicles are retold by Sigüenza through baroque narrative devices, these nuns' stories are made American by becoming part of the complexity of *Parayso Occidental*. They are woven into the history, bearing witness to the role of God in the two convents' foundations and, by extension, to the Conquest of America. When their texts are included verbatim, these women authors are given full credit, although their words are still locked in by Sigüenza's careful narrative strategy.

I have offered examples of the tinkering Sigüenza performs on passages that almost, but not quite, meet his standards for historical rhetoric. Cyclical, religious time gives way to secular dating in order to keep the women's texts "in line" on the straight and narrow. This attempt at such limitation leads to the polyphony of narrative voices that twists *Parayso* into a baroque history. The situation becomes more acute in the instances of wholesale rewriting of the nuns' texts, such as the scene of the archbishop's dawn Mass. Here the clashing of historical and literary languages, simmering in the cases where only dates are changed boils over. Rewriting the vida-*relación* causes a rhetorical crisis: interventions by the historian and editor are not enough to convert these texts into material acceptable for a history.

Furthermore, the biographical content of the vidas suggests a narrative closer to literature, particularly that of the picaresque and of Cervantes. Thus, to write a credible history using Marina de la Cruz's vida, Sigüenza uses Pedro de la Mota as his foil. What de la Mota has left out in style and detail, Sigüenza provides, doing what should have been done in the first place by correcting the errors of an untutored priest. But it gives the criollo free reign to balance the mystical quality of the nun's visions with his own version of historical time: excess detail that will bring the narrative back to a chronological progression. This shifting between the nuns' texts, with their cyclical time frame, and Sigüenza's rewriting happens so quickly that the two texts cannot be separated anymore in the reading of *Parayso Occidental.* As in the nuns' writing, subjective time and objective time blend in a narrative that draws from various historical and literary models of discourse. In this way the vidas become *Parayso Occidental,* shaping it with their difference.

The texts omitted by Sigüenza are eliminated, as I have indicated, to make the vidas conform to the history's overall discursive plan. Sigüenza makes it clear that Mariana's story has been severely cut, and, indeed, her 165 pages are reduced in *Parayso* to two chapters of eleven pages total. Sigüenza's text concentrates on the facts of Mariana's life (facts easily compressed into a chronological progression), leaving out the bulk of her account of the actual foundation. That story, of course, is one of political intrigue, jealousy, rivalry, and passion that is a far cry from the "delicious Paradise of virtue" Sigüenza would portray the cloister to be.

Whereas *Parayso's* Inés de la Cruz writes the story of her interior life, Mariana's *Relación* resembles more Sigüenza's Libro Primero in its depiction of colonial bureaucracy and politics. As I have said, Inés's extant manuscript tells that same story, but Sigüenza did not use it. Inés's *vida* as quoted in the history lends itself more readily to Sigüenza's narration precisely because of its picaresque, literary aspects, which fit into the strategies he has devised for dealing with cyclical time, including his own interventions and a baroque layering of voices. Its overall emphasis is on the nun herself, following her story in more or less chronological order wtih a few digressions.

Mariana's text shows the nuns as strong outside the convent as well as within it. These women participated fully in the social institutions important to them and knew how to lobby on their own behalf. Moreover, as I described earlier, they were intimately involved in the conflicts rampant among the peninsular and criollo groups. Two citations that Josefina Muriel has edited, and that Sigüenza leaves out entirely, attest to this issue:

Mis hermanas y deudas que eran hartas, me ayudaban a atribular diciéndome para qué me metía en aquellas novedades que Dios me había traído desde pequeña a aquella religión donde era amada de todas, y dándome talentos para vivir en su compañía con gusto, que dejase a la Madre Inés de la Cruz, que era propiedad de gachupinas ser noveleras, amigas de hacer ruido, ambiciosas para ganar fama y que hiciese caso de ellas, razones que me afligían por saber yo sus santos deseos y pura intención. . . .
Llegó la noticia de nuestro padre provincial y visitador fray Tomás de San Vicente que se trataba de esta fundación, y reprobándola decía en ocasiones que no en sus días, que mientras él fuese prelado no consentiría fundasen convento de religión que profesa tanta perfección criollas regalonas y chocolateras, que traeríamos tres o cuatro criadas cada una que nos sirviesen. (Muriel 1982, 69)

My sisters and others in the convent added to my tribulations, asking me why I was getting involved in all those new things, that God had led me from the time I was a child to the rule of that convent where

I was loved by all, giving me talents to live in their company with pleasure, and that I should forget Madre Inés de la Cruz, that it was the
way of *gachupinas* to be looking for novelties, that they were fond of
making trouble, ambitious to gain fame and be noticed, arguments
that pained me because I knew of her saintly desires and pure intentions . . .
The news reached friar Tomás de San Vicente, our provincial
priest and *visitador*, that we were planning this foundation, and dis-
approving it he said on different occasions that as long as he was the
prelate he would not give his consent that a convent professing such
a perfect rule be founded by chocolate-loving, spoiled criollas, who
would each bring along three or four servants to wait on us.

Sigüenza leaves out the conflict of national identity within
the convent in order to present the New World Paradise in an
idealized manner, according to his own vision. Since the entire
history is dedicated to the Spanish King, this particular conflict
was not a topic the criollo writer wished to include outside the
context of his own familiar, patriotic arguments. Moreover, the
gossip and politicking of the nuns fit neither into the factual
nor the religious categories; thus they have no role in the en-
hancement of this history and are rejected.

Here I would consider again the episode of Inés's vida in
Parayso describing her passage to America. As the citation from
Mariana recalls, Inés was a *gachupina*, the disparaging criollo
term for a resident of Mexico born in Spain, as was Marina de
la Cruz, her mentor. The Convento de Jesús María was
founded for criollas such as Mariana de la Encarnación and,
therefore, Inés and Marina did not really belong in the institution at all. Yet Sigüenza manipulates their life stories to the
advantage of his history, emphasizing not only the good fortune of the New World in receiving such saintly women, but
also the luck of these future nuns in arriving on American soil.

Marina was brought to Mexico by her first husband, who
wanted to make himself rich and saw little opportunity in
Spain. Although Marina feared the danger and distance of the
trip, and did not want to leave her family or her country, she
went along dutifully. It was her husband's, and thus God's, will
that Marina come to America, where indeed she did obtain material success compared to her life in Spain. Marina is God's instrument; much as God favors the New World with her
immigration, she is blessed by this virgin Paradise. The impli-

cation is that her obedience to her husband is a virtue that has been handsomely rewarded because after his death (and that of her second husband as well) Marina will become a nun.

Inés, too, is brought to Mexico by others, in this case her parents. She comes not only willingly, but joyfully, expecting not a Paradise but a pagan hell that will intensify her desire for Christian martyrdom. In many ways, this is a self-fulfilling prophecy, but it is not so much satisfied in the outer world of the secular "siglo" as within the convent itself. Inés finds plenty of sin to battle against among her unreformed sisters, and their resistance to her efforts to wipe out all traces of physical desire and pleasure makes her happier still. Inés's life is lived according to the ascetic model, in direct imitation of Teresa of Avila and Marina de la Cruz, and like Marina her suffering takes place in a supposed Paradise.

What Sigüenza's history attempts with these two vidas of Spanish nuns is an absorption of their life stories into his American narrative. These accounts tell of the encounter of European women with a new world, and also of the conquest of spirit over flesh. The antieroticism we first saw in Marina's biography reaches a fever pitch with Inés's obsessive insistence on erasing the body to enhance the soul. Her desire to be considered a "mala muger" (fol. 132v) reflects a strict moral code and the regulated position of women within it. Although male ascetics, too, wish to eliminate desire, clearly the female authorship of this account opens up a different possibility for Sigüenza's use of the narration in his larger scheme.

The Carmelites are examples for Concepcionista nuns to follow in 1684; at the same time, their conquest of sin within themselves and their communities echoes the criollo's preoccupation with the other Conquest, that of the New World. The story of how two European-born women find salvation in Mexico fits perfectly in the theme of a western Paradise of superior virtue. The purity of their endeavor is possible only in an untouched, virgin territory ripe for Christianization.

Thus the locking up of the nuns' texts by the criollo history parallels Sigüenza's rewriting of the chronicles of Conquest – the classics of the sixteenth century – in the way it uses baroque language and overlay. Sigüenza y Góngora does not so much alter the nuns' own words as he does the greater historical context surrounding them. It is evident that he has accomplished a careful editing job in order to emphasize certain themes: the virginity of the New World Paradise and of the women inhabiting it, and the zeal with which they maintain that purity. The control of female sexuality in *Parayso Occidental* is achieved through both stern moralizing and the closing of temporal gaps left in the text.

To these religious women who wrote about their lives and personal experience, control of sexual desire was a crucially important issue. Their choices emerged from the codes of the society surrounding them, which offered very few alternatives for women of the criollo or Spanish-born privileged classes. As Inés relates so clearly, the line separating a good woman from a bad one could be crossed instantly and irrevocably because of mere appearance, regardless of fact. The importance of public ceremony and superficial impression in the colonial period has been well described by Leonard (1959) and Paz (1982); in Inés de la Cruz's obsession with good and evil, these outward circumstances are melded with a subjective perception of reality.

To be sure, the interior life of mystics and visionaries serves as their primary source of faith and the wellspring of their absolute moral conviction. Interior and exterior worlds merge; the decision to deny the body and its pleasures is made on behalf of another ecstasy rooted in a different, cyclical sense of time. The choices made by nuns who were also mystics, such as the Carmelite founders, were informed by a kind of communion with God not shared by the majority of their sisters (as is evident from the latter's reaction to attempted reforms).

The cyclical time of their perceptions works in tandem with the colonial milieu to create the narrative of the vidas, a blend of chronicle and autobiography incorporating the eternal time frame of the mystic with the surrounding restrictions of New Spain's religious orthodoxy. To this project the nuns bring a mandate to put into words what they have experienced directly. The writing process thus becomes both frustrating in its limitations and pleasurable in the power of the images that memory evokes. The wavering of the narrative from subjective to objective discourse, from cyclical to narrative time, reflects the lives of women cloistered from the outer world yet still a part of it, participating in politics and making history.

Carlos de Sigüenza y Góngora, a criollo historian writing the history of the founding of a colonial Mexican convent, has other rhetorical preoccupations with which to contend. He must combine the nuns' cyclical narration with the strict laws of history in order to claim authority for his text; he must somehow absorb their vidas into his own book. The nuns' texts, with their conflict between the limitations of written words and the indescribability of experience, resonate with another rhetorical confrontation: that of the chronicles of Conquest with the reality of the New World. Sigüenza would take both these undefined forms and through baroque narrative strategies establish authority over the texts of convent and American history. The Conquest of America by Europe is bettered by the conquest of sin and desire that enables the planting, and cultivation, of an occidental Paradise, recorded in the language of the *barroco de Indias.*

In the process of editing and embroidering the nuns' writing, Sigüenza would change its sense of time and restrict the actions of colonial women as authors of their own lives and history. By closing up the nuns, and their texts, behind convent walls, the criollo history would have both women and writing conform to another set of rules. But the difference of the nuns' texts overflows those boundaries, goes beyond the walls set around it, and creates the baroque narrative of *Parayso Occidental.*

Epilogue

In August of 1982, as a graduate student embarking on dissertation research, I found myself in Mexico City searching for the archive of the Convento Real de Jesús María, on which Sigüenza y Góngora had based his *Parayso Occidental*. In the Archivo de la Nación, however, the file listed as that of the convent's foundation proved to be an eighteenth-century manuscript copy of none other than *Parayso Occidental*. Caught in a labyrinth of scholarly repetition reminiscent of Borges, I decided to look for something more material and solid: the convent itself.

Walking through the teeming, narrow streets to the east of the Zócalo, I located the Iglesia de Jesús María, a simple church open for worship and in the process of a government-sponsored restoration. Next to it was the façade of the old convent with its Latin inscription over the entryway, a building crumbling with age and neglect. That door was locked: continuing on to the end of the block, I rounded the corner to see if another existed. It did: past the shop windows of a Viana chain store, I was able to enter. There, the original colonial architecture of arched walls surrounding a central patio stared down on sale-priced reclining chairs and stereo equipment, on the buyers and sellers of modern technology and comfort.

That trip to Mexico – the first of several related to this project – was fruitful to my research, but not exactly in the way I had planned. In 1982 I came away convinced of the power of literary language to create its own text apart from archival data or evidence, and of the need to read colonial texts in all their multiple meanings in order to work toward a new Spanish American literary history reflecting those many facets. I wished to read old texts through the prism of contemporary literary theory and, in 1982, that was still a bold, uncommon enterprise.

The intervening years have brought substantial changes to the field of colonial Latin American studies. The frenzy of preparation for the Columbian quincentenary and a more generalized interest in colonialism and post colonialism cutting across academic disciplines have pushed forward work on colonial texts in particular. The renovation the field of Latin American colonial literature has undergone in less than a decade has placed it, I believe, at the forefront of Hispanic studies today, for as critics we are posing radical questions that challenge all sorts of standard ideas regarding genre, canon, and literary history.

In this study of Carlos de Sigüenza y Góngora, I have focused on the seventeenth-century *barroco de Indias* as a part of a colonial culture in the process of great change. I say part, rather than reflection, response, or manifestation, because baroque texts were actors on the scene of change. Baroque history, in particular, was a major player in the establishment of a distinct mixture of factual chronicle and subjective testimony that, through the centuries, has come to characterize the Latin American narrative. When we read works such as *Parayso Occidental, Infortunios de Alonso Ramírez,* or Freyle's *El carnero,* we are witnessing the evolution of a new way of narrating past events that, sometimes quite consciously, uses the illusions of language to report the truth. The criollo condition of colonial subjectivity spawned a patriotism that desired to rewrite the American past in such a way that the chronicles of Conquest would tell their own New World story, rather than that of the Spaniards. To accomplish this feat, more than an unconscious will to skip over the violence of the sixteenth century was required; an overhaul of the language of history was also necessary.

Parayso Occidental is especially valuable for us as critics today. The process of thinking through the place of women in colonial culture forces a challenge to what I think of as the blood-and-guts canon of colonial literature. Predicated on the assumption that the wars of Conquest and the struggle for independence define colonial historical narrative, this way of interpreting the past ignores the voices of other groups that use other discourses, in this case the voices of women. In this regard, much more research is needed on the ways in which the history written by women in colonial America – history composed as spiritual life stories, letters, and other nontraditional forms – participated in the reshaping of narrative discourse in the New World.

More research on Sigüenza y Góngora as a baroque historian would also be an important contribution to colonial studies. In this book my goal has been to break down the image of Sigüenza as a modern thinker, and in that way to consider his era and culture from a different angle. Narratives such as *Libra astronómica, Theatro de virtudes políticas, Triunfo parténico,* and *Infortunios de Alonso Ramírez,* and the epic poems *Oriental planeta* and *Primavera indiana* are all understudied and waiting for new approaches.

As I have written here about colonial historiography and posited connections between the sixteenth and seventeenth centuries, I have constantly been reminded of the Romantic literary historians of the postindependence nineteenth century. Their reading of colonial narrative as a basis for national or regional tradition has been passed down through the decades and only in recent years has begun to be questioned. Although I wish to see baroque historiography situated in a historical context that has its own past and future, I resist the invention of a colonial legacy for present-day fiction stretching backwards like a smooth road. History has been invented and reinvented time and again in Latin America, beginning with the rewritings of the chronicles of Conquest: baroque narratives are a part of that story we can only regard as undefinable according to the standards of European national traditions.

And so I have become convinced that documents and archives do have a crucial role to play in the work of a literary historian and critic who deals with the distant past. I have sought to read Sigüenza y Góngora's narratives historically. Inevitably, though, I position myself in my own current critical context of feminist, poststructuralist thought. Like a colonial patio bedecked with the artifacts of modernity, my own inquiry is indelibly marked by its layers of experience and interpretation, concerned in particular with a questioning of history as a yardstick for truth both in Sigüenza's era, and in my own.

Appendix A
Prologo al letor

No ha sido otro mi intento en este Libro sino escrivir historia   1
observando en ella sin dispensa alguna sus estrechas leyes. Assi lo
hazen quantos despues de haver leydo las antiguas, y modernas
con diligencia, hallan ser las que solo se aplauden las que son
historias. Es el fin de estas hazer presente lo pasado como fue enton-   5
ces, y si entonces no se exornaron los sucesos humanos con adornos
impertinentes de otros asuntos, como puede ser plausible en
la historia lo que por no ser en ella à proposito suele causar à
los que la leen notable enfado? Comprobar lo que se habla con autoridades de la Escritura, y de Santos Padres es muy bueno para   10
quien haze Sermones, ò persuade en tratados espirituales à seguir
las virtudes, y detestar los vicios, que es en donde sirven semejantes apoyos plausiblemente, como tambien los de otros Autores
aunque profanos, y Poetas en lo que se requiere que assi se escriva
que suele ser lo que de su naturalesa pide florido estilo, y que   15
Yo tambien he practicado en algunos papeles mios, que se han em-
presso: y aunque me huviera sido en estremo facil embarazar
el texto, y ocupar los margenes de este libro con semejantes cosas,
siendo mi asunto el escrivir historia de mugeres para mugeres,
claro està que hiziera muy mal en hazerlo assi, y mas si me persua-   20
diera (como otros hazen) a que necessitaban los Doctos de mis marginales anotaciones, pues no ignoro el que de ordinario las desprecian
los varoniles ingenios, que son los que cuydan poco de Poliantheas.
   Por lo que toca al estilo gasto en este Libro el que gasto
siempre; esto es, el mismo que observo quando converso, quando   25
escrivo, quando predico, assi por que quizas no pudiera executar
lo contrario si lo intentase, como por saber haver perdido algunos
tratados por su lenguage horroroso, y nimio lo que merecian de
aplauso por su asunto heroyco. Escrivir de una difunta el "que en
vez de mostrar palidas tristezas, ò marchitas perfecciones se son-   30
roseaba de rojas colores, ò coloria de rosas carmesies, las quales alin-
daban, mas de lo que puede encarecerse, la cara apacible de la difunta
yerta," y servir todo este circunloquio para dezir que conservaba despues de muerta los mismos colores que quando viva, que
otra cosa es sino condenar un Autor su libro (y mas formandose   35
todo el de semejantes periodos) à que jamàs se lea; y no queriendo
tan mal a este mio, que guste ver por el lo que de otros dizen,

aseguro el que se hallaran los orizontes, las estrellas, y los
coluros en los Autores que escriven de esfera; en los Lapidarios
40 los chrysolitos, los topacios, y los carbuncios: los ambares, y
almizcles en los Guanteros: los jazmines, los claveles, y mira-
flores en los jardines, y todo esto con mucho mas en los que se
presumen imitadores de Fray Hortensio Paravicino, y D. Luis de
Gongora, y como quiera que no es esto lo que se gasta en las co-
45 munes platicas, debiendo ser el estilo que entonces se usa el que se
debe seguir quando se escriven historias, desde luego afirmo el
que no se hallarà el cathalogo de essas cosas en la presente, porque
sè que es este el escollo en que peligran muchos.
   En su verdad, puedo afirmar no haver perdonado para conseguir-
50 la diligencia alguna, leyendo quantos libros impressos podian
contener algo para mi asunto; pero todos necessitan de emmienda,
como dirè adelante, y assi ocćurì al archivo del Real Convento,
cuyos papeles se me entregaron, y tambien varios quadernos de
autos, y cedulas . . . no ay [historia] sino la que aqui se dirà, sacada
55 de los mismos papeles originales que se escrivieron entonces, y que
refiero en parte.

Appendix B

A la magestad de Don Carlos II
Nuestro Señor Emperador de las
Indias y Rey de España

Enoblecieron los augustissimos progenitores de V.M. su Imperial   1
Ciudad de Mexico con el Convento Real de Jesus Maria; mejorando
en el su magnificencia aquel delicioso Parayso, con que en las
niñezes del mundo se engrandeciò el Oriente: porque si aquel
se componia de lo que experimentò la voracidad del tiempo por   5
vegetable; el que en el contexto deste volumen le ofresco à V.M. se
forma de flores, que se han de immortalizar por racionales en el
mismo Empyreo: si en aquel triunfò de la original pureza la
primera culpa: en este tiene pacifica habitacion la divina gracia: si
en aquel conducidos de la inobedencia se enseñorearon de la   10
humana naturaleza todos los vicios; en este la reducen à su ser
primitivo las virtudes todas: y si de aquel desterrò un Cherubin à
una sola muger, que lo habitaba, por delinquente; en este viven
como Serafines abrazadas en el amor de su Esposo innumerables
Virgines.   15
  Mejoras son estas, que, en parangon de el Oriental Parayso, no
solo le grangean al Occidental del Convento Real de Jesus
Maria antelaciones bastantes, sino que tambien le forman à los
gloriosissimos progenitores de V.M. panegyricos, que desde oy
llevara la immortal Fama de gente en gente: Y con razon muy justa;   20
porque si para engrandecer Dios la Monarquia Austriaca les entregò
las sombras de este Ocaso à sus triunfantes armas, credito fue de
la sabiduria del prudentissimo Felipe, Salomon de España,
retornarle à Dios este beneficio engrandeciendole, y dilatandole el
Reyno de sus escogidos no con otra cosa que con empeñarse en   25
debelar perfectamente las sombras de la infidelidad, con que se
infamaban estas provincias desde su antiguo origen. Empressa es
esta que sabe el mundo, y aun por esso es conveniente el que no
ignore sus circunstancias para elogiarlas.
  No podian ahuyentarse tantas sombras sino con muchas luzes, ni   30
era suficiente para triunfar de todo un Ocaso, sino el Oriente todo;
con que afanandose su discretissimo zelo en que sojusgasen
los resplandores del Evangelio à las denegridas tinieblas del
gentilismo equivocò el Ocaso con el Oriente, trasladando quanto
havia de claridad en el Oriente al obscuro Ocaso: Y como quiera   35
que el primer conocimiento que tubieron de Dios los primeros
hombres se consiguiò entre las delicias del Parayso, de cuya posesion

fueron despojados por su grave culpa; para que aquel en esta
Occiseptentrional America se conservase estable, por preciso tubo
40 el prudentissimo Rey ilustrar su Imperial Metropoli de el nuevo
mundo con el mejorado Parayso, que para obsequiar à V.M. con sus
fragancias me sirviò de asunto.

Y aunque es verdad no haver salido de èl las primeras luzes de la
Fè, à que les debe este Ocaso el blazonarse Oriente (por ser funcion
45 que solo fia la Iglesia Catholica à varoniles animos) con todo, no es
dudable ser el Convento Real de Jesus Maria el lugar desde donde
se recabò, y recaba de el Altissimo el que ilumine con los
resplandores de su noticia, y mantenga en el conocimiento de su
divinidad à las nuevas gentes; y desde donde con exercicios santos
50 se le solicitan, y consiguen a la Española Monarquia felicidades, y
duraciones.

Notes

Introduction

1 Some of the most eloquent writing on this topic is cited in the Bibliography, including the works of Gallop, Jardine, Miller, and Moi.

2 The most influential anthologies in Spanish (or in English with Spanish texts) are those of Anderson Imbert and Florit (1970), Englekirk et. al. (1968), and Anderson and Flores (1974). Although each takes a somewhat different posture toward the colonial period, their overall approaches fit into these two tendencies. It is also important to mention in this context Emir Rodríguez Monegal's two-volume anthology of Latin American literature in English translation (1977), which includes a large colonial section and has had a significant impact on the North American reading public.

A more recent collection is that of Raquel Chang Rodríguez and Malva E. Filer (1988), which does much to include new scholarship on the colonial period in the vision it offers. Nevertheless, even this collection includes examples of the imposition of modern literary forms on colonial texts, such as the unqualified identification of Sigüenza's *Infortunios de Alonso Ramírez* as a novel (7–8). Similarly, Evelyn Picón Garfield and Iván A. Schulman's 1991 textbook characterizes *Infortunios* as an antecedent to the novel (138).

Although all these anthologies are used primarily in the North American academy, I contend that they reflect the state of thinking in Latin America as well, and indeed are instrumental in shaping the canon of colonial texts in both Americas. Anderson Imbert and Florit (1970), for instance, is listed in the bibliography of Margarita Peña's *Descubrimiento y conquista de América: Una antología general*, published in Mexico in 1982 and meant for a student readership.

3 The 1982 volume of essays published in Spain as *Historia de la literatura hispanoamericana: Época colonial*, edited by Luis Iñigo Madrigal, contains an important study of the colonial chronicles by Walter Mignolo, as well as broader chapters on individual writers and genres. See also the 1989 collection edited by René Jara and Nicholas Spadaccini, and the journals *Dispositio* 14 (1989), *Revista de Crítica Literaria Latinoamericana* 14 (1988), and *Revista de Estudios Hispánicos* 23 (1989) for collections of articles on the colonial period.

4 The *Cambridge History of Latin American Literature*, presently being compiled and edited by Roberto González Echevarría and Enrique Pupo-Walker, will go far in the work of breaking down the received ideas of colonial literature and challenging exclusive canons.

5 Of particular note in this context, concerning the baroque in Spain, are Otis Green's monumental *Spain and the Western Tradition* (1963–6) and Helmut Hatzfeld's *Estudios sobre el barroco* (1964). These are but two of the "classic" texts on the subject, and they serve as examples of a literary criticism reaching beyond the strictly textual. Heinrich Wölfflin's *Renaissance and Baroque* remains an essential text for understanding the evolution of the term "baroque" as applied to European art. In Chapter 1 I discuss the bibliography concerning the Hispanic baroque in more detail.

Chapter 1

1 My source is the 1993 edition of *Guía Roji's Ciudad de México*.

2 Some exceptions published since 1980 (besides those I discuss in this chapter) are the articles by Arrom (1987), Chang Rodríguez (1982), Gimbernat de González (1980), González Pérez (1983), Johnson (1981), Moraña (1990), and Ross (1988). It should be noted that the majority of these studies, in turn, concentrate on *Infortunios de Alonso Ramírez*. Among recent book-length studies in which Sigüenza is paired with Sor Juana is Catalá (1987).

3 Part of *A Mexican Savant* was originally published in 1927 as an article in the journal *Hispania* (Leonard 1927). This same article was also the seed for what may be the best-known of all portraits of Sigüenza, the chapter "A Baroque Scholar" in Leonard's 1959 *Baroque Times in Old Mexico*.

4 All translations, unless noted, are my own.

5 Also from this period are Leonard's 1932 edition of *Alboroto y motín de los indios de México*, printed in English translation in *A Mexican Savant* (1929) as "Letter to Admiral Pez," and the facsimile edition and translation of *Mercurio volante* done by Leonard in the same year.

6 Collected editions of the *Obras históricas* (1944) and *Relaciones históricas* (1940), plus new printings of *Triunfo parténico* (1945) and *Glorias de Querétaro* (1945) date from this time. The Spanish publisher Espasa-Calpe's first printing of *Infortunios* dates from 1941.

7 And also, in this case, another sentiment current in the 1940s: anti-Semitism. Describing how the area of Mexico City where Sigüenza's boyhood home had stood (on the Estampa de Jesús María, near the Convento de Jesús María) had of late fallen on hard times, Rojas Garcidueñas disparages the presence of Jewish immigrants: "calles donde alternan antes magnificas y hoy maltratadas iglesias con carnicerías que ostentan la estrella de David y rótulos en yidish" [streets where churches, magnificent in the past and

neglected today, alternate with butcher shops boasting the Star of David and signs in Yiddish] (15).

8 Such a coupling of the two figures had been used before 1959 as a device for portraying the *barroco de Indias*, notably in an article by López Cámara (1950).

9 In 1959 and 1960 there was another small publishing "boom" of editions of Sigüenza's works, including an excellently annotated version of *Libra astronómica*, edited by José Gaos and published by the Universidad Nacional Autónoma de México (UNAM).

10 Roberto González Echevarría explores this in his 1987 article on Sarduy, which also discusses the relationship between Lezama and Sarduy's theories of the baroque.

11 This is explained very clearly in the anthology *Poesía hispanoamericana colonial* (Chang Rodríguez and de la Campa 1985, 34–5).

12 I quote from Margaret Sayers Peden's fine 1988 translation, *Sor Juana, or, The Traps of Faith*. The first page number is from the translation; the second from the 1982 Spanish edition.

In this quote, the English phrase "a prevalent doctrine held, more or less consciously" communicates a meaning somewhat different from the Spanish "Una doctrina común que, más o menos difusa, se encuentra." But the implication, in the English, of conscious or unconscious intention on the part of these writers further underscores my observation of Paz's concern with existential, symbolic issues rather than material ones.

13 Other critics who have written along these lines, although their work does not rely on Maravall's, are Leonardo Acosta ([1972] 1985) and Jaime Concha (1976). Concha's formulation is particularly suggestive, all the more so for being one of the earliest critiques of an idealistic view of the colonial period.

14 As in the work I have already discussed by Leonard, Pérez Salazar, and Rojas Garcidueñas: see also Sibursky (1965).

15 For the subject of the cult of Guadalupe, one of the most suggestive analyses is that of Jacques Lafaye in his 1974 study *Quetzalcóatl y Guadalupe*.

16 See also Miguel A. Sánchez Lamego, 1955, *El primer mapa general de México elaborado por un mexicano*.

17 Such a heterogeneity of culture is coming to light through the efforts of scholars in Mexico who are cataloging the literary contents of documents in the National Archives that are related to the Inquisition. Works such as Solange Alberró's 1988 book also broaden our view of these underground aspects of colonial society.

Chapter 2

1 Adorno (1988b) provides an especially useful synthesis of these ideas with a short bibliography. The articles collected by her and Walter Mignolo in a recent (1989) special issue of *Dispositio* (XIV:

37–38) dedicated to "Colonial Discourse" present a weightier treatment of the subject. In that issue Mignolo proposes a further refinement of colonial discourse to what he calls "colonial semiosis" in order to reflect a diversity of semiotic interactions beyond alphabetized oral or written discourse. For my purposes in studying Sigüenza's written texts and their models, "discourse" is the term of choice.

2 I refer in particular to Paz's *Las trampas* (1982), Stephanie Merrim's edited volume *Feminist Perspectives on Sor Juana Inés de la Cruz* (1991), which effectively carries Paz's project into new areas, and to articles by Luciani (1987) and Perelmuter-Pérez (1983).

3 I refer here to Pupo-Walker 1982a, Zamora 1988, and González Echevarría 1990 on El Inca; to Merrim 1982 and Myers 1990 on Oviedo.

4 I take my information on Solís from Luis A. Arocena's authoritative 1963 study, *Antonio de Solís, cronista indiano.*

5 Arocena also discusses the general diffusion of Machiavelli's *The Prince* among seventeenth-century historians. It would be interesting to read Sigüenza's *Theatro de virtudes* in this light.

6 Walter Mignolo (1982) has also touched on these changes as seen in the work of Solís and two earlier seventeenth-century chroniclers: Alonso de Ovalle (*La histórica relación del Reino de Chile* [1646]) and Lucas Fernández de Piedrahita (*Historia general del Nuevo Reino de Granada* [1661])(92–6).

7 Besides the studies on El Inca and Oviedo mentioned in note 3, a key source for the understanding of the rhetoric of history in the Renaissance is Struever 1970.

8 Studies on Bernal Díaz include Adorno 1988a and González-Echevarría 1983.

9 The narratives of Indians, whether written, pictorial, or oral, centered on the catastrophic changes wrought by Conquest from the time of initial encounter. I am not addressing this topic here, but it is currently very much discussed by literary critics and anthropologists. Some recent studies include Adorno 1986, Castro-Klarén 1989, MacCormack 1989, and Zapata 1989.

I have written a more extensive treatment of the narratives of this period in a contribution, "Historians of the Conquest and Colonization of the New World, 1550–1620," to the forthcoming *Cambridge History of Latin American Literature.*

10 See Zamora 1988, chap. 6, 129–65, for a discussion of Inca Garcilaso's use of utopia in his 1609 *Comentarios reales.*

11 Line references are to the text provided in Appendix A.

12 This line of reasoning is continued in Laura Benítez Grobet's *La idea de historia en Carlos de Sigüenza y Góngora* (1983), where the author defines modernity as a dialectical process of crisis and contradiction. History serves in the interest of science as the vehicle whereby ideas can be expressed scientifically, i.e., critically. My point is that by recognizing *Parayso Occidental* as history, it be-

comes clear that for Sigüenza science serves history rather than the other way around.

13 Nelson (1973) mentions another group of historians that may have influenced Sigüenza: the Bollendist fathers of the early seventeenth century, a group of Flemish Jesuits who set out to restyle and reorder medieval saints' lives in accordance with unadorned truth (42). Sigüenza displays a similar concern with the authenticity of his sources, but does not reject the notion of style in historical discourse.

14 Folio references, recto or verso, are to the first edition of *Parayso Occidental* (1684). I am presently engaged in the preparation of the first modern edition of this text, which consists of 206 numbered folios plus the preliminary "Dedicatoria," official statements of permission, the "Prologo," and a table of contents.

15 Line references are to the text in Appendix B.

16 See, for example, E. R. Curtius, [1953] 1973, *European Literature and the Latin Middle Ages,* chap. 10; Joseph E. Duncan, 1972, *Milton's Earthly Paradise: A Historical Study of Eden;* and A. Bartlett Giamatti, 1966, *The Earthly Paradise and the Renaissance Epic.*

17 There is an obvious analogy here with Inca Garcilaso de la Vega's comparison of Cuzco with Rome in the *Comentarios reales.* Garcilaso also devotes the first six chapters of the fourth book of the *Comentarios* to the virgins who maintained the Incan Temple of the Sun. However, the purpose of Garcilaso's history is different from that of Sigüenza's, for it centers on a demonstration of the generally civilized character of a pre-Conquest Incan culture known intimately to the author. Sigüenza's criollo, syncretic ideology is one of appropriation, where certain Indian customs, such as the consecration of virgins, are appreciated for their exemplary quality as exceptions to the general rule of barbarism.

18 According to Irving Leonard, 1959, *Baroque Times,* 200–1.

19 See Warner, 1976, *Alone of All Her Sex,* 32, 48.

20 For criollas of an intellectual bent – as we know from Sor Juana's testimony – the convent offered comparative freedom, autonomy, and the chance to pursue goals beyond the constrictions of marriage and family. I review the issues involved in defining the cultural milieu of the convent in Chapter 5.

21 I have also explored this issue in my article (Ross 1988) on Sigüenza's *Alboroto y motín de los indios de México,* where I draw on Marshall Brown's argument in his 1982 essay "The Classic Is the Baroque." Brown dissects Heinrich Wölfflin's *Principles of Art History,* showing how the Hegelian concepts of essence and existence are identified with classic and baroque, respectively.

Chapter 3

1 The importance of the book and writings as religious or philosophical metaphors is explored in Curtius [1953] 1973, 302–47. Al-

though Sigüenza y Góngora did not employ the concept of *libro* as a trope in the manner of Calderón or other Golden Age poets, I consider it here as a symbol of the cosmic order that his criollo history strives to achieve.

2 This is Sigüenza's view; in truth, women played a far broader role in colonial society. See Luis Martín 1983, especially 9–34. On the subject of the importation of women to the New World, see Mac-Lachlan and Rodríguez 1980, 229–48, and Varner 1968.

3 Rachel Phillips (1983) comes to much the same conclusion as Todorov: that *la Malinche* disturbs the clear dichotomy of Indian versus Spaniard with her third mixed component. Phillips's essay, however, has a historical framework that recognizes differences in pre- and postindependence points of view.

4 As described in Lavrin (1983) 1991, Martín 1983, and Muriel 1946.

5 See Nelson 1973.

6 This account is one of the few documents cited by Sigüenza still known to be in existence, in the form of an 1823 manuscript copy of Mariana's *Relación* located in the collection of the Perry Castañeda Library at the University of Texas at Austin. This text is described in Muriel 1982 and I wish to thank Professor Muriel for calling my attention to the document before her book was published. I refer to the *Relación* more specifically in subsequent chapters of this book; rather than making textual comparisons with *Parayso Occidental* at this point, my objective is to concentrate on the narrative strategies of Sigüenza's history.

7 My references to narrative technique in Cervantes follow the suggestive analysis of El Saffar 1975.

8 See Bacigalupo 1981 for a discussion of the years 1521–1610; Israel 1975 for 1610–70.

Chapter 4

1 Lavrin ([1983] 1991) notes that several papal decrees during the first half of the seventeenth century "obliged all biographers of religious persons to disclaim support of any author's assumption of sanctity or divine intervention until and unless it was backed by the church. The material printed had to be understood as an example of virtue for the faithful" (80).

2 The bibliography on the picaresque is rich and extensive; I mention here those studies most pertinent to *Parayso Occidental*. In the context of thinking through the relationship of the picaresque to the vida, I found to be especially helpful Guillén's 1971 essay, which discusses autobiographical models, and Rico 1970 on issues of narrative perspective. González Echevarría's 1980 article, besides discussing the colonial *relación* as a rhetorical model for the early modern novel, gives an admirably succinct summary of the principal critical literature up to 1980. González Pérez takes

the most advanced stance to date on Sigüenza's possible manipulation of the picaresque in his 1983 study of *Infortunios de Alonso Ramírez*.

In my view Sigüenza's narration of the nuns' vidas within the framework of his history owes its picaresque quality not to a modern, intentional making of fiction, but rather to the fact that confessors and nuns alike used the well-defined rhetoric of the *relación* as a vehicle for writing spiritual biography or autobiography. In this regard González Echevarría's work has been key for my analysis. However, what has been most enlightening for my reading of *Parayso Occidental* is recent work on gender studies in the picaresque, as discussed in note 4 of this chapter.

3 The Judeo-Christian tradition of prescriptive writing for women begins with the Bible, of course, and continues all through the Middle Ages, leading into such Renaissance works as Vives's tract. Warner's *Alone of All Her Sex* (1976) is an exhaustive source of information on the subject of the figure of the Virgin as a model for women and girls. Another book that discusses didactic literature written for noblewomen is Putnam's *The Lady* ([1910] 1970).

4 Recent critical work on the female picaresque – Spanish novels of the Golden Age with *pícaras*, or female outlaws, as protagonists – has related the rise of that type of narrative to the regulation of prostitution (Cruz 1989). The depiction of the "liberal" female sexuality of the pícara, a character invented by male writers for a male audience, actually represents the increased control exerted over women living outside the bounds of society (Friedman 1987).

Cruz (1989) speculates on the roles of both nuns and pícaras within such a repressive context: "Gender studies of these two radically different texts thus reveal the ways in which prostitution and religious orders functioned as a means of gender control in the Renaissance, their potential for subversion, and the differing limitations imposed upon women by both systems" (198). This aspect of the manipulation of the pícara by male authors is most suggestive when considering how Sigüenza casts nuns such as Marina within the narration of his overarching history.

5 Lafaye ([1974] 1987) discusses the evolution of the term *nación* in New Spain of the seventeenth and eighteenth centuries, pointing out that it was used in the biblical sense of "tribe" more than the modern one of "country" (172–75). I believe that Sigüenza means to criticize his own Spanish (including criollo) group for its lack of historical consciousness.

6 One of Teresa's constant themes in her *Vida* is the inability of *entendimiento*, of knowledge or understanding, to comprehend the ineffability of divine visions and to describe them with language. I address this problem further in chapter 5.

7 The most complete study of *El carnero* to date is Herman 1978. See also González Echevarría 1990.

8 See Ross 1988 for a treatment of this text in the context of baroque historiography.

9 Although Sigüenza cites this as Psalm 113, verse 9, in the Revised Standard Version of the Bible, the latter passage reads: "He gives the barren woman a home, making her the joyous mother of children." The passage quoted in *Parayso Occidental* is from Psalm 115, verse 1. One may only speculate as to why Sigüenza's mistake (not noted in his list of corrections) echoes so precisely the text's search for a paternal role.

Chapter 5

1 See Alberró 1988 on the Inquisition and the topic of magic or witchcraft; Gonzalbo 1987 on the education of women in New Spain.

2 I would like to acknowledge conversations with Alice Kaplan regarding this point that have been especially useful to my argument.

3 The historian Jodi Bilinkoff is working on this question with regard to Spanish religious women. I thank her for sharing her work-in-progress with me.

4 Asunción Lavrin, private conversation, 1991.

5 This short manuscript is cited in Mureil (1982) with the date of 1625; Sigüenza's reference is dated 1629. In my own consultation of the manuscript I found the date to be ambiguous, with the last number either 5 or 9. In either case, it is not the same one used in *Parayso Occidental*. I would like to thank Manuel Ramos and the nuns of the Convento de San José for making possible my access to the convent archives in Mexico City.

6 Some of the classic texts on this subject are included in Kelly 1984. Regarding Latin American history, see Lavrin 1989 and Gonzalbo 1987.

7 The handwritten 1823 copy of the *Relación* consists of 165 faintly numbered pages. It is generally quite clear, although some lines are illegible, as I indicate in my reading of the text.

8 Sigüenza's *Infortunios de Alonso Ramírez* (1690) is also divided into seven parts. Alan Soons 1976 notes that this may have its roots in the model of the *Spiritual Exercises* of Ignatius of Loyola (201–5). In my view, it was Sigüenza's rewriting of Inés's *vida-relación* along picaresque lines that provided an immediate model for the writing of *Infortunios*. It is possible that Loyola's tract was the religious inspiration for both, but in the actual writing, it was the vida that served as the crucial source (Ross 1992).

9 This part of the *Relación* is included in Muriel 1982, 65–6.

Bibliography

I. Editions of the works of Carlos de Sigüenza y Góngora

No complete, collected edition of Sigüenza y Góngora's works exists. The most detailed and exhaustively researched listing of all extant materials, both printed and in manuscript, is found in Irving A. Leonard's *Don Carlos de Sigüenza y Góngora: A Mexican Savant of the Seventeenth Century.* This 1929 work has been reissued in Spanish translation as *Don Carlos de Sigüenza y Góngora: Un sabio mexicano del siglo XVII* (1984), with an updated bibliography.

Other sources for consultation are the volume *Seis obras,* edited by William G. Bryant, Jaime Delgado's 1960 introduction to *Piedad heroyca,* and Elías Trabulse's *Los manuscritos perdidos de Sigüenza y Góngora.*

Alboroto y motín de los indios de México. Mexico City, 1692. Ed. Irving A. Leonard. Mexico City: Talleres Gráficos del Museo Nacional de Arqueología, Historia y Etnografía, 1932.
    Included in *Relaciones históricas* and *Seis obras.*
Glorias de Querétaro. Mexico City, 1680; Querétaro: Ediciones Cimatario, 1945.
Infortunios de Alonso Ramírez. Mexico City, 1690.
    Madrid: Espasa-Calpe, 1941.
    Ed. J. S. Cummins and Alan B. Soons. London: Támesis, 1985.
    Ed. Lucrecio Pérez Blanco. Madrid: Historia 16, 1988.
    Ed. Raúl Crisafio. Milan: Arcipelago Edizioni, 1989.
    Included in *Obras históricas, Relaciones históricas,* and *Seis obras.*
Libra astronómica y philosóphica. Mexico City, 1690.
    Ed. Bernabé Navarro. Mexico City: Universidad Nacional Autónoma de México, 1959.
    Included in *Seis obras.*
Mercurio volante. Mexico City, 1695.
    Ed. Irving A. Leonard. Los Angeles: The Quivira Society, 1932; reprinted, New York: Arno Press, 1967.
    Included in *Seis obras* and *Obras históricas.*
Obras, con una biografía. 1928. Ed. Francisco Pérez Salazar. Mexico City: Sociedad de Bibliófilos Mexicanos.
    Includes *Piedad, Primavera, Relación, Theatro,* and *Trofeo.*

Obras históricas. 1960. Ed. José Rojas Garcidueñas. 2d edition. Mexico City: Porrúa.
    Includes *Infortunios, Mercurio, Relación, Theatro,* and *Trofeo.*
Oriental planeta evangélico. Mexico City, 1700.
    Included in *Poemas.*
Parayso Occidental, Plantado y Cultivado por la liberal benefica mano de los muy Cathólicas y poderosos Reyes de España nuestros señores en su magnifico Real Convento de Jesus Maria de Mexico. 1684. Mexico City: Juan de Ribera.
Piedad heroyca de don Fernando Cortés. Mexico City, 1693?.
    Ed. Jaime Delgado. Madrid: José Porrúa Turanzas, 1960.
    Included in *Obras.*
Poemas de Carlos de Sigüenza y Góngora. 1931. Ed. Irving A. Leonard. Madrid: Biblioteca de Historia Hispano-Americana.
    Includes *Oriental planeta, Primavera,* and other poetry.
Primavera indiana. Mexico City, 1662, 1668, 1683.
    Included in *Obras* and *Poemas.*
Relación de lo sucedido a la Armada de Barlovento. Mexico City, 1691.
    Included in *Obras, Obras históricas,* and *Relaciones históricas.*
Relaciones históricas. 1940. Ed. Manuel Romero de Terreros. Mexico City: Universidad Autónoma de México.
    Includes *Alboroto, Infortunios,* and *Relación.*
Seis obras. 1985. Ed. Wiliam G. Bryant. Caracas: Biblioteca Auacucho.
    Includes *Alboroto, Infortunios, Libra, Mercurio, Theatro,* and *Trofeo.*
Theatro de virtudes políticas que constituyen a un príncipe. Mexico City, 1680.
    Included in *Obras, Obras históricas,* and *Seis obras.*
Triunfo parténico. Mexico City, 1683. Prologue by José Rojas Garcidueñas. Mexico City: Ediciones Xóchitl, 1945.
Trofeo de la justicia española. Mexico City, 1691.
    Included in *Obras, Obras históricas,* and *Seis obras.*

II. Works cited

Abreu Gómez, Ermilo. 1931. "Estudio preliminar." In *Poemas de Carlos de Sigüenza y Góngora,* ed. Irving A. Leonard, pp. 13–37. Madrid: Biblioteca de Historia Hispano-Americana.
Acosta, Joseph de, Padre. 1590. *Historia natural y moral de las Indias.* Mexico City: Fondo de Cultura Económica, 1940; reprinted 1979.
Acosta, Leonardo. 1985. "El barroco de Indias y la ideología colonialista." In Acosta, *El barroco de Indias y otros ensayos,* pp. 9–52. Havana: Casa de las Américas. (Article originally published in *Unión* (Havana), Sept. 1972.)
Adorno, Rolena. 1986. *Guaman Poma: Writing and Resistance in Colonial Peru.* Austin: University of Texas Press.

———. 1988a. "Discourses on Colonialism: Bernal Díaz, Las Casas and the Twentieth-Century Reader." *Modern Language Notes* 103 (March): 239–58.

———. 1988b. "Nuevas perspectivas en los estudios literarios coloniales hispanoamericanos." *Revista de Crítica Literaria Latinoamericana* 14: 11–27.

Alberró, Solange. 1988. *Inquisición y sociedad en México 1571–1700*. Mexico City: Fondo de Cultura Económica.

Anderson, Helene, and Angel Flores. 1974. *Masterpieces of Spanish-American Literature*. Vol. 1, *The Colonial Period to the Beginnings of Modernism*. New York: Macmillan.

Anderson Imbert, Enrique, and Eugenio Florit. 1970. *Literatura hispanoamericana: Antología e introducción histórica*. Vol. 1. Rev. ed. Orlando, FL: Holt, Rinehart, & Winston.

Arenal, Electa, and Stacey Schlau. 1989. *Untold Sisters*. Albuquerque: University of New Mexico Press.

Arocena, Luis A. 1963. *Antonio de Solís, cronista indiano: Estudio sobre las formas historiográficas del barroco*. Buenos Aires: Editorial Universitaria de Buenos Aires.

Arrom. J. J. 1987. "Carlos de Sigüenza y Góngora: Relectura criolla de los *Infortunios de Alonso Ramírez*." *Thesaurus* 42: 386–409.

Bacigalupo, Marvyn Helen. 1981. *A Changing Perspective: Attitudes toward Creole Society in New Spain (1521–1610)*. London: Támesis.

Bakewell, Peter. 1971. *Silver Mining and Society in Colonial Mexico*. Cambridge University Press.

Balbuena, Bernardo de. 1603. *La grandeza mexicana*. 2d ed. Mexico City: Porrúa, 1975.

Benítez Grobet, Laura. 1983. *La idea de historia en Carlos de Sigüenza y Góngora*. Mexico City: Universidad Nacional Autónoma de México.

Beverley, John. 1987. "Barroco de estado: Góngora y el gongorismo." In Beverley, *Del Lazarillo al Sandinismo: Estudios sobre la función ideológica de la literatura española e hispanoamericana*, pp. 77–97. Minneapolis, MN: Prisma Institute.

Bilinkoff, Jodi. 1989. *The Avila of Saint Teresa: Religious Reform in a Sixteenth-Century City*. Ithaca, NY: Cornell University Press.

Brown, Marshall. 1982. "The Classic is the Baroque: On the Principle of Wölfflin's Art History." *Critical Inquiry* 9: 379–404.

Castro-Klarén, Sara. 1989. "Dancing and the Sacred in the Andes: From the *Taqui-Oncoy* to 'Rasu-Niti.'" *Dispositio* 14: 169–85.

Catalá, Rafael. 1987. *Para una lectura americana del barroco americano: Sor Juana Inés de la Cruz y Sigüenza y Góngora*. Minneapolis, MN: Prisma Institute.

Chang Rodríguez, Raquel. 1982. "La transgresión de la picaresca en los *Infortunios de Alonso Ramírez*." In Chang Rodríguez, *Violencia y subversión en la prosa colonial hispanoamericana*, pp. 85–108. Madrid: José Porrúa Turanzas.

Chang Rodríguez, Raquel, and Antonio R. de la Campa, eds. 1985. *Poesía hispanoamericana colonial.* Madrid: Alhambra.

Chang Rodríguez, Raquel, and Malva E. Filer. 1988. *Voces de Hispanoamérica: Antología literaria.* Boston: Heinle & Heinle.

Ciudad de México: Area metropolitana y alrededores. 1993. Mexico City: Guía Roji.

Columbus, Christopher [Cristóbal Colón]. [1498] 1946. *Los cuatro viajes del Almirante y su testamento.* Madrid: Espasa-Calpe.

Concha, Jaime. 1976. "La literatura colonial hispanoamericana: Problemas e hipótesis." *Neohelicon* 4: 31–50.

Cruz, Anne J. 1989. "Studying Gender in the Spanish Golden Age." In *Cultural and Historical Grounding for Hispanic and Luso-Brazilian Feminist Literary Criticism,* ed. Hernán Vidal, pp. 193–222. Minneapolis, MN: Institute for the Study of Ideologies and Literature.

Curtius, E. R. 1953. *European Literature and the Latin Middle Ages.* Trans. Willard R. Trask. Reprint Princeton, NJ: Princeton University Press, 1973.

Delgado, Jaime. 1960. "Estudio preliminar." In his edition of Sigüenza y Góngora, *Piedad heroyca de Hernán Cortés,* pp. xi–cviii. Madrid: José Porrúa Turanzas.

Duncan, Joseph E. 1972. *Milton's Earthly Paradise: A historical Study of Eden.* Minneapolis: University of Minnesota Press.

El Saffar, Ruth. 1975. *Distance and Control in Don Quixote: A Study in Narrative Technique.* Studies in Romance Languages and Literatures, No. 147. Chapel Hill: University of North Carolina Department of Romance Languages.

Englekirk, John E. et al. 1968. *An Anthology of Spanish-American Literature.* 2d ed. New York: Appleton Century Crofts.

Florescano, Enrique, and Isabel Gil Sánchez. 1976. "La situación económica y social hasta 1750." In *Historia general de México,* vol. 2, pt. 1, pp. 185–98. Mexico City: El Colegio de México.

Franco, Jean. 1989. *Plotting Women: Gender and Representation in Mexico.* New York: Columbia University Press.

Friedman, Edward H. 1987. *The Antiheroine's Voice: Narrative Discourse and Transformations of the Picaresque.* Columbia: University of Missouri Press.

Gallop, Jane. 1982. *The Daughter's Seduction: Feminism and Psychoanalysis.* Ithaca, NY: Cornell University Press.

Gaos, José. 1959. "Presentación." In Sigüenza y Góngora, *Libra astronómica y filosófica,* ed. Bernabé Navarro, pp. v–xxv. Mexico City: Universidad Nacional Autónoma de México.

Giamatti, A. Bartlett. 1966. *The Earthly Paradise and the Renaissance Epic.* Princeton, NJ: Princeton University Press.

Gilbert, Sandra M., and Susan Gubar. 1979. *The Madwoman in the Attic: The Woman Writer and the Nineteenth-Century Literary Imagination.* New Haven, CT: Yale University Press.

Gimbernat de González, Ester. 1980. "Mapas y texto: Para una estrategia del poder." *MLN* 95: 388–99.

Gonzalbo, Pilar Aizpuru. 1987. *Las mujeres en la Nueva España: Educación y vida cotidiana.* Mexico City: El Colegio de México.

González Echevarría, Roberto. 1976. "José Arrom, autor de la Relación acerca de las antigüedades de los indios (picaresca e historia)." In González Echevarría, *Relecturas: Estudios de literatura cubana,* pp. 17–35. Caracas: Monte Avila.

———. 1980. "The Life and Adventures of Cipión: Cervantes and the Picaresque." *Diacritics* 10: 15–26.

———. 1983. "Humanismo y retórica en las crónicas de la conquista." In González Echevarría, *Isla a su vuelo fugitiva: Ensayos críticos sobre literatura hispanoamericana,* pp. 2–25. Madrid: José Porrúa Turanzas.

———. 1990. *Myth and Archive: A Theory of Latin American Narrative.* Cambridge University Press.

González Pérez, Aníbal. 1983. "*Los Infortunios de Alonso Ramírez:* Picaresca e historia." *Hispanic Review* 51: 189–204.

Green, Otis. 1963–6. *Spain and the Western Tradition.* 4 vols. Madison: University of Wisconsin Press.

Guillén, Claudio. 1971. "Towards a Definition of the Picaresque Genre." In Guillén, *Literature as System: Essays toward the Theory of Literary History.* Princeton, NJ: Princeton University Press.

Hatzfeld, Helmut. 1964. *Estudios sobre el barroco.* Madrid: Gredos.

Herman, Susan. 1978. "The *Conquista y descubrimiento del Nuevo Reino de Granada,* Otherwise Known as *El carnero:* The *corónica,* the *historia,* and the *novela.*" Ph.D. diss., Yale University.

Inés de la Cruz. [1625]. *Fundación del convento de San José.* Archive of the Convento de San José de México, Mexico City.

Iñigo Madrigal, Luis, ed. 1982. *Historia de la literatura hispanoamericana.* Vol. 1, *Epoca colonial.* Madrid: Cátedra.

Israel, J. I. 1975. *Race, Class and Politics in Colonial Mexico: 1610–1670.* New York: Oxford University Press.

Jara, René, and Nicholas Spadaccini. 1989. "Introduction: Allegorizing the New World." In *1492–1992: Re/Discovering Colonial Writing,* ed. Jara and Spadaccini, pp. 9–50. Minneapolis, MN: Prisma Institute.

Jardine, Alice. 1985. *Gynesis: Configurations of Woman and Modernity.* Ithaca, NY: Cornell University Press.

Johnson, Julie Greer. 1981. "Picaresque Elements in Carlos de Sigüenza y Góngora's *Los infortunios de Alonso Ramírez.*" *Hispania* 64: 60–7.

———. 1983. *Women in Colonial Spanish American Literature: Literary Images.* Westport, CT: Greenwood Press.

Juana Inés de la Cruz. *Obras completas.* Mexico City: Porrúa, 1975.

Kelly, Joan. 1984. *Women, History and Theory: The Essays of Joan Kelly.* Chicago: University of Chicago Press.

Kristeva, Julia. 1981. "Women's Time." Trans. Alice Jardine. *Signs* 7: 13–35.

Lafaye, Jacques. 1974. *Quetzalcóatl y Guadalupe: La formación de la conciencia nacional en México.* Mexico City: Fondo de Cultura Económica, 1987.

Lavrin, Asunción. 1972. "Values and Meaning of Monastic Life for Nuns in Colonial Mexico." *Catholic History Review* 58: 367–87.

———. 1976. "Women in Convents: Their Economic and Social Role in Colonial Mexico." In *Liberating Women's History*, ed. Bernice A. Carroll, pp. 250–77. Urbana: University of Illinois Press.

———, ed. 1989. *Sexuality and Marriage in Colonial Latin America.* Lincoln: University of Nebraska Press.

———. 1991 [1983]. "Unlike Sor Juana? The Model Nun in the Religious Literature of Colonial Mexico." In *Feminist Perspectives on Sor Juana Inés de la Cruz*, ed. Stephanie Merrim, pp. 61–85. Detroit: Wayne State University Press.

Leonard, Irving A. 1927. "A Great Savant of Seventeenth Century Mexico: Don Carlos de Sigüenza y Góngora." *Hispania* 10: 399–408.

———. 1929a. *Don Carlos de Sigüenza y Góngora: A Mexican Savant of the Seventeenth Century.* Berkeley: University of California Press.

———. 1929b. *Ensayo bibliográfico de Don Carlos de Sigüenza y Góngora.* Mexico City: Imprenta de la Secretaría de Relaciones Exteriores.

———. 1949. *Books of the Brave.* Cambridge, MA: Harvard University Press.

———. 1959. *Baroque Times in Old Mexico: Seventeenth Century Persons, Places, and Practices.* Ann Arbor: University of Michigan Press.

———. 1984. *Don Carlos de Sigüenza y Góngora: Un sabio mexicano del siglo XVII.* Trans. Juan José Utrilla. Mexico City: Fondo de Cultura Económica.

Lezama Lima, José. 1957. "La curiosidad barroca." In Lezama Lima, *La expresión americana*, pp. 43–81. Havana: Instituto Nacional de Cultura.

López Cámara, Francisco. 1950. "El cartesianismo en Sor Juana y Sigüenza." *Filosofía y Letras* 39: 107–31.

Luciani, Frederick, 1987. "Octavio Paz on Sor Juana: The Metaphor Incarnate." *Latin American Literary Review* 15: 6–25.

MacCormack, Sabine, 1989. "Atahualpa and the Book. "*Dispositio* 14: 141–68.

MacLachlan, Colin M., and Jaime E. Rodríguez. 1980. *The Forging of the Cosmic Race: A Reinterpretation of Colonial Mexico.* Berkeley: University of California Press.

Maravall, José Antonio. 1975. *Culture of the Baroque.* Trans. Terry Cochran. Minneapolis: University of Minnesota Press, 1986.

Mariana de la Encarnación. 1641. *Relación de la fundación del Convento antiguo de Santa Teresa.* MS G 79. Perry-Castañeda Library, University of Texas at Austin, 1823.

Martín, Luis. 1983. *Daughters of the Conquistadores: Women of the Viceroyalty of Peru.* Albuquerque: University of New Mexico Press.

Martín de Córdoba. 1500. *Jardín de las nobles donzellas, Frey Martín de Córdoba: A Critical Edition and Study.* Ed. Harriet Goldberg. Studies in Romance Languages and Literatures, No. 137. Chapel Hill: University of North Carolina Department of Romance Languages, 1974.

Méndez Plancarte, Alfonso, ed. 1944. *Poetas novohispanos: Segundo siglo (parte primera).* México City: Universidad Autónoma de México.

———. 1945. *Poetas novohispanos: Segundo siglo (parte segunda).* Mexico City: Universidad Nacional Autónoma de México.

Merrim, Stephanie. 1982. "The Castle of Discourse: Fernández de Oviedo's *Don Claribalte* (1519) or " 'Los correos andan más que los caballeros.' " *MLN* 97: 329–46.

———, ed. 1991. *Feminist Perspectives on Sor Juana Inés de la Cruz.* Detroit: Wayne State University Press.

Mignolo, Walter. 1981. "El metatexto historiográfico y la historiografía indiana." *MLN* 96: 358–402.

———. 1982. "Cartas, crónicas, y relaciones del descubrimiento y la conquista." In *Historia de la literatura hispanoamericana,* Vol. 1, ed. Luis Iñigo Madrigal, pp. 57–116. Madrid: Cátedra.

———. 1989. "Afterword: From Colonial Discourse to Colonial Semiosis." *Dispositio* 14: 333–7.

Miller, Nancy K. 1982. "The Text's Heroine: A Feminist Critic and Her Fictions." *Diacritics* 12: 48–53.

Moi, Toril. 1985. *Sexual/Textual Politics: Feminist Literary Theory.* New York: Methuen.

Moraña, Mabel. 1988. "Barroco y conciencia criolla en Hispanoamérica." *Revista de Crítica Literaria Latinoamericana* 28: 229–51.

———. 1990. "Máscara autobiográfica y conciencia criolla en *Infortunios de Alonso Ramírez.*" *Dispositio* 15: 10–17.

Muriel, Josefina. 1946. *Conventos de monjas en la Nueva España.* Mexico City: Santiago.

———. 1982. *Cultura femenina novohispana.* Mexico City: Universidad Autónoma de México.

Myers, Kathleen A. 1990. "History, Truth and Dialogue: Fernández de Oviedo's *Historia general y natural de las Indias* (Bk. XXIII, Ch. LIV)." *Hispania* 73: 616–25.

———. Forthcoming. *Becoming a Nun in Seventeenth-Century Mexico: An Edition of the Spiritual Autobiography of María de San Joseph.*

Needham, Joseph. 1958. *Chinese Astronomy and the Jesuit Mission: An Encounter of Cultures.* London: The China Society.

Nelson, William. 1973. *Fact or Fiction: The Dilemma of the Renaissance Storyteller.* Cambridge, MA: Harvard University Press.

Paz, Octavio. 1972. "Literatura de fundación." In Paz, *Puertas al campo,* pp. 15–21. Barcelona: Seix Barral.

————. 1982. *Sor Juana Inés de la Cruz o las trampas de la fe.* Mexico City: Fondo de Cultura Económica.

————. 1988. *Sor Juana, or, The Traps of Faith.* Trans. Margaret Sayers Peden. Cambridge, MA: Harvard University Press.

Peña, Margarita. 1982. *Descubrimiento y conquista de América: Una antología general.* Mexico City: Secretaría de Educación Pública/Universidad Nacional Autónoma de México.

Perelmuter-Pérez, Rosa. 1983. "La estructura retórica de la *Respuesta a Sor Filotea*." *Hispanic Review* 51: 147–58.

Phillips, Rachel. 1983. "Marina/Malinche: Masks and Shadows." In *Women in Hispanic Literature: Icons and Fallen Idols,* ed. Beth Miller, pp. 97–114. Berkeley: University of California Press.

Picón Garfield, Evelyn, and Iván A. Schulman. 1991. *Las literaturas hispánicas: Introducción a su estudio,* Vol. 1. Detroit: Wayne State University Press.

Picón Salas, Mariano. 1944. *De la Conquista a la Independencia.* Mexico City: Fondo de Cultura Económica, 1975.

Porqueras Mayo, Alberto. 1957. *El prólogo como género literario: Su estudio en el Siglo de Oro español.* Madrid: Consejo Superior de Investigaciones Científicas.

Pupo-Walker, Enrique. 1982a. *Historia, creación y profecía en los textos del Inca Garcilaso de la Vega.* Madrid: José Porrúa Turanzas.

————. 1982b. *La vocación literaria del pensamiento histórico en América.* Madrid: Gredos.

Putnam, Emily James. 1910. *The Lady: Studies of Certain Significant Phases of Her History.* Chicago: University of Chicago Press, 1970.

Ramos Medina, Manuel. 1990. *Imagen de santidad en un mundo profano.* Mexico City: Universidad Iberoamericana.

Rico, Francisco. 1970. *La novela picaresca y el punto de vista.* Barcelona: Seix Barral.

Rodríguez Freile, Juan. 1638. *El carnero.* Medellín: Editorial Bedout, 1973.

Rodríguez Monegal, Emir. 1977. *The Borzoi Anthology of Latin American Literature.* 2 vols. New York: Knopf.

Rojas Garcidueñas, José. 1945. *Don Carlos de Sigüenza y Góngora, erudito barroco.* Mexido City: Ediciones Xóchitl.

Ross, Kathleen. 1988. "*Alboroto y motín de México:* Una noche triste criolla." *Hispanic Review* 55: 181–90.

————. Forthcoming. "Historians of the Conquest and Colonization of the New World, 1550–1620." In *Cambridge History of Latin American Literature,* vol. 1, ed. Roberto González Echevarría and Enrique Pupo-Walker.

————. 1992. "Gender and Genre in *Infortunios de Alonso Ramírez.*" Unpublished manuscript.

Said, Edward. 1978. *Orientalism.* New York: Pantheon.

Sánchez Lamego, Miguel A. 1955. *El primer mapa general de México elaborado por un mexicano.* Mexico City: Instituto Panamericano de Geografía e Historia.

Sarduy, Severo. 1972. "El barroco y el neobarroco." In *América Latina en su literatura,* ed. César Fernández Moreno, pp. 167–84. Mexico City: Siglo XXI.

———. 1974. *Barroco.* Buenos Aires: Sudamericana.

Siburský, Saúl. 1965. "Carlos de Sigüenza y Góngora: La transición hacia el iluminismo criollo en una figura excepcional." *Revista Iberoamericana* 31: 195–207.

Simpson, Leslie Byrd. 1975. "El siglo olvidado de México." In Woodrow Borah, *El siglo de la depresión en Nueva España,* pp. 141–54. Mexico City: Secretaría de Educación Pública.

Soons, Alan. 1976. "Alonso Ramírez in an Enchanted and a Disenchanted World." *Bulletin of Hispanic Studies* 53: 201–5.

Struever, Nancy S. 1970. *The Language of History in the Renaissance.* Princeton, NJ: Princeton University Press.

TePaske, John, and Herbert S. Klein. 1981. "The Seventeenth-Century Crisis in New Spain: Myth or Reality?" *Past & Present* 90: 116–35.

Teresa of Avila [Teresa de Jesús]. 1577? *Libro de las fundaciones.* Buenos Aires: Espasa-Calpe, 1950.

———. 1562. *Libro de su vida.* Mexico City: Porrúa, 1979.

Todorov, Tzvetan. 1985. *The Conquest of America: The Question of the Other.* Trans. Richard Howard. New York: Harper Colophon.

Trabulse, Elías. 1974. *Ciencia y religión en el Siglo XVII.* Mexico City: El Colegio de México.

———. 1988. *Los manuscritos perdidos de Sigüenza y Góngora.* Mexico City: El Colegio de México.

Varner, John G. 1968. *El Inca: The Life and Times of Garcilaso de la Vega.* Austin: University of Texas Press.

Vives, Juan Luis. 1948. *Instrucción de la mujer cristiana.* Buenos Aires: Espasa-Calpe.

Warner, Marina. 1976. *Alone of All Her Sex: The Myth and the Cult of the Virgin Mary.* New York: Random House.

Weber, Alison. 1990. *Teresa of Avila and the Rhetoric of Femininity.* Princeton, NJ: Princeton University Press.

Wölfflin, Heinrich. 1932. *Principles of Art History.* Trans. M. D. Hottinger. Mineola, NY: Dover. 1950.

———. 1964. *Renaissance and Baroque.* Trans. Kathrin Simon. Reprint. Ithaca, NY: Cornell Unversity Press, 1984.

Zamora, Margarita. 1988. *Language, Authority and Indigenous History in the Comentarios Reales de los Incas.* Cambridge University Press.

Zapata, Roger A. 1989. *Guamán Poma, indigenismo y estética de la dependencia en la cultura peruana.* Minneapolis, MN: Institute for the Study of Ideologies and Literature.

Index